History

By Miles Jupp and available from Headline

Egg and Soldiers:
The Childhood Memoir of Damien Trench

History

Signed by the author

HEADLINE

Miles Jupp
History

HEADLINE

Cataloguing in Publication Data is available from the British Library

Hardback ISBN 978 1 4722 3995 2

Prin ... S.p.A.

Headline's ... policy is to use papers that are natural, renewable and recyclable
products and made from wood grown in well-managed forests and other
controlled sources. The logging and manufacturing processes are expected
to conform to the environmental regulations of the country of origin.

HEADLINE PUBLISHING GROUP
An Hachette UK Company
Carmelite House
50 Victoria Embankment
London EC4Y 0DZ

www.headline.co.uk
www.hachette.co.uk

'Somewhere in our history, the future's shining bright'

TOM MCRAE, 'All That's Gone'

PART ONE

May 1998

1

'It's just one afternoon, Clive.'

'Is it, though? It always ends up being a whole day.'

'Yes, but a fun day.'

'But will it be fun?'

'Clive, if you approach it as a fun day, then it will be a fun day.'

Iain Dixon was fifty years of age, tall and whippet thin, with thick grey hair and a noticeable lack of concern for the views of others. He was childless, often single, and had taught art and design at the same unremarkable private school for a quarter of a century. Why it was felt by the powers that be that this would make him a suitable person to take on the role of careers officer was something that was never adequately explained. But nevertheless, one afternoon a week he would sit behind the desk in the school's small careers office and languidly describe to the teenagers sitting opposite him the narrow courses that their lives would follow, and the paths of least resistance that would take them there. If his views were ever challenged, Dixon would simply look back at them with a serene expression and say, 'It is, of course, all *entirely* up to you.'

It was this very same facial expression, almost as much as the man's envious build, that was currently infuriating Clive Hapgood. Clive was only thirty-eight years old, but a stone heavier than he had been a decade ago, and had hair that, though still just about more brown than it was grey, was somehow neither as thick nor as curly as it used to be. Of the many things that gnawed away at Clive like Highland ticks, the most pressing was how to stop this smirking, disingenuous fool from persuading him to play for the staff cricket team this Sunday.

'Iain, can I think about it? I'd have to make a few calls. I'm not sure I'm free.'

'I'll put you down as a probable.'

'I really don't think Helen will like it.'

'Tell her to come. Bring the children. It'll be fun.'

Clive and Helen had been married for twelve years, and they had two daughters: Sarah, eleven, and Katie, eight. They lived in a mid-terrace house not far from his place of work, and too many of his history students walked past on their way to and from school for him to ever feel truly at ease. Once a group of fifteen-year-olds walked by as he was dropping a clutch of empty wine bottles into the rubbish bin next to his front step and they laughed at him. Another time he had heard boys laughing and joking outside his front door, and when he went outside, he found that his scrappy, narrow front garden had been decorated with pages from a pornographic magazine. Those, too, went into the rubbish bin. He thought he recognised the miscreants' voices, but what was the point of pursuing the matter? It would only be more fuss.

'Iain, I'm not sure that a Sunday is really the best day for my family. It's our one chance to be together.'

'Well, can't you be together at the cricket? We won't start until twelve. You've most of the morning free to wash the car or read the papers. You could grab breakfast somewhere?'

'I grab breakfast in my own kitchen. And I don't spend Sundays washing my car, Iain. And I barely have *time* to read the Sunday papers, let alone turn out for your—'

'It is, of course, *entirely* up to you.'

The staffroom was filling up now. Perhaps Iain could turn his attentions elsewhere and leave Clive to drink coffee.

The jug sitting on the hot plate under the filter machine was already half empty, he saw, and there was a queue forming.

'Anyway,' said Iain, 'you look like you're anxious to get your morning coffee, Clive. You're down as a probable.'

Clive gave what he hoped was a non-committal smile and set off in the direction of the coffee machine and his head of department, Robert Icke, who was at the back of the queue. Icke's latest crime was to clamp down on the amount of use his department members made of the photocopier. Clive was about to tap him on the shoulder and discuss the matter when someone at the front of the queue gave an almighty howl.

'Oh Jesus Christ! Bloody hell!'

The queue broke up and Clive could see the figure of Wally Davis, bent double and sucking on two of his fingers while jumping up and down. Those who had been in the queue, Icke among them, took this opportunity to push past and get to the coffee while Wally, his face reddening, clamped his eyes shut and tilted back his head. Clive put a hand on Wally's shoulder.

'OK, Wally?' he asked.

'Jesus, that was hot.'

'Let's get you away.'

Clive helped Wally up to his full height of five foot three and walked him over to a wooden armchair in the corner. Wally, perhaps to compensate for his unimposing height, always wore jackets made from an incredibly heavy tweed that added considerably to his girth and restricted his movements, with the result that he struggled to sit back all the way into the chair, and instead had to perch on its front edge in the manner of a self-conscious Humpty Dumpty. The jackets also meant that Wally was always too hot, whatever the weather, and permanently marked with perspiration. He wiped at his forehead with a cuff and looked sadly around.

'Why do people have to jostle like that? Of course I'm going to spill hot coffee on myself if people are rubbing up against me. I've always thought someone might get seriously hurt. It would be me, wouldn't it?'

The first two fingers of Wally's right hand were dark red and mottled with white lumps, and appeared to be swelling even as Clive watched. He would need medical attention, although the school nurse's brusque bedside manner would only break Wally's morale further. In any case, the low urgency with which she offered medical help hardly qualified her as an emergency service. Wally himself seemed less concerned about the physical aspects of his injury than the behaviour of his colleagues.

'It's unseemly. Don't you think?'

'Yes,' said Clive. 'But then, it's always been like this, hasn't it?'

'Doesn't make it right.'

'Why don't I get something for your hand?'

Clive shuffled over to the sink, under which he vaguely recalled once seeing some Savlon and plasters. He got down on all fours to open up the cupboard, but as he did so several bottles of cleaning fluid tumbled out, bringing with them a profusion of browning J-cloths and an assortment of parched washing-up sponges. Removing an ageing, perished plunger, he saw a red box behind the U-bend that could be a first-aid kit, and so also took out two old Jif bottles and a wooden box of shoe polish. The U-bend was quite tight against the back of the cupboard, and so Clive had to reach as far as he could just to lay his fingers on the box. Then, to get sufficient purchase on it, he had to lower his shoulders and roll onto his side so that he could hook his arm around the back. He could now get a decent grip on the box but was unable to pull it towards him, so he tried instead to punch the box through the gap to collect it from the other side. His third punch saw some success, at which point he heard a voice say, 'Everything all right, Clive? This all seems rather desperate.'

The remark, made by Frampton's headmaster, was intended to be jovial. Clive paused to glance over his shoulder and saw that he was looking up at Julian Crouch's pinstriped trousers. His moustached but otherwise Roman-looking face was the best part of six feet away.

'Hello, Headmaster,' said Clive.

'You look as if you're trying to burrow your way out. Things can't be that bad, can they?'

Clive chuckled politely and then continued trying to push the first-aid box through.

'I'm just trying to get a first-aid kit. Wally Davis has burnt himself,' he explained as the box finally came loose. He poked his arm around to the other side and then stood up, holding the first-aid box triumphantly.

'Well done, Clive. You've left yourself with rather a lot of tidying up to do, of course.'

Clive surveyed the cupboard's useless contents, now arranged at his feet. There was a bar of green Fairy soap that must have been older than he was. Clearly it all belonged in a bin but Clive, like everyone else before him, was just going to shove it all back in and shut the doors.

'Everything else going smoothly, Clive?'

'Well, the lower sixth are . . .'

'Excitable?'

'Tiring.'

The headmaster gave Clive an admonishing look. Like everything that the headmaster said or did, he intended this to be taken humorously, though it was meant entirely literally.

'Tiring? For a young man like you? You're supposed to be dynamic. You seem happy enough rolling about on the floor of the staffroom.'

The head laughed and Clive did his best to join in, despite always finding their interactions as bothersome as they were chilling.

The headmaster's laughter ended as abruptly as it had begun, and the possessor of the school's most perennially straight back strode off towards the coffee machine. Clive shoved the various crumbling cleaning materials back in the cupboard, then opened the box and found it empty.

*

'No plasters or anything, I'm afraid. But I thought it might help if you lowered your fingers into this.'

Clive passed a glass of water to Wally and sat in the next armchair along. He was never quite sure if the chairs were coffee-coloured by design or through years of hot spills. Wally tried to force his fist into the glass, but his hands and fingers, much like the rest of him, were stubby and didn't fit in. He gave up and instead sipped the tepid water.

'Do you think someone might make another pot of coffee?' Wally asked.

'Robert looks like he's having a go.'

Robert Icke had fitted a new filter into the machine and was now very slowly and deliberately filling it in accordance with the handwritten instructions affixed to the side. He then took great care as he transferred the old filter towards the bin to ensure that no coffee seeped onto his crisply ironed short-sleeved shirt. He always wore a short-sleeved shirt, something Helen had once told Clive she found annoying. Clive was more irritated by the way Icke whistled, and the irksome waft of his scented moisturiser.

Wally gave a little lop-sided smile. 'He's another one.'

'Robert?'

'Never speaks to me. Worse than the head.'

'I'd happily never have to speak to either of them. Still, at least Icke knows something about teaching, which is more than you can say about Crouch.'

'He can't have taught a lesson for years, can he? He's basically an administrator.'

'He's a sort of meeter-and-greeter, really. Likes the formal wear. Handing out prizes at the end of the year. I saw him showing some parents around in the quad yesterday; he was being unbelievably suave. He pointed me out to them and said, "Young Clive there is scurrying off to teach the historians of tomorrow." Sick-making.'

'I hate suave people,' said Wally sadly as he looked down at his blistering fingers. 'Oh God.'

'Why don't I get us both a coffee?' said Clive. But just as he stood up, Crouch began to strike the side of his cup with a teaspoon. Everyone fell silent as the headmaster strode into the middle of the room. Clive lowered himself back onto the arm of his chair.

'Thank you, everyone. I don't want to keep you from your morning coffees for long. There are only a couple of things I have to say.' As he spoke, he turned expansively from side to side so as to take in all corners of the room and to connect with his entire audience of around fifty or so.

'The first thing I wish to do is to introduce to you all to Flora Wilson. Where are you, Flora?'

A tall, slim woman with dark hair took a step forward from a group huddled by the noticeboards and gave a cheery, confident wave. Early forties, Clive reckoned.

'Thank you, Flora. There she is. Miss Wilson is here for a few weeks to observe us for the last . . .' He searched for a suitable word for a moment, and having found it, made full use of its plosive possibilities, '. . . for the last *portion* of this summer term, before joining the Frampton staff *permanently* in the autumn as part of our excellent history department.'

Wally flashed a quizzical look and Clive shot back a look of complete innocence. Who was leaving?

'I'm sure that you can all be relied upon to be as charming and helpful as ever, but *please* do all that you can to make her feel as welcome as is humanly *possible*.'

As each plosive struck Clive's inner ears with full force, he was reminded of last night's drinking. Four glasses of red wine. Not a heavy session, but ill-disciplined for a Wednesday night. *Portion. Permanently. Please. Possible.* Still two left in the chamber.

'If you see her wandering the corridors looking lost, do set her on the right *path*.'

As the last word of Crouch's most recent utterance ricocheted around the room, Clive wondered why nobody had told him that there was going to be a new member of staff in his department.

'The other thing I have to do is remind you that our staff cricket side – so capably and enthusiastically run by Mr Dixon – have a match this Sunday against . . . who is it against again, Mr Dixon?'

'Welbrook,' said Iain smoothly.

'And are they an intimidating outfit?'

'A walk in the park,' said Iain. The headmaster found this expression priceless. Clive, meanwhile, slid backwards on the arm of the chair to try and get more comfortable, but felt the back of his trousers snag on something.

'A walk in the *park*!' Bang. The chamber was now empty. 'Our team are, however, a few short. I myself am unable to help as my wife and I are out of the country this weekend at a wedding. But it would be wonderful if a few more of you could volunteer your sporting services to Mr Dixon. I am sure that it would be quite untoward of us to enlist Miss Wilson so early in her Frampton career – though she's doubtless an absolute tearaway fast bowler!'

Crouch laughed so loudly at his own remark that Clive was sure he felt some wax in his ear dislodge.

'Mr Hapgood has apparently keenly offered his services only minutes ago, so please don't be shy about following his excellent example.'

He beamed at Clive, and then performed a little bow to the assembled staff to indicate that his morning oration was over.

'Playing cricket? On your day off?' said Wally, as the hubbub resumed.

'Hopefully not. I'm going to try to persuade some other people to play so that I can pull out.'

Clive made to stand, but found that he had not yet managed to work his trousers free of whatever it was that they had snagged on. He leant forward but could feel the fabric pulling, and so attempted instead to manoeuvre his posterior gently about in the hope of releasing it.

'Have you got an itch, Mr Hapgood? You are a victim of events this morning, aren't you?'

The headmaster turned to Flora Wilson.

'I thought perhaps you ought to meet Clive Hapgood. Clive is a fellow historian. You'll be working side by side, I imagine.'

'Robert Icke's told me all about you,' said Flora as she offered her hand. 'Pleased to meet you.'

Clive, still perched, took her hand and shook it warmly. He tried to stand as he did so, but the negotiations between his trousers and the chair's arm were yet to reach a successful conclusion.

'I would stand,' said Clive, 'but I've got a bit of an issue with my . . .'

'You're far too young for back trouble, Mr Hapgood,' beamed the headmaster.

'It's a problem with my trousers, actually.'

'Ah,' said the headmaster. 'Marvellous.'

He held out his hands like a priest over the gifts, gave an assuming smile and turned on his heel. Wally stood up and proffered his own hand, remembered too late that it was it was burnt, and so simpered when it was taken.

'I'm Wally,' he winced. 'Wally Davis. Welcome to Frampton, Miss Wilson.'

'Yes, it's actually Mrs Wilson.'

'Oh. Well, in that case, congratulations,' said Wally.

'Ha. Not for long. I'm in the process of getting a divorce.'

'Commiserations, then,' said Wally.

Clive had spent the last few exchanges struggling to get free and now felt just a few crucial millimetres of thread from success. A gentle lean towards Wally was all it took and he at last felt some fresh air between his chinos and the chair. He stood up gratefully.

'Thank you,' said Flora. 'It's fine. It's for the best. It's partly why I'm changing schools. I've been given leave for the moment. My husband and I currently work at the same school.'

'Right. Any children involved?'

'In the school?'

'Sorry. No. Your husband and you?'

'No.'

'I'm divorced,' said Wally.

'I'm sorry to hear that,' Flora said.

Clive, who had learnt that a conversation with Wally about his divorce was something to be avoided at all costs, tried to change the subject.

'You're here to observe us, are you?' he asked. 'I have to say, I didn't actually know we were having a new teacher in the department.'

'No one told you?'

'No. Not your fault, of course. And I'm delighted that we'll have the extra support. Well, not support. Actual manpower. Not manpower, obviously. Another set of hands. More boots on the ground. Another member of staff, that's all I mean.'

'I know what you mean,' said Flora kindly.

'Thanks. Too tired to bloody think properly. I need a holiday. This term seems to have gone on for ever, and we're not quite halfway through it yet. It'll be much easier with you around. Unless someone's leaving? Is someone leaving?'

'No, I don't think so. Apparently history's becoming so popular at A level that they've had to expand the department.'

'Right. Well, that's a relief. Thought I might be getting the sack without being told.'

'They haven't told you?'

Clive found himself genuinely laughing. Wally suddenly sighed with despair.

'Oh God,' he said. 'I've got the ruddy lower sixth in five minutes! Where does morning break disappear to? I've not even managed to have a coffee. Right. Better get my armour on. Nice to meet you, Miss . . . er, Flora.'

Clive and Flora watched Wally walk sadly away.

'He seems nice,' said Flora.

'He's fine,' said Clive. 'He's just absolutely terrified of teaching.'

'What's Wally short for?'

'What's he short for?'

'His name. Is it Walter? Quite old-fashioned.'

'He's called Duncan. It's just that the students started calling him Wally and it . . . sort of caught on.'

2

'This Sunday?'

'Yes.'

'Will it take *all* day?'

'Just the afternoon. I thought that maybe you and the girls might like to come along and watch.'

Helen snorted. She had been even less thrilled about Clive giving up his one day off than he was, and unimpressed by his impassioned defence that he had been forced into it. Clive chewed his supper and tried another tack.

'It works well cold, doesn't it? Lamb? With the ratatouille?'

Helen poured them each a second glass of wine and then sat down again. They had stopped eating at the same time as their daughters a few weeks ago. Clive came home from school after seven o'clock most nights, and Sarah and Katie were ravenous by five. Besides, Helen felt, this meant that she and her husband were more likely to spend some time alone together each day.

'You did go up and see the girls when you got in, didn't you?' Helen asked.

'Of course. They're reading. Said they'd turn their own lights out.'

'I'll go up in a bit. Make sure they have. You can tell them that you're not going to be around on Sunday though.'

'Look, I'm sorry. One more week after Sunday and then it's half-term.'

'For which we have no plans.'

'I'll think of something. I said I would. Wouldn't you all like to come down to the match? For a bit?'

'I was planning a picnic. The gardens are open at Telling-thorpe. The Frasers usually put in an appearance.'

'The Frasers?'

'The Frasers own the house, Clive.'

'And do we know them?'

'Well, no. But it would be nice to. We might all get on.'

'I hardly think a pair of aristocrats will have any interest in some teacher and a part-time—'

'Frampton's a very prestigious school, Clive. Don't do yourself down.'

'Right. Why don't you have the picnic at the match?'

'We could do. But only so the girls actually get to see you. And so that I can.'

Clive took a sip of his wine and swallowed another forkful of ratatouille. The coldness of the lamb only served to underline just how hot the ratatouille was.

'I don't *want* to play, Helen. I've been pressured into it. Honestly.'

Helen looked at her husband and tried to work out how he'd let himself get into this position. Did he secretly want to play?

'Is playing for the staff cricket team the sort of thing that might earn you a promotion?' she asked.

'No.'

'Then why on earth are you doing it?'

'I told bloody Dixon that I could possibly play, and then he told the head that I was definitely playing, and then the head told everyone in morning break.'

'I think you'd really like Tellingthorpe.'

'I'm not sure that if I have one day off I necessarily want to spend it haring around the gardens of a country house in the hope of meeting some aristocrats who may or may not like us.'

'Clive, don't be ridiculous. We'd be going there to spend time together. For you to spend time with the girls. It's about doing things as a family. We like spending time with you.'

'I see.'

'And if we happened to bump into the Frasers, that would just be a little bonus. You should feign an injury.'

'And then turn up at school with a limp on Monday?'

Helen smiled at him. 'Yes. Or I'll put your arm in a sling if you like. The council have sent me on endless first aid courses. I'm sure I could.'

Clive still looked depressed, so Helen said, 'Maybe it's good for you to show a bit of willing.'

'It's not being willing. It's basically conscription.'

'The headmaster knows you'd be doing it. So that's good. I've told you before, he undervalues you. I'd like that to change. I'm sure you would, too.'

'He spoke to me today as if I was some sort of competition winner.'

'What does he know? He doesn't even know how to dress like a headmaster. Looks like a hedge fund manager.'

'I'm not bothered about how he dresses.'

'These things are important, Clive—'

'I'm bothered about how he treats people. And . . .' Here Clive suddenly became so animated that he had to put his fork and glass down so that he could really point and gesticulate. '. . . *And* they've just appointed a new history teacher without even telling me. I didn't even know they'd advertised a position.'

'Why? Who's leaving?'

'No one, apparently. The department's just growing. Don't you think they should have told people?'

'Did they tell the others?'

'Frobisher didn't know anything about it. Rogers said he thought he remembered it being discussed as a possibility.'

'So it's not personal then. I do like that you all refer to each other by your surnames.'

Clive thought about this. 'We do, I suppose. It's just habit now. As if we're all suspended in time. But then the entire private education system *is* suspended in time. We didn't used to do that at Uxbridge.'

It always amazed Helen how nostalgic Clive was about Uxbridge. He had been so stressed there that she had worried about him constantly. The problems there had seemed so much greater than those at Frampton.

'Anyway,' said Clive, 'how was your day? How are the offices of Frampton Council? Presumably the whole building shakes with the relentless march of progress?'

Helen smiled at this. 'Well, we've just got a defibrillator. And we call each other by our first names. And even more excitingly, we're not expected to turn up to things on a Sunday. They should give you a night off in lieu. Couldn't someone else wander around the boarding house making sure that people are doing homework?'

'We call it prep.'

'It doesn't matter what it's called. Couldn't someone lesser be supervising it?'

'There's an enormous discrepancy between the regard in which you think I should be held and the regard in which I am actually held.'

'Well, there shouldn't be. And there won't be. I'll see to it.'

'How?'

'I just will. Perhaps I'll corner a few people at this match. Lay on some charm.'

'You don't need to launch an offensive, but do come. It'll be nice weather. And it will be a chance to catch up with some of the teachers that you've not seen for a while.'

'It will be a chance to have Iain Dixon smiling at my chest.'

Helen knew that she was right. Not just about Iain Dixon's barely concealed lust for all women, but about the school too. Clive should have been held in higher regard by them. She saw how hard they made him work. And she knew that he felt compromised simply by working there in the first place. Despite having been privately educated himself, he and all his contemporaries at teacher training had pledged allegiance to the comprehensive system. Then they all qualified and many of them immediately found that their ideals collided with reality. One by one they started dropping out of state schools and applying for cosier jobs at schools with large grounds and libraries and cricket pitches and smaller classrooms. Teaching the entitled just seemed easier than teaching the disillusioned and the uninterested. It was a source of great pride to Helen that Clive had been the last to succumb. He had done six years at the Uxbridge comprehensive, but it had felt like twelve. All around him his colleagues had been dropping like flies: stress, depression, anxiety. And they could barely afford to live. They had already had Sarah, Katie was on the way. Finally Helen had tried to persuade him that his principles were getting in the way of security, comfort and strong mental health. She left educational supplements lying open on the kitchen table with various advertisements for teaching positions circled in red pen. Clive eventually took the hint. He started reading about history posts at the sort of schools he really hoped that he had left behind and would never see again: ancient establishments in small market towns in green-sounding counties, with pupils in school scarves scurrying to and from lessons to the sound of a striking bell, teachers in academic wear, buttresses, quads, bicycles with wicker baskets, the sound of clarinets and cellos from upstairs windows. Wouldn't this be a nicer world for the girls to grow up in? Helen asked.

For a month Clive called in sick and drove all over England and Wales for interviews. He drove for miles. He soon realised that he liked being on the road and out of school. When he was behind the wheel of a car he felt free. He was driving through parts of the country he'd never been to, to towns he'd never heard of. He was eating in strange pubs. Smoking in lay-bys. It was as if Helen had ordered him to take a sabbatical. He wasn't trying to shout down forty fifteen-year-olds. He would have been happy just going to job interviews like this for ever, he thought. Which was just as well, because the interviews certainly weren't resulting in any job offers. Some schools sent him letters kindly explaining about the unusually high standards of the applicants; others he never heard from again.

But then suddenly along came a letter from Frampton. At first he hadn't been able to remember which one Frampton even was. They had all been so similar. Cheshire? Devon? He had had to study the AA map. Wiltshire. That was it. He had eaten a pub lunch in Hungerford, been kept waiting for three-quarters of an hour and then the interview only lasted ten minutes. He'd declined the offer of a tour of the school; he would have already seen it all before. It would probably be fine. They would all have probably been fine. But it was Frampton who actually wanted him. So they turned up in August with one daughter in the back seat, another in the womb and a new life to begin. A 300-year-old school in the middle of a small market town. Helen was delirious. Clive, dizzy with change, was happy too.

But all that was eight years ago. In London, Clive had taught history from Monday to Friday and, tough though it had been, that was that. Frampton, though, was a boarding school. There were 800 pupils. All boys. The timetable covered the day from seven in the morning until nine o'clock at night. There were lessons on Saturdays. There were clubs

and societies. Teachers had to be attached to a boarding
house and spend an evening a week on duty. Teachers who
were good at sport had to teach sport. Teachers who were
bad at sport had to supervise the boys who were bad at
sport. Boys needed to be taken on outings. Teachers had
to drive minibuses to take boys to sports matches, theatres,
concerts. It was all-consuming. But boys needed to be kept
busy, their parents had to be kept happy and the school
needed things to boast about in its magazine: good A levels,
successful sports sides, garlanded musicians. Helen thought
that she'd persuaded Clive to take a peachy job in a rural
idyll, but Clive now behaved as if he was stuck in a cross
between an academic hothouse and a sausage factory.

As Clive had been tasked with more and more pastoral
responsibilities, Helen had at first encouraged him. But now
it had become increasingly clear to Helen that these additional assignments weren't getting Clive anywhere and only
made him miserable. She was always asking why he didn't
say no to things when he was asked if he could do them.
Sympathy gave way to resentment. And, in turn, resentment
could give way to anger. She despaired of how Clive always
responded to being asked if he could do something as if it
was a direct order to do it.

'Why can't you be more like Wally?' she once asked him.

'Divorced and frightened?' Clive asked. Being more like
Wally was exactly what he didn't want.

'Wally says no to things,' Helen said.

This much was true. Wally would be asked if he could do
something and reply that he couldn't on grounds of ability
or suitability or, more often, because he needed to get home
and let his dogs out. Still, he seemed a strange sort of hero.

Clive got up to clear the plates.

'I'll do that,' said Helen. 'You go up and see the girls
again.'

Out in the hallway, the girls' schoolbags were all packed at the foot of the stairs, ready for the next day. Next to them, Clive's battered leather briefcase looked somehow oafish. He stepped over the bags and went up to the girls' room to find the bedside lights on but both girls fast asleep in Sarah's bed, Katie snuggled up against her older sister. Katie's night-time reading book was still open in Sarah's hand. Clive carefully slipped it out, replaced the bookmark and then put the book on Katie's bedside table. He peeled back Katie's duvet in readiness for transporting her sleeping form. It was harder to peel back Sarah's duvet to get Katie out, because Sarah liked to pull it up around her shoulders and trap the edge under her armpit. Despite the peaceful look on her face, her arms were clamped into position and it was a struggle to prise it from her. But if he left them in the same bed, they'd both be bound to wake. And if Katie ever woke in the night, it meant that her parents would also be woken by the sound of their bedroom door slowly scraping over the rough carpet. Then Katie would wriggle into the middle of their bed and that night's sleep would effectively be over. Somehow Clive managed to scoop up Katie and carry her, his knees bent, across to her bed and lay her down. That was always when he felt the weight: not picking them up but putting them down. Even Katie was almost too heavy to carry far now. He gave her a little kiss on the temple and then looked at her light-brown hair splayed out across the pillow. She gave a little grunt. Then he pulled Sarah's duvet back over her, and she stirred a little and pulled it back into place under her arm. He kissed her too. Then he turned out both lights, stepped noiselessly from the room, and returned to the kitchen and Helen.

'More wine?' he asked her.

'I'd better not.'

'Do you want to do anything this evening?'

'I want to have a bath.'

Clive went upstairs, brushed his teeth and slipped into bed. By the time Helen had come back from her bath, he too was lying asleep with an open book on the pillow next to him.

3

Clive was out of the front door by quarter past seven the next day. The others were yet to stir. He had to be on duty in the refectory by twenty past but it was only a short walk. He pulled back the front gate and turned left. A further frustration of living this close to school was that it meant he was the first to be called upon if someone was late or hadn't shown up. Last week he'd been called from his supper to do evening duty in the place of someone who had hay fever. When they first arrived it had seemed an advantage to be so close to work and not to have to thread his way through the Uxbridge morning traffic. Wally lived nowhere near the school, probably a twenty-minute drive out of Frampton in a little village with a pub that did food, and plenty of woodland where he could walk his mastiffs. *He* never had to do refectory duty.

The row of Victorian terraced houses Clive walked past were mostly still dark, although a few commuters were walking the other way, towards the train station. How early must they have had to get up? They always looked immaculate. Nice suits, light summer overcoats, hair brushed and dried. Clive's was still wet from the shower, the occasional drop landing on his neck as he scurried across the street that divided his block from the one that was taken up by the school. He could see its vast stone frontage now: a high stone wall with battlements and Frampton's name and motto inscribed over the grand archway. A few uniformed boys and the odd teacher soon appeared. There were two boarding houses on the main school site, including the one that Clive was attached to, but a further six were dotted around that end of the town. Breakfast was served from twenty-five past seven until five past eight precisely, but some pupils – especially the ones from overseas – arrived early, perhaps because they were eager to get away from the often unsympathetic atmosphere of the boarding houses.

'Morning, Sir.'

'Morning.'

Clive didn't remember being chirpy when he was fourteen but a lot of the boys habitually were. They'd had the best part of the academic year to conquer their homesickness, he supposed. As he turned into the arch there came a honk from behind. Iain Dixon's ludicrous old Mercedes was also turning in, sending the boys scattering.

Iain braked and wound down his window.

'Morning, Clive. Sunday's weather's looking really splendid.'

'Are you on duty?' asked Clive. 'Have I got my day wrong?'

'I'm just here to get a good parking space. Going to walk into town and have breakfast at a café. Great news you're joining us on Sunday.'

Iain wound up his window again and drove off into the quad. An hour to himself in a café sounded dreamy, thought Clive. And it would be an experience entirely wasted on Iain, who could spend as much of his life being solitary as he pleased. A few children began to run around the quad to the refectory on the other side, but Clive hollered to them. 'Breakfast doesn't start until twenty-five past! And no running in the quad!'

No running in the quad. What a ridiculous phrase that would have seemed to him ten years ago, and now here he was barking it at people outside a buttressed chapel. He might as well have been bellowing at them to keep off the grass or mind out for the geraniums. As he passed the side door to the chapel, it suddenly swung open to reveal the chaplain standing there, blinking into the light.

'Morning, Mark! You been in there overnight?'

'Yes. I've been kicked out by my wife. Had to snuggle down in a pile of vestments.'

'I see.'

Mark Taylor, an achingly relaxed bachelor in his late forties, was dressed in a white T-shirt and a pair of tracksuit bottoms adorned with the name of his Oxford college down one leg.

'I had to get up early and do some bloody admin,' he explained. 'Marking. Photocopying. All the balls I got into this game to avoid. You playing in this cricket match?'

'Reluctantly. You?'

'Yes.'

'Well, that's a relief.'

When he had first arrived at Frampton, Clive, who generally found all church people sinister, had been suspicious of Mark. He didn't seem to say much in the staffroom, and Clive had mistaken his languor for diffidence. One morning break, though, the headmaster had been five minutes into a quite unwarranted discourse about 'the uniqueness of the Frampton Character' when Clive had looked up to see the chaplain mouthing the word 'Christ' and rolling his eyes. Clive then stifled a laugh loud enough to catch the headmaster's attention, and when the headmaster started up again, the chaplain began to mime vigorously sawing at his own wrists before snapping straight into a look of benign fascination.

'I've seen a lot of grand, tedious sermonisers in my time but that man really is the apotheosis of the oeuvre,' he told Clive over a drink that night.

'Some people say he means well,' said Clive.

'Ye-e-e-es,' said Mark, uncertainly. 'That's what people generally say about people who are completely lacking in self-awareness. Do you need another?'

They had become regular drinking companions from that day on, and Mark often came round to his and Helen's home. He never mentioned religion unless somebody else brought it up and, though his sexual orientation and history were unclear, he was completely insouciant about Helen's attempts to pair him up with a number of local divorcees. These matchmaking endeavours had included a council administrator who still seemed incredibly raw about her recent marital collapse, and who had drunk so incredibly heavily that Helen had asked Mark to walk her home while the main course was still on the table. Mark had attempted to do so, only for the lady in question to insist that he walked her to the home of her soon to be ex-husband, after which Mark returned to the dinner table and announced that if anything was going to happen between the two of them, it was probably still a bit early.

'I'm glad you're playing too,' said Clive. 'I'm really not looking forward to it.'

'It'll be fine.'

'Yes, but you can play a bit.'

'Well, I'm all right,' said the man who had once kept wicket for Worcestershire seconds. 'But it's been a while.'

'It's the fielding I hate.'

'We'll get it out of the way quickly and then there'll be a barbecue or something. You'll have to put up with Iain telling you what to do for an afternoon first, of course, but then we can have some fun.'

'Helen's not pleased.'

Mark looked at his watch.

'You on breakfast duty?' he asked.

'Yes.'

'Again?'

'Again indeed.'

'Well, I'll come and join you in a bit. Just have to go and change into my dog collar. Crouch doesn't like me wandering about like this.'

Mark jogged off towards his cottage, and Clive carried on around the quad towards the refectory, where a queue of boys had already formed. Clive walked past them, nodding politely in response to a few of the 'Morning, Sir's that came his way, then headed through the double doors, down a tiled corridor and into the serving area, where some of the kitchen staff were wheeling the last of the racks of trays into place. The brightly lit counters were piled high with eggs and bacon and hash browns, and there were vast mountains of toast that would soon be soggy with the steam that rose from the huge catering warmers on which they were piled.

The head of catering popped his head out of a door and flashed Clive his bright butcher's grin.

'Morning, Mr Hapgood!'

'David.'

'You again, is it?'

'Me again, I'm afraid. You all ready?'

'It's a bit early but yes, we're good and ready. You can go and let the animals in.'

'Thanks, David.'

Clive walked back down the corridor and held open one of the double doors to let the boys in, then nipped back down to the service area to get to the coffee machine.

Unfortunately a tall boy with black hair and a pockmarked neck had got there first and Clive waited in line behind him as the machine whirred and puffed before eventually dispensing the boy's drink. But when it had done so, the boy simply put the cup on a tray next to him and then placed another empty cup under the machine. When this drink had been delivered, he began the process again.

'Excuse me,' said Clive. 'How many drinks are you getting?'

The boy turned around.

'Oh, sorry, Sir.'

Clive recognised him now. Davies. Clive had taught him history once but he'd be doing his A levels now. The machine dispensed another drink, and Clive saw that Davies already had another empty cup lined up.

'How thirsty are you?'

I'm getting drinks for my whole table, Sir. There are six of us.'

'It's just that there's a queue,' said Clive, indicating himself.

'Well, that's the point of our system, Sir. It's to avoid queuing.'

'OK. Fine. Carry on.'

When Davies had departed with his tray of cups, Clive finally had a chance to put his own cup under the machine. There was now a long queue behind him, but once his drink had been forcibly dispensed he found himself sliding a second cup under the machine and pressing the button for another milky coffee.

'Sorry,' he said to the boy behind him. 'Saves queuing.'

*

The redbrick refectory building – the gift of a benefactor on the occasion of some centenary or other, which presumably serendipitously coincided with someone's sudden need to register a tax loss – was far too young to blend into its surroundings and yet already old enough to be no longer fit for purpose. The school had doubled in size since it was built, and thus its capacity was insufficient. There were only one hundred and eighty tables and so the times that the inhabitants of different boarding houses could eat had to be staggered. Large queues formed outside and in. Clive often marvelled at how a building with so many windows could possibly be so dark. He found eating there to be unendurable, not least because once he had food on his tray came the agony of not knowing where to sit. There was a stage at one end with a long table on it, which was intended for staff to dine at, but it was generally only used at lunch or supper and Clive would have felt silly going up there and sitting down on his own. Sometimes it could be fun to sit down with a few of the boys, but only if invited, which hadn't happened today. Instead he took up position in a corner with his twin cups of coffee, but they were still too hot and had become a ludicrous impediment. He raised one to his lips and blew on it to try and cool it down, then took a small but nevertheless agonising sip.

It was rare that anything happened at breakfast, but it was necessary to be there in case something did. As breakfast wore on the clamour grew louder and louder, but not to the point where one could have reasonably requested them to be quiet. It was just white noise, the soundtrack to him having to be up an hour early in order to impassively observe nearly 200 upper-middle-class teenagers all eating at once.

He decided to get some toast, possibly jettisoning the ridiculous extra cup of coffee on the way, and so began walking back along the side of the stage towards the entrance to the serving area. As he did so he saw a small boy come wobbling through the entrance carrying a tray piled far higher than it ought sensibly to have been. Some boys really were unlucky, he thought. Lots of children arrived at the school with their voices already broken and growth spurts well underway. Others, like this one, arrived in an obviously still prepubescent state and stayed that way for much of their first year, sticking out like sore thumbs, partly because of their diminutive statures – their blazers too long at the sleeve, their over-large uniform trousers flapping about at their heels and constantly needing to be pulled up at the waist – but also because of their shrill voices and an innocent gloss to their skin and hair that adolescence had yet to take the sheen off. Clive recognised instantly that here was the sort of boy who attracted rough and unhelpful behaviour like a magnet. Frampton was one of those schools that insisted to its parents that it had no problem with bullying whatsoever, but the only sense in which this was really true was that it was institutionally tolerated. Big people were cruel to small people. Sporty people were cruel to unsporty people. Even people who were only reasonably intelligent could be cruel to dim people. This was generally looked upon by those whose job it should have been to stamp out such behaviour as Darwinism manifest.

One of the headmaster's innovations a couple of years ago was to insist that the school developed a bullying policy.

'There isn't a problem with bullying,' he had told his staff. 'But it might be worth putting a structure in place so that in the event of any instances of bullying coming to light, completely out of the blue, then the school will be in a position to deal effectively with those responsible and sympathetically with those who are the victims. We will be protecting both them and ourselves.'

Everybody in the staffroom that morning break had nodded earnestly and gone back to their coffee. Then two days later the headmaster announced that he had asked Richard Crawford DipEd (Physical Education) to front the 'bullying task force'. Crawford's expertise in this department was mainly as an exponent. He made skinny boys do shuttle runs until they were sick, and he called the over-weight boys 'Fatty'. Now he had the chance to pull more pupils, and indeed the occasional staff member, to one side and give them a rollicking, to let them know that he was onto them. 'How would you like it if someone did that to you? Eh?' he'd scream at people, his face inches from theirs, his hand having found its way instinctively to their collar to clutch it in a tight grip.

But Richard Crawford DipEd (Physical Education), like all men who appear strong, had a weakness. In his case, he liked stopping girls from the nearby comprehensive in the street and chatting to them. Sometimes they'd go to cafés with him and chat there. About all kinds of things. And sometimes their fathers, who didn't care how big and strong he thought he was, would knock on his front door and quietly ask him just what the fuck he thought was going on. Word got back to the school. We should hold an internal investigation, the school said. We should call the police, the fathers said. Look, the school reasoned, the last thing anybody needs in a situation like this is any kind of fuss. Fuss, the fathers said, would be just the beginning. The threat of police involvement hung over Crawford for just too long. One morning he took himself off to the sports fields and when he came back, he and his tracksuit were covered in mud and he couldn't stop crying. Once his eyes were dried and his tracksuit had been laundered, he was encouraged to apply for a job in a completely different part of the country, armed with exemplary references. Crawford headed off to the north-east and the Frampton College Bullying Policy Task Force was dissolved.

And all this was just one of the reasons why Clive became so cross when he realised that this small boy's tray was so ridiculously overburdened because bigger boys kept dashing up to him and piling more items of crockery and cutlery onto it. He was still a good twenty feet from the boy when he saw another pupil approach him from behind and place two full cups of hot drink on the tray, on top of an upturned and already precarious plate.

'Oi!' Clive shouted. 'Stop that!'

The guilty pupil sniggered and ran off, to be rewarded with high fives and claps. Clive rushed towards the boy to help but, with a cup of coffee in each hand, was unable to offer meaningful assistance. The weight of the tray became too much. The mound of crockery and glassware began to slip as the boy lost his grip, and then the entire lot hit the floor with an almighty crash. Much of it broke or shattered instantly. A plate fell, spinning, hit the floor and continued to spin on its rim as the boy slumped, reddened and humiliated, to his knees. The room fell silent for a moment, the only sound in the room that of the plate slowly circling on the tiled floor.

There was, in the refectory at Frampton, a traditional response to the sound of a plate hitting the tiled floor and spinning. The moment that sound reached the ears of the boys they would hush entirely until only the noise of the plate could be heard, and would wait, however long it took, for it to stop. When it did they would begin to make an 'ooh' sound. It would start quietly and then gradually become louder as the 'ooh' slid up the scale, singing in unison until at last they reached the magic, optimal note at which point they would, as one, bellow the word 'wanker'. The unfortunate person who had dropped the plate would have to absorb their blithe holler, sometimes looking amused, sometimes looking glum, and always looking embarrassed. It was a test. Those who managed to laugh it off were respected and those who were crushed by it were mocked. Whenever the headmaster made his preposterous remarks about the Frampton Character, this was the sort of behaviour that Clive always thought of. Even if it happened at lunch-time, when the place was full of teachers, no action was ever taken. The entire building would have had to be disciplined. Instead it was just accepted by the staff. Decent, civilised members of staff, people that Clive would chat to about normal, sensible things, would just sit it out and look on with a wry detachment.

Clive had been in the room hundreds of times when this had happened, but he had never before been standing so close to the subject of this ritual. The student in question just looked ashen. Why should this poor boy be expected to laugh it off? And why should Clive just stand by and accept it? He simply wasn't going to. The chatter in the room started up again but Clive, who found himself standing next to the steps up onto the stage, clambered up them and set down his two still scaldingly hot coffee cups on the edge of the staff dining table. There was a gong next to the table, and Clive picked up the mallet that leant against it and began striking the gong. The striking of the gong was always a symbol that an announcement was going to be made to those dining, and so the room hushed once more. But silence wasn't what Clive wanted to achieve; he wanted to show he was angry. He struck the gong a second time, then a third and a fourth and a fifth. He kept on striking it until every eye in the place was on him, by which time he had struck it ten times. Then he hit it five times more in rapid succession, before slamming down the mallet and marching to the front and centre of the stage.

'What in the name of hell do you think you are all *doing*?' he asked them.

Hundreds of wide eyes looked back at him.

'Hmm? What the hell do you think you're doing? Why do you all do this? Why?'

Still the eyes stared.

'I'll tell you why. It's because some of you are just dis-respectful. That's why. Mindlessly disrespectful. This boy hasn't done anything wrong. He's had an accident.'

Clive ignored the titters here.

'And he's had it because of you. I saw people piling stuff on his tray. I saw who you were and I know your names.'

In fact, Clive had only seen one of the perpetrators and wasn't entirely sure he'd recognise him again, but he was on a roll now.

'Your parents pay a lot of money for you to come to this school because they believe – ridiculously in some cases – that it is money well spent, that by coming here you'll get some sort of advantage in life. They believe that you'll get some sort of head start, and then be able to spend the rest of your life lording it over other people. Well, if you want to lord it over other people – and some of you so clearly do – then you need to earn that right. Shouting at someone like that – what the bloody hell's that supposed to achieve? Does it show that you're a better person purely because you've not suffered the misfortune of being badly treated?'

By this point more boys had come into breakfast car-rying trays and were all standing numbly by the doorway, wondering what on earth they were interrupting.

'No, I'll tell you what it shows. It shows that you are severely lacking in compassion. In empathy. In kindness. And it shows something else too. The fact that you *all* shouted shows that some of you are simply not able to think for yourselves. Just because the person next to you joins in with this sort of behaviour, does that mean that you should? Of course it doesn't. But you do it anyway. Because you don't have the wherewithal, the guts, to make your own mind up about things. Some of you who shouted out then were being true to yourselves. That's the way you've always been happy to behave and probably always will. You're like that instinctively. Probably brought up to behave that way, some of you. But some of you aren't like that at all. Some of you wouldn't normally behave like that. And you – you're the ones I'm really angry with. The people who are pretending to be something they're not just because they want to be part of something and are afraid to be different. You're the ones who can change. Of all the people in life to copy, why choose the loud, mindless idiots? When you're allowed to be different? When you can choose to be better people?'

The boy who had dropped the tray was now quietly picking up the cups and bits of broken plates with the help of one of the kitchen staff. During the last few lines of Clive's speech, Mark Taylor – now attired in a suit and dog collar – had entered the room by the door next to the conveyor belt for the trays and slowly made his way onto the stage via the steps at the other end in a gesture of solidarity. Clive, having started this impromptu critique, was not quite sure how it should now end.

'Don't just mindlessly join in with all that rubbish like a load of . . .' What could he say? Robots? Nazis? No, no, no. '. . . a load of *sheep*.' No, that didn't sound strong enough. 'Or Nazis. Like robotic Nazis.'

Clive still wasn't quite sure he had found the right tone, but thought it best to move on.

'I have been teaching for quite a few years now, and I can tell you this: none of the loud people have come to anything. Ever.'

'You're talking quite loudly,' came a voice from one of the tables at the back, although Clive couldn't pick out which one.

'That is as maybe,' said Clive.

Mark, correctly sensing that Clive was now floundering somewhat on the stump, spoke up.

'Mr Hapgood is quite right. Think on. And now get on with your breakfast.'

The boys started to talk amongst themselves again, largely, Clive rightly imagined, about him. He suddenly felt drained, a feeling that always descended on him after a tantrum, and he sat down on the nearest chair. Mark came up to his end of the table and joined him.

'Well then,' he said as he sat down. He pointed at the coffees. 'One of these for me?'

'Absolutely,' said Clive.

They both sipped in silence.

'That was pretty strong stuff,' said Mark. 'Are you OK?'

*

Twenty minutes later, the boys who had been in the room during Clive's outburst had all left, and he and Mark were now sitting at the staff table with a hall full of completely different boys sitting below them. Mark had fetched them each a second excruciatingly hot coffee.

'Excuse me, Sir?'

Clive looked to his right and saw that the diminutive victim of the earlier loutishness was standing at his elbow. So small and slight was the boy that he had made it up the stairs and across the stage without Clive or Mark even noticing.

'Hello,' said Clive. 'Are you all right?'

The boy nodded back at Clive. 'I'll be fine,' he said. His eyes were moist at the corners but he was doing his best to look valiant. 'I just wanted to say thank you, Sir.'

'Ah,' said Clive. 'I was worried that I might have made it worse.'

'Three people have already come up and said sorry to me, so I don't think so. Thank you.'

'My pleasure,' said Clive. 'Er . . . I'm so sorry, I've forgotten your name.'

'Findlay, isn't it?' said Mark. 'Jonathan Findlay?'

'That's right,' said the boy.

He put out his hand and Clive shook it.

'Good to meet you, Findlay. And if anyone else gives you any trouble, you come and find me, OK?'

'Yes, Sir. Thank you, Sir.'

Findlay made his way back down the steps and towards the doors.

'How on earth,' said Clive, 'could someone send a child so small and delicate as that to a place like this?'

'Like the wings of a butterfly,' said Mark.

4

At the end of breakfast Clive took himself next door to the staffroom. Sometimes there was some bread by the little toaster in there. And sometimes by the toaster was little Wally Davis. Despite living the furthest away of all members of staff and never being on breakfast duty, he was often the first to arrive. Clive thought that Wally could only cope with the staffroom when it was empty of nearly all others.

'Ah, you're in early,' said Wally, as Clive strode into the room.

'Refectory duty. Any toast?'

'There's a few slices left in the bag, I think. I just had a couple of pieces with marmalade.'

'There's marmalade?' asked Clive.

'Oh. Well . . .' Wally looked a little sheepish now. 'I, er, bring my own in. You can have some if you like. It's Tiptree.'

He reached into one of the side pockets of his heavy tweed jacket and held up a miniature pot like a specimen jar. 'I get them when I stay in hotels.'

'You stay in hotels a lot, do you?' asked Clive, in surprise. Perhaps Wally went to hotels with ladies.

'Only when I go to see my mother. She's in a residential home in Poole. There's a little hotel I stay in. It's not much. But they let you bring dogs. And the breakfasts are good.'

The thought of the marmalade's flight from the sad and dog-filled breakfast room put Clive off.

'It's all right. I'll just have margarine.'

Wally placed the little pot in his opposite pocket with his other hand, catching his injured fingers as he did so.

'Oh damn. Bloody thing.'

'Oh yes. How's your hand?'

Wally held it up. The first two fingers were bound with a prodigious quantity of bandage. 'Still very sore. I've put a lot of cream on it. The bandage is there as a precaution really. Had to hold both dog leads in the one hand when I took them out.'

Clive located the bread by the toaster and popped two slices in. 'What time do you get up, Wally?'

'Six. For the dogs, you see. I try to give them a good hour. Then another hour when I get home. Good way to unwind, isn't? I feel bad leaving them at home. They can look terribly plaintive.'

Clive nudged the dial on the toaster, which seemed to have stopped turning.

Wally let out a tortured sigh. 'I've got the lower sixth again,' he said. 'First bloody thing.'

'What's wrong with yours? Mine are just a bit noisy.'

'Mine are frankly unnerving. There's something going on under the surface. Yesterday they asked me where I got my socks from.'

'And what did you say?'

'I said that it wasn't any of their business where I get my socks from. But they made it pretty clear that they weren't going to do any work until I'd told them. So I told them that they were a Christmas present from my mother and then they all laughed at me. One of them said, "Does she comb your hair as well?"'

Clive laughed.

'Why are you laughing?'

'It's just that socks are a funny thing to get as a present, I suppose.'

'What's funny about socks?'

'Well, you know. As a present. Socks are something you'd buy for somebody when you didn't know what else to get them. She is . . . compos mentis, isn't she?'

'She's completely compos mentis, thank you. It's me that's mentally degenerative.'

'That's working here, probably.'

'She's never really got over my divorce, sadly. We're very close. And she knows that I get through socks.'

'It's probably all the dog walking,' said Clive.

Wally sat down in an armchair. 'I wonder what they'll ask me today?' he said. 'What washing powder I use?'

'What sort of washing powder do you use?'

'Non-biological. Other kind makes me flare up.'

'Do you ever get cross, Wally? With people? To their faces?'

'I get frustrated, but I try not to show it.'

Clive gave up waiting for the toast to brown, took it out and went and sat down next to Wally.

'I got cross just now.'

'At home? Why? I always think you must have a lovely life. Helen. The girls. Jane never wanted children.'

'At breakfast. When they all shouted "wanker".'

'I've had that done to me. Nobody did a thing.'

'I just lost it. I stood up and shouted at them.'

'At the boys who did it?'

'At everyone.'

'And how did it feel?'

'It felt . . . *embarrassing*, I suppose. And Mark was there. He saw it. Looked as baffled as the boys.'

'I'd love to be like Mark,' said Wally. 'He's so calm. What do you make of that Flora?'

'She seems nice. I wouldn't have minded knowing that she'd been appointed. I mean, wouldn't you expect to be told if there was going to be someone new in your department?'

'Nobody ever tells me anything,' said Wally, with eyes like glass.

As Wally slipped ever further into dread at the prospect of facing down the lower sixth, Clive continued to munch on his breakfast. The bread was barely toasted enough for there to be any sound of crunching as he bit into it, but Wally occasionally broke the silence with his little sighs that bordered on whimpers.

*

'You seemed quite cross this morning, Sir,' said a fourth former called Jones in Clive's last period before break.

'I was cross,' said Clive. 'I don't like that behaviour and I'm in a position to do something about it.'

'Why don't you just go along with it, Sir? Everybody else does.'

Clive said, 'We've just spent the last fifteen minutes discussing Rosa Parks and the influence of her actions on the American Civil Rights cause and you ask me, "Why don't you just go along with it?"'

'It's hardly the same, Sir,' said an inane boy called Mason, who wore expensive glasses and fancied himself as something of a professorial character. 'Rosa Parks was standing up for something.'

'I know it's not the same,' Clive said. 'The whole point about Rosa Parks, Mason, is that she didn't stand up. She refused to. Shall we continue?'

'Are you still angry?' asked Jones.

'No. I'm very happy. What could be more delightful than spending my last period before morning break teaching a class as bright and talented as yourselves? I can hardly believe my luck.'

*

41

The staffroom during Friday morning break was generally subdued, as they all still had to get up and come to work the next day. Saturday's break, by contrast, would be tinged with elation. Clive had managed to get the first cup of coffee from the machine and first dibs on the newspaper. Wally came over, looking relieved.

'They were all right, actually,' he said, squeezing into the chair next to Clive's. 'No silly questions about socks.'

Across the room Mark was deep in conversation with Iain, presumably about Sunday's cricket match.

'You've not been roped into this cricket match, have you?' Clive asked.

'No. Wouldn't mind being asked though.'

'Would you play?'

'I can't give up a Sunday. The dogs would go spare.'

'Why don't you bring them along? There's talk of a barbecue.'

'Mmm. I'd rather just have the day away from this place, I think. And I couldn't guarantee that the dogs would behave. If they see a ball, they always try and chase it, and the smell of meat makes them go a little loopy. I think we'll just head into the woods and have a bit of a sniff around. Oh God.'

The headmaster had cleared his throat to signal the commencement of his daily oration. Despite the fact that everyone was quietening down, he banged his teaspoon on the rim of his coffee cup anyway.

'Thank you, everyone. Not too many notices today, you may be relieved to hear. Mrs Jones is taking twelve members of the lower sixth to Stratford tomorrow afternoon for a matinée *performance* of *Hamlet*, so there will be some absences from sport. Speaking of which, another reminder about Sunday's game. There are still some *places* up for grabs, I understand. Is that correct, Mr Dixon?'

'Just one,' said Iain.

'Well,' said the headmaster. 'Somebody had better volunteer. I wouldn't want to have to forcibly coerce anybody!'

Wally stirred uneasily and sank lower into his chair.
Mercifully, Mrs Jones herself had just arrived late to break
and was now blocking the sightline between Wally and the
headmaster.

'And hopefully some of you who aren't *playing* will be
able to turn up and support our side. Ah, a latecomer,' said
the headmaster. 'I can't imagine what could *possibly* keep
you from your morning coffee, Mrs Jones. I have just made
mention of your trip tomorrow. I trust everything is sorted?'

'Yes, Headmaster. All sorted.'

Mrs Jones sounded a little flustered. She was normally
a quite breathless individual, but today there was something even more panicked about her. She was a short and
robust-looking woman who tended towards brightly coloured
clothes, usually matching, and worn with an accompanying
silk scarf. Sometimes she wore a shade of lipstick that matched
her skirt and jacket, and she always wore leather high-heeled
shoes that made a terrific sound as she bustled about the
place. Today she was in subdued turquoise. Though she could
be a more formidable figure than her breathlessness implied,
her nose would run when she was particularly stressed.
She was dabbing forcibly at it now with a paper tissue.

'Wonderful. Well, do have a good time. Actually, speaking of which, there is one more thing: school trips. Various
boys, or rather their *parents*, are taking rather a long time
to fill in their *permission* slips regarding travelling to abodes
other than their own over the half-term holiday and I wonder
if . . .'

Clive took advantage of the cover provided by Mrs Jones
to return to his newspaper as the headmaster droned on. He
had already read the front page and so peeled it open at a

random page as quietly as he could manage. Years of discreetly reading the newspaper while at various school events had stood him in good stead. He started to read a comment piece reflecting on the upcoming first anniversary of Hong Kong being returned to the People's Republic of China. Had this been a success? Clive liked his history a bit older. Easier to make a judgement. He had to teach Vietnam and that seemed a bit recent. Far better to get your head down and wait for a few centuries to pass. Much like the school had done. He read on. Citizens of Hong Kong still had to apply for travel permits in order to visit mainland China. What kind of atmosphere was such a policy going to—

'Clive?'

Clive suddenly came to.

'Is Mr Hapgood actually here? I'm sure I saw him when I first came in.'

'He's here,' said Mrs Jones, standing aside to expose Clive, newspaper wide open in front of him, to the rest of the room. Clive tried to snap the paper shut but the pages weren't lined up properly.

'Ah, Mr Hapgood. There you are. Hiding behind a newspaper it would seem, although I do hope that my eyes deceive me.'

'I'm just trying to fold it,' said Clive.

A single sheet had got loose and Clive couldn't fold it without bits sticking out. Wally, next to him, found this excruciating.

'I was just saying, Mr Hapgood, that I'd like to speak to you for a few moments. Before you go back to the classroom. And after you've finally managed to fold your newspaper, of course.'

The rest of the staffroom giggled at Clive and the headmaster turned 180 degrees on his heels to signal the end of his oration.

Wally was enormously relieved on Clive's behalf.

'You've got off lightly there. Reading while he was talking. Dear oh dear.'

'I don't know what he wants to talk to me about yet.'

Clive stood up and dropped the scrappy-looking newspaper onto his chair and sought out the headmaster. He wanted to get his talk with Crouch out of the way as soon as possible. The headmaster was now deep in conversation with Robert Icke, so Clive could only hover near them. Their exchange didn't sound as if it was ending any time soon.

'Yes, I did watch it. We both did,' the headmaster was saying. 'We thought it was hilarious.'

'I'm so glad,' Icke said. 'I thought it would be up your street.'

Clive had managed to avoid Icke in the history department this morning, and so this was the first time that he'd caught a whiff of today's aftershave. It wasn't unpleasant but nor was it subtle. A hint of orange peel, perhaps. Bit Christmassy for the time of year.

'Hello, Clive.'

It was Flora. She already looked very at home.

'Flora, hello. How are you getting on? You don't think you've made a terrible decision?'

'Not yet, but then I've only had to watch other people work. How long have you been here?'

'Eight years.'

'And where were you before?'

'State school. Uxbridge. Enjoyed it actually.'

'I'll be coming and watching one of your lessons soon, I think. Robert – Mr Icke – has drawn me up a timetable of lessons to go to.'

'Well, he's a very organised man.'

He said this quietly but the volume at which Icke and

Crouch were speaking made being overheard a remote possibility.

'Yes, he seems so. He interviewed me last term.'

'Last term? We weren't told about you until this week. Not that I have a problem with it. Great appointment. I'm just surprised it was kept a secret.'

Flora looked awkwardly around. 'It was probably for my sake,' she said. 'I didn't want to hand in my notice until the end of last term. I wanted to leave it as late as possible for my ex to find out that I was going.'

'So we're your escape plan?'

'Exactly.'

'Frampton was our escape plan, originally.'

'And did it work?'

'Well, I didn't really feel as if I needed to escape. But our daughters are very settled here. My wife likes it.'

'What does she do?'

'She works part-time. For the town council. Not as dull as it sounds, actually. I mean it's not heart-stoppingly exciting. Although they have just got a new defibrillator. So if it was, they'd have the means to cope.'

Flora laughed and then said, 'My ex was involved with the local council. He'd come back all excited, talking about flood prevention or something.'

'Helen doesn't have to get too involved in the actual political side of it. Luckily.'

'What do you have to see the headmaster about? Have you been naughty?'

'Oh, probably. I'm just waiting for him and Icke to stop discussing aftershave or whatever.'

'It is quite strong, isn't it? Christmassy, I thought.'

'I thought that,' said Clive. 'When have you got to come and see one of my lessons?'

'Start of next week. Civil rights, I think.'

'That's right. Well, I'll try and make it a good one.'

'Make it a normal one.'

'They're normally good,' said Clive, a little wounded.

Flora rolled her eyes at him. 'I didn't mean it like that. I'm sure they are. I meant that I want to see how the children normally behave.'

'They're normally spellbound,' Clive assured her.

Icke and Crouch's conversation seemed to be winding down now, and teachers were drifting from the room. The headmaster, without turning, addressed Clive.

'Clive. That little word I wanted to have.'

Flora tiptoed away, but the headmaster didn't move from where he stood and so Clive was forced to go and take the spot on the carpet vacated by Icke. It was a feeble power move, but it irked Clive.

'Headmaster?'

'It's not a big thing, Clive. But word has reached me that you got a little cross in the refectory this morning.'

'I did, yes. But I'm fine now.'

'It's not actually you I'm worried about, Clive.'

'No?'

'I think some of the boys were rather taken aback.'

Clive bit his lip and allowed the headmaster to continue.

'*Apparently* you shouted at them.'

'Well, they were all calling a boy a wanker for dropping his tray.'

'Clive, that happens every week.'

'Yes, well . . .'

'And I think the best thing to do is just draw a discreet veil over it. If we *punish* everybody who shouted it, we'd have to *punish* the whole school. I mean, even the *prefects* do it.'

Clive reeled from these rapid plosives but said, 'It's bullying. If we don't call it out, then we're complicit.'

The headmaster scoffed.

'Oh, Clive. Bullying! It's some boys having a bit of a laugh.'

'It was a lot of big boys having a laugh at the expense of someone small.'

'My real concern is what you said to them. You mentioned the fees. And Nazis, I think somebody said. Bit uncouth.'

'The fees or the Nazis?'

'The fees business. Doesn't do to remind them of it. It's best disregarded. It helps normalise their school experience. And the Nazis? A bit de trop, don't you think?'

'I think they were worse than that.'

'To bring them up, I meant.'

'Perhaps I went a little overboard,' Clive said, apologetically.

'Best to make sure we're on the same *page*.'

As Clive jogged out of the staffroom and across the quad to the history block, the bell for the start of the next lesson was already sounding.

*

Clive managed to make it home earlier than usual that night, and he suggested that they all eat together as a family. He and Katie walked into town to pick up fish and chips. There was a long queue at their preferred shop but he judged the wait worthwhile.

'Why don't we go to the other one, Daddy? There's never a queue at that one.'

'It's not as good,' said Clive. 'Why don't you get a can out of the fridge?'

'Isn't that stealing?'

'Not if I pay for it when we get to the front.'

'So until you pay for it, then it is stealing?'

'Yes. OK. If that'll make it more fun.'

'A lot more fun,' said Katie and skipped over to the fridge for a can of Tango.

The other place never does have a queue, thought Clive. The other place was older and the service wasn't as good. The man who ran it was embittered. Probably about the fact that the people of Frampton didn't enjoy his fish and chips as much as they enjoyed the ones made by a Turkish man. He and Mark had lazily gone into the other one after a drink recently and the man had moaned about the success of this place. 'It's not right,' he'd said. 'He steals my customers.' He's not stealing customers, thought Clive. He's serving them. And his chips aren't shit.

'Hello, Sir,' said a quiet voice. It was Jonathan Findlay.

'Oh hello. You all right?'

Findlay was in his home clothes now, looking more grown-up than he did in uniform. He was with a few of the other boys of similar stature, all slouching in their hoodies. Some sort of surf-wear brand.

'Yes, thank you.'

'Didn't fancy the refectory?'

'Not really.'

'Best out of there, I think. Those your friends?'

'Well, kind of.'

Katie was noisily slurping her drink.

'Hello,' said Findlay to her.

She gave him a shy look.

'This is Katie,' said Clive.

'Hello, Katie,' he said.

'Katie, say hello to Findlay.'

She said nothing, but smiled at him.

'And thanks again for this morning, Sir.'

'Any time. Any time. Look, if you ever need someone to talk to, my number's in the school book. Or there's the chaplain, of course.'

'Thank you, Sir.'

Findlay gave a shy smile and then went to the back of the queue with his friends.

*

Katie opened up the packets of fish and chips on the kitchen table and Clive called upstairs to the others.

'Coming!' shouted Sarah as she galloped down the stairs.

Helen walked down not long after.

'You did go to Marmaris, didn't you?'

'We did.'

'Mushy peas?'

'Heaps of them.'

Helen took two long-stemmed glasses down from the shelf and a bottle of white wine from the fridge.

'Why don't we all do something together tomorrow night?' said Clive.

'Like what?' said Sarah.

'We could go and see a film. Drive to Newbury, maybe. Or Swindon.'

'What's on?' asked Helen.

Clive picked up a copy of the *Frampton Advertiser* from the sideboard and found the listings page.

'We could see *Dr Dolittle*? Or something called *Can't Hardly Wait*.'

'My friend saw *Can't Hardly Wait*. She said it was *really* good,' offered Sarah.

'"Jocks, headbangers and misfits go wild in this graduation party romp. Certificate 12,"' read Clive. '*Dr Dolittle* is a PG. There we are then. "Eddie Murphy is a doctor who can talk to animals."'

'Well, that doesn't sound very good,' said Helen.

'It'll be fun,' said Clive. 'Anyway, we'll all be together. If it's awful, then we can find it awful together.'

'And we can have popcorn,' said Katie.

'Exactly,' said Clive. 'We can have popcorn.'

'I might bring some wine in my handbag,' said Helen.

'You drink too much wine,' said Sarah.

5

Clive left the house the next morning with an easy ten minutes to spare before his first lesson of the day. He was carrying a couple of empty bottles from the night before and deposited them in the bin in the front garden. One of them had been only half full when the evening began, so that wasn't so bad. As he heard the satisfactory clink of the empty bottles on the bin's metal floor he was greeted with a 'Hello, Sir' from the street. It was Mason, the cheeky fourth former he'd taken so much personal satisfaction in shutting down in class yesterday.

'Hello, Mason.'

'Big night was it, Sir?'

Clive sighed at him. 'It was a quiet night. With my family. Who are all having breakfast together while I have to head out and teach the likes of you.'

'Only joking, Sir.'

'Those were jars by the way. Not bottles. We eat a lot of marmalade. Especially on Fridays.'

Mason trotted off and Clive opened his gate and turned left, letting it clang shut behind him. He ambled along the street to the school's entrance and started across to the history department. As he did so he saw Mrs Jones coming the other way.

'Morning, Elizabeth.'

'Oh, Clive. Hello.'

She was in navy blue today, an unusually taciturn colour choice for her, and as he got closer he saw that her eyes were wet with tears.

'I can't stop,' she sniffed and bustled on past him towards the archway and out of sight.

Mark Taylor was next. 'Have you seen Elizabeth Jones?'

'That way,' Clive said, pointing out her direction of departure. 'Everything all right?'

'She's just had some bad family news, apparently. Thought I might see if I can help.'

'You'll have to be quick. She was moving at a pace.'

Mark jogged on and Clive turned into the quad, which was already alive with teachers and pupils all making their way to their first lessons of the day. The headmaster liked people to be at their desks and ready to start by the time the bell rang.

*

Twenty minutes later Clive was standing in front of his whiteboard when there was a brisk knock on the door. Before he could even open his mouth to say, 'Come in,' the door had already opened and the headmaster had entered the room.

It was sometimes hard to know just how much esteem the pupils held the headmaster in. Yes, he was the important one who made all the big decisions, but he was also rather aloof from proceedings as far as the boys were concerned. He hadn't taught for years and was so rarely seen in any of the teaching blocks (this morning's sudden and surprising appearance being an exception) that he had about him an almost other-worldly quality. He was a figure that they would see at chapel or at the very occasional school assemblies they had, usually at the start and end of each term. At the end of this term they would all get to see him in action at Speech Day. This was an event that marked the conclusion of the school year, for which an enormous marquee would be erected somewhere in the school grounds. Attendance was compulsory for all pupils and staff, and the parents attended in droves. Depending on the weather, the tent would either be muggy or sweltering, and everybody would sit in neat rows through speeches by the headmaster and then perhaps a visiting dignitary or maybe a former pupil of the school. At some point 'Jerusalem' would be sung with a gusto that suggested that the society that Blake had once envisaged was somehow best embodied by those associated with Frampton College. The staff were all required to sit on the vast stage behind those speaking and were under strict instructions to beam along cheerfully with proceedings as well as to laugh in all the right places. On that day the headmaster would be in his element, showing off his gauche public-speaking skills and making the parents laugh at stories and anecdotes they had presumably heard before. But then they were the sort of people who liked to laugh at things they'd heard before. The headmaster's speech was essentially an annual reminder of the distinctive qualities of the Frampton Character, a description that grew alarmingly in length year on year. At last year's event, kindness, patience and tolerance were just three of the virtues that he insisted were absolutely unique to people who had passed through Frampton College. Once the speeches were over, a lengthy prize-giving ceremony would start, in which seemingly hundreds of children had to file up and receive awards and trophies: the House Drama Cup, the Most Improved Rugby Player, the Intermediate Percussion Prize, the Ainsleigh Cup for Fortitude and so forth. Then everybody would sing the school song before decamping outside and picnicking competitively. Everybody and everything was on show, and the whole thing – the longest period of time that any parent would have spent on school property in the last 365 days – gave the least representative impression of the school's usual atmosphere that could possibly have been achieved. Events like that were where pupils actually saw the headmaster the most. He was like a distant figurehead, a mascot. Many pupils probably related to him in the same way as people who worked for Admiral Insurance related to the actor who played Nelson in the television adverts.

'Headmaster, good morning.'

'Mr Hapgood, a word? Out in the corridor.'

Crouch left the room, and Clive followed. The door had barely shut behind them when Crouch said, 'Clive, I don't know if word has reached you yet, but I'm very sorry to say that Elizabeth Jones – from the English department . . . ?'

'Yes, yes.'

'Bit of bad news. Mother died. Terribly sad.'

'Right.'

'I'm sure you heard that Mrs Jones was due to spend this afternoon taking a party of boys from the lower sixth to see *Hamlet* at the RSC. It's had terribly good notices. Tickets are like gold dust apparently. Arabella and I *adore* the theatre. But, of course, we so rarely have the time. It would be enormously helpful if you could go in her place.'

*

'*Hamlet*!' exclaimed Helen. 'You'll be there all bloody afternoon. And evening. It's about four hours long. And it'll feel like longer.'

'I know, I know,' said Clive.

He was using the payphone mounted on the wall outside the entrance to the staffroom. Clive had thought phoning would be easier than telling her face to face. From the staffroom Clive could hear the headmaster beginning his morning oration.

'Well, this is going to mess up our plans for the evening. Isn't it? Did it occur to you to say no, Clive? Can't you ask someone else to do it?'

'Crouch asked me personally.'

'He'd respect you more if you stood up to him. Not being all bendable, like this.'

'I wasn't being bendable,' Clive said. 'I told him we had plans.'

'You show too much willing for no reward. You should start showing some resistance. I would hate to think that you're going soft.'

I'm practically liquid, Clive thought.

'If you're late back, we'll just go without you,' Helen added.

Before she had returned the receiver to its cradle, Clive could heard her say the words 'ruddy man'. He replaced the receiver at his end, then instinctively pressed his forehead against it and held the position for some moments. When he returned to the staffroom the headmaster, who had in fact been the subject of Helen's last remark, was still speaking.

'Anyway, I must dash. Off to *Paris*, as I think I might have mentioned. My godson's wedding. Tomorrow. In a restaurant. All very modern.'

The headmaster turned on his heel and made for the door.

'Good man, Clive,' he said as the two passed each other. And then, for the second time that morning, the headmaster patted Clive's shoulder.

'Bon voyage,' said Clive quietly.

6

The keys for the minibus had to be collected from the school office. The headmaster's assistant, Linda, handed them over gleefully.

'Have a wonderful time, Clive. I envy you.'

'You can take them if you like.'

'I'm not insured to drive a minibus,' she said.

Clive pocketed the keys and walked over to the back of the science block, where the minibuses could be found. A cluster of boys was already waiting there for him.

'Hello, everyone. Thanks for being so prompt.'

Two boys that he took for history A level were among the waiting group. Joe Clarke was a bright and languid boy with thick blonde hair that fell in a big swoopy fringe that had to be continually swept or flicked back. Beside him stood Michael Hicks, shorter and with greasier hair, who considered himself artsy and creative: did a lot of plays, was probably in a band. He had dreadful skin that Clive sometimes found himself staring at in lessons. Hicks somehow wore it as a badge of honour. It probably suited the outsider image he so carefully cultivated. He had a 'Vote Labour' lapel badge, which he'd been wearing around school in celebration since the previous May, although Clive didn't know if he wore it so proudly when he was back home with his financier parents in Virginia Water.

'Hello, Sir,' said Clarke. 'We were all just talking about Mrs Jones.'

'Yes, very sad. Are we all here?'

Clive took out a list from his pocket. There were twelve names on it.

'Still waiting for Matthew Dunster,' said Clarke.

'Dunster. All right. Well, the rest of you get in.'

Clive unlocked the driver's door and opened up the double doors at the back. The boys all leapt in excitedly. Clive got in and adjusted the mirrors. The rear-view one was next to useless, offering him only a view of the boys shoving each other.

'Seat belts, everyone. Anyone know where Dunster is?'

'Toilet, probably,' a voice called back.

Clive put the key in the ignition and checked the tank. They'd need to stop on the way back. Then he heard another boy scrambling into the back of the bus.

'Sorry I'm late, had to go back to my house to get my wallet. And then I needed to go the toilet. And then . . . Oh hello, Sir.'

'Hello, Dunster.'

'Where's Mrs Jones, Sir?'

'She's had a bereavement, I'm afraid. Could someone shut the doors please?'

Dunster tried to pull the doors to, but without success.

'I don't think it can be done from the inside, Sir.'

Clive turned off the engine, undid his seat belt and got out of the minibus. Dunster was buckling up, and Clive glimpsed a packet of Marlboro Lights sticking out of the side pocket of the boy's blazer as he slammed the doors shut.

*

The first time that Clive had been asked to drive a school minibus he had been completely terrified. He'd only been teaching at Frampton for a fortnight when he was asked to drive a sports team to an away fixture. He'd stuck in the left-hand lane doing sixty the whole way but still managed to arrive in a sweating mess. Another teacher had driven them home again. Now his only fear was whether he'd get home in time to go out with his family. It was a pretty journey, as these things went, up past Cirencester and then onwards through Stow-on-the-Wold.

'Can we have some music on, Sir?'

'If you like.'

Hicks passed forward a CD and Clive pushed it into the slot. Electric guitars and a voice that sounded hurt came through the speakers.

'What are we listening to?' Clive called back.

'Radiohead.'

'Right.'

'*OK Computer*, it's called. Came out last year.'

The boys all knew the lyrics. It was good, Clive thought. Nice to drive to. Several tracks in, something about the music made Clive feel as if his head was filling with smoke: all the distortion, crossed with a sort of plinky-plonk melody. Then the song flattened out into more of a soundscape with long, slow notes. It gave him an out-of-body feeling.

'Do you like this, Sir?'

'Yes. It's . . . interesting. I liked those lyrics: "Arrest this man, he talks too much."'

'It's "he talks in maths". That one's called "Karma Police".'

'Oh, I see. Still. Good. Would Mrs Jones have let you listen to this?'

'Probably not. I think she's a bit more Radio 4, Sir.'

The journey took just under an hour and a half. If the play was over by four, he'd be able to . . . No, four was too early. Half past? What if it was five? He could still be home by twenty to seven. That would leave enough time to get to Swindon.

Clive parked the minibus and they walked into the theatre with ten minutes to spare.

'Is it all right if we go outside?' asked Dunster.

'What for?'

'Just . . . some air.'

'Fine.'

When Dunster and a few others returned five minutes later they were all sucking on Polos and absolutely reeked of cigarette smoke.

'Got some air, did you? Hope you had time for a Marlboro Light as well?'

Dunster attempted an innocent expression.

'Let's try not to treat each other like idiots, shall we?' said Clive.

Twelve of the tickets were for one row and there was a single seat a few rows back, which Clive took. The boys all took their seats at the end of a row and Clive found his seat, ten in from the aisle. Clive was between two pensioners who had both brought shopping with them. The lady to his right was reading the programme and snapped it shut when Clive tried to read it over her shoulder. Then the lights went down and the play started. Clive had never seen *Hamlet* before, or even read it, but enough of it had seeped into popular culture for him to feel familiar with some of the characters and its general air of gloom. It was not Clive's thing at all though. Not least because Hamlet himself was completely incapable of letting slip any chance to bang on.

'Arrest this man,' thought Clive. 'He talks too much.'

*

At the interval an usher told Clive it would all be over by quarter to five. Perfect. If he could get the boys straight back onto the minibus, they would be home in good time. He went outside the theatre and found a payphone to call Helen on.

'How's it going up there?'

'It's staggeringly tedious, but the good thing is it's over before five. We'll all leap straight back in the bus and be on the road by five and I should be with you by twenty to seven. Then we can all go straight out to Swindon.'

'The girls want to go to Newbury.'

'All right then, Newbury. Have you checked the times?'

'Yes, we can make a screening if you're here by twenty to seven. We'll have to have supper at home.'

'Shall I call again when the play's finished?'

'No, just come home.'

Clive walked back into the theatre and stood in the foyer. The boys were nowhere to be seen but had probably nipped out of another door to go and smoke. As long as I don't see them, they're fine, he thought. And as long as that's all that they're doing. But then what other trouble could they get up to in Stratford? Ransack a branch of the Edinburgh Woollen Mill? Clive spent the last of his change on a tub of vanilla and returned to the auditorium just as the bell was ringing in the foyer. His row all had to slowly stand to let him past. He squeezed by them, stepping over their shopping bags, until he came to his seat. Then, just before he sat down, he looked forward and saw that a few rows in front of him there were twelve empty seats.

'I'm so sorry,' he said to the people to his left, and they all slowly started standing up again as he clambered past them and made a dash for the exit, just as the lights were going down.

'Is there anyone out there?' he whispered to an usher.

'Foyer's empty,' she said. 'The second half is starting right now, Sir.'

'Can you let me out please?'

'We will have to wait until an appropriate moment in the performance before readmission.'

The lady opened the door and Clive stepped out into a totally empty foyer. He looked up and down, ran up any stairs he could see and down them again. Then he looked into the toilets in the foyer. One cubicle was engaged.

'Hello?' called Clive, banging on the door.

'Hello?' a voice boomed back at him. It clearly belonged to someone of retirement age rather than a schoolboy. 'This one's engaged. Sorry.'

'I beg your pardon,' said Clive. 'The play's started again by the way,' he added.

'I'm not here for a play. I'm here to do this.'

'Right you are,' said Clive and ran back out into the foyer. There was an usher standing by the entrance.

'Have you seen twelve boys?'

'Twelve boys?'

'Pupils of mine. We're on a school trip. They've gone missing.'

'I don't think so. Not since the second half started. Sorry.'

Clive went out of the front doors and did a complete lap of the building. Next he tried the two pubs nearest the theatre. It was still too early to raise the alarm with the school, so instead he walked to a newsagent and paid for cigarettes and matches with a cheque. If Helen and the girls smelt anything, he could blame it on the boys. Then he returned to the theatre's front steps and smoked eight cigarettes in a row, after which he did one more lap of the building and then returned to smoke two more. There was nothing to do but wait. They'd be sitting happily in a pub somewhere, smoking and drinking, and laughing about not having to sit through the second half. If they were so desperate to sod off, they could have just told him and he would happily have taken them all back to school earlier.

They could have concocted a little lie together about technical difficulties or a bomb scare, and his evening would have been saved.

Finally the thought struck him that an hour had now passed since he'd realised that twelve boys were missing and unaccounted for, so he went into the theatre and asked someone from the box office if he might use the phone. He worked through all the names on his list and rang all of their housemasters to inform him that the boys had absconded. They could deal with the disciplinary side of this. Clive just wanted to get home.

Once the calls were made he sat on the front steps again, smoking more cigarettes down to the filter and then grinding them out furiously on the steps. There was a little pile of stubs in front of him which he scooped up using his ticket and dropped into a bin. It was probably the third most depressing moment of his week.

As quarter to five neared, Clive scanned the horizon for signs of the boys returning from their little jaunt. He wondered if he might conceal himself somehow and then step out and surprise them just when they thought they had got away with it. Perhaps he'd just meet them in the foyer and say nothing, then just casually ask what they thought of the second half on the way home and try and force a confession. Or perhaps he should wait until they were all in the back of the minibus and had their seat belts on, and then absolutely lose his shit with them. That might be more cathartic.

He returned to the foyer in time to hear the applause beginning for the curtain call. It was long and booming, a howling tumult of, if the first half was anything to go by, wild over-appreciation. He could hear feet drumming on the floors and the odd whistle. Then the doors from the auditorium opened and the audience began to stream out. Clive stood his ground as the crowd swarmed around him, still keeping an eye on all doors back into the foyer. They'd timed it wrong, the boys. There was no way they could even attempt to make it look as if they'd been in the theatre if they arrived now.

'Hello, Sir! That was fantastic, wasn't it? Really good.'

Clive spun round to see Joe Clarke. He was sweeping that big fringe out of his eyes and beaming wildly.

After Clarke came Michael Hicks. 'What did you think, Sir?' Hicks asked.

'I thought it was . . . interesting.'

The boys gathered around him.

'Do we have to go straight back to school, Sir?' asked one.

'Have we got time to have a look around Stratford?' said another.

Clive said nothing but eyed them all suspiciously. 'Where were you all?'

'For the second half, Sir?' said Clarke. 'We noticed an empty row of seats right near the front. We asked an usher and she said there was another school group that hadn't turned up. Said we could sit there.'

'We did look for you,' said Hicks. 'There was a space for you but we couldn't find you anywhere. We wondered if you'd decided not to see the second half.'

'Me?' said Clive. 'No, no. Just a bit late back to my seat. It was all very good, I thought. Right. To the minibus.'

*

'Can we put the CD on again?'

Clive had been anxiously looking at both the clock and the petrol gauge for the last twenty minutes. There had to be a garage soon. And he'd see if they had a phone. Perhaps one of the boys would lend him some change. If he could get in touch with at least one of the housemasters he had spoken to, then they could spread the word that there'd been a little mix-up. No need for the boys to know anything about it. He'd have to be quick though.

Clive turned on the stereo again and pressed play. As soon as the lyrics kicked in, the boys all joined in. There were some good voices among them, but none of them could match the beautiful fragility of the singer on the CD. It didn't seem to Clive to be the sort of music that one was meant to sing along to, but who was he to deny them their fun? At last he saw a petrol station up ahead, flashed his indicator and pulled into the left-hand lane.

Clive joined a queue for a pump. It was the wrong queue, as it turned out. There was only one car in front, but its occupant, once he had paid for his petrol, also took the opportunity to rearrange the contents of his boot and change his shoes. Clive rested his forehead on the steering wheel until the ordeal was finally over.

He moved forward, then put the handbrake on and got out. It took some effort to prise open the flap and unscrew the fuel cap. He took out the petrol dispenser, waited for the display to go back to zero and then started filling the tank. He looked at his watch. There was still at least an hour of the journey to complete. He was really pushing it now. Perhaps he shouldn't call the housemasters. He could just explain to the boys what had happened and then let them do the telling. They'd probably enjoy it. Clive didn't even mind being the butt of the story, as long as he got home in time to avoid the full force of his wife's exasperation. He'd rather be humiliated at work than at home. He looked at the meter on the pump. The fuel tanks on these minibuses were massive. Did he really have to fill the whole thing up? Technically that was the school policy, but that would take an age. It was still only half full. He resisted the temptation to stop there and carried on pumping. Then he looked down and noticed the little sign on the inside of the flap. It was a yellow sign with black writing on it that spelled out the words 'DIESEL ONLY'.

Oh, he thought.

He stared at the sign and froze, still holding tightly onto the nozzle and pumping petrol into the tank. Then he snapped out of it and released his grip. Then he took the nozzle out and replaced it on its stand, before he knelt down on all fours next to the minibus, lowered his head gently onto the tarmac and began to scream.

*

It was long past eight by the time Clive finally parked the minibus back behind the science block. The boys ran off cheerfully to enjoy what was left of their Saturday night and Clive trudged back home. The lights were all off, so he turned them on one by one as he walked through the silent house. There was a note left on the kitchen table in Katie's handwriting: 'SOORY DADDY WE JUST HAD TO GO.'

He picked up the phone and dialled Mark's number.

7

'You really should have come, Daddy,' said Sarah.

'Mummy took us out for PIZZA,' shouted Katie.

'Lucky you. How was the film?'

'Kind of stupid,' said Sarah. 'But also great.'

'Mainly great,' said Katie. 'But also silly. I liked the silly bits best.'

'You would have hated it,' said Helen, placing a full cafetière down on the table.

'Still. I'd have liked to be there,' said Clive.

'Well, we'd all have liked you to be there,' she said. 'Your dressing gown's open, by the way.'

Clive readjusted his gown and tried to butter his toast, but it was torn by the firmness of the butter. He pushed his plate back in defeat and got up to fetch a glass of water. When he'd got back from his drink with Mark the house had once again been in darkness. He and Mark had stayed in the Dragon until closing time and then gone back to Mark's house to drink whisky and listen to music. He'd still made it home by midnight. Mark would already have drummed the hangover out of his system on his morning run and be getting ready to preach. Clive, though, felt like he had a head full of shrapnel. He had not dared turn any lights back on when he'd returned home the second time and had crept as quietly up the stairs as he could manage before looking in on the girls and then undressing on the landing so as not to disturb Helen. He had turned the door handle silently and then tiptoed around the room in as wide an arc as possible in an effort not to collide with the bed on the way to his side. He'd peeled back the duvet and slipped into the bed.

'Are you going to brush your teeth?' Helen had asked, breezily.

'Oh yes,' said Clive. And got out of bed again.

'Turn a light on. You'll crash into something.'

He'd found the switch for the bedside light and gone to the bathroom to brush his teeth. After he'd spat out his mouthwash he had stood looking at himself in the bathroom mirror for some time, staring at the way his tummy now bulged a little over the waistband of his boxer shorts. Sideways on he looked better somehow, but only if he made himself stand up straight. He examined his hairline for a minute or two and tried sweeping his hair left and right across his forehead to see if either worked better. Messy, that was best. Let what curls were left do their magic. It was quite grey at the sides now, but still the right colour on top. The girls said it was silver at the back, and he was happy to take their word for it. There was a bottle of aftershave next to the tooth mug on the little shelf, so he instinctively picked it up and gave himself a couple of brief squirts at the base of his neck.

Helen was sitting up in bed when he went back to their room, writing her diary.

'Have you had a dreadful day?' she said.

'Awful,' said Clive.

'Sorry I was cross with you on the phone. It all just seemed so . . .'

'Preventable?'

'Yes. Come on.'

She closed her diary, put it under her pillow and then slid back down under the duvet and rolled onto her left side. Clive got in on his side and they both turned out the lights. He moved as close to Helen as he dared.

'That's better,' she said. 'You smell nice now.'

She reached behind her and pulled Clive's arm across her, positioning his hand on her stomach. Clive still marvelled at the slight softness of her belly, its unchanging shape over the years, and pulled closer. He planted a soft kiss behind her ear. When she didn't resist he kissed her again, for longer this time and further down her neck.

'Just hold me,' she said.

And so he did, until she took his hand again and placed it under her nightdress so the flat of his hand now touched the skin of her belly.

'I'm sorry I've been so hopeless,' he whispered.

'Don't talk about it,' she said.

His dick was hard now, pressing against her buttocks. Helen reached around and positioned it between her thighs. She eventually took his hand away and then rolled over to face him. He could just about make out her features in the dim light that came through the gap in the curtains. She kissed him on the lips, almost formally at first, and then again more softly, pressing her lips gently against his. Then his tongue was in her mouth and she rolled over on top of him. She sat up and pulled her nightdress over her head so that he could see the outline of her breasts. He took them in his hands and craned up to kiss them both in turn, his tongue lingering over each nipple before he brushed them with his lips. She pushed him down again and then rolled off him and onto her back. Clive knelt next to Helen now and ran a line down across the centre of her chest with his finger, before coming to rest on her pubic hair. He began to stroke her as she took his dick in her hand. She let out a moan as he felt her become wet and she gripped him more tightly. Then her normal voice returned and she said, like a surgeon asking for a scalpel, 'Condom.'

Clive, still in Helen's grip, leant over to the bedside table, pulled open the drawer and started scrabbling around. He switched on the light. The drawer was empty.

'There aren't any,' he said quietly. There had been some in there, he was sure of it.

Helen let go of him.

'Oh for God's sake,' she said.

'Sorry,' said Clive, and then lay down beside her.

They did what they could, but it wasn't as good. It never was.

'I'll get some tomorrow,' said Clive.

Helen fell asleep within minutes. Clive just lay there, thinking about the condoms that were no longer in the drawer and wistfully recalling the events of a holiday that now seemed a very long time ago. He needed to do something about half-term. Book them a holiday. That would fix things.

*

It had been Helen's idea. They had already had five days on Corfu, and beautiful as all the views out to sea were, Helen could not keep looking out at those vast swathes of the Aegean Sea without wanting to travel across them, to get somewhere else. A slightly dusty black saloon taxi had dropped them outside the port, just above the Old Town, and they had joined a queue that was longer than they had both been hoping of holidaymakers keen to see the islands of Paxos and Antipaxos. Passports, to their surprise, had to be shown and they were led up a gangplank to a ferryboat with tight rows of white plastic seats on the deck and a smoky lounge below with weathered, brown banquettes. Greek music played tinnily through tannoy speakers that looked far too small for their purpose, and would only stop to make way for lengthy descriptions of the areas that they were passing through delivered by a tour guide who was as enthusiastic as she was audible. Sitting out on the deck, though, facing each other and with a white canopy above them, they could just about block out all the hubbub and read their novels, occasionally glancing up to look at the sea and the land around them, or to gaze into each other's eyes and share moments of silent companionship. They could have entire conversations about the passengers around them with just a tilt of the head or a knowing flick of an eyebrow: the teenage boy to one side who prattled on and on to his parents about his favourite digital watches; the middle-aged sisters from Derby who disagreed about the root cause of their mother's unhappiness; the recently retired man from Ullswater who had once got sunstroke on a picnic in 1974 and whose wife was not quite yet ready to let him forget it.

'It sounds like that picnic will feature quite strongly in his eulogy,' Clive whispered to Helen.

'Or her inquest,' Helen giggled.

They returned to their novels and felt good about life.

In a bay near Antipaxos the ferry moored, and the passengers were invited to climb down the ladder at the back of the boat to swim, or even, if they were so daringly inclined, to jump from the lower decks. It was the queue for the ladder that convinced Helen to jump after she had emerged from the tiny loo in her bikini; for Clive it was a desire to impress his wife. Helen had slung one leg then the other over the railing and executed a dive without fuss, arms stretched into a point and her legs and body straight as a pencil as she coolly entered the water twelve feet below. Clive climbed over the railings rather more nervously, and then gingerly turned himself around to face outwards, always with both hands firmly clasping the rail.

'Just dive!' Helen called up to her husband teetering anxiously the edge of the drop. 'You can do it!'

Clive smiled, took a gulp of air, held his nose and then dropped feet first. He saw a beautiful bright blue horizon travelling upwards in front of him for all of three milliseconds and then all he could see were the bubbles as he shot beneath the water. Then he was suddenly still for a moment before slightly rising to the surface and emerging exultant into the sun and the open air. Helen wrapped her arms around him, then they swam laps of the boat and paddled to the rocks at the water's edge. They had time to drip-dry out on the bow deck and dress again before the ferry set off for Paxos and a longer stop-off.

'We leave again in two and a half hours,' they were told as they disembarked. 'If you are not back by then, we leave without you.'

They had lunch at the quietest restaurant they could find, sitting outside in a shaded alley. Plates of fried seafood and a bottle of rosé, then two coffees. Helen had been scandalously funny as they ate, doing impressions of their fellow passengers and then opening up the pudding menu and reading it out loud in an imperceptible mumble through cupped hands as if she was the mournful tour guide, before paying the bill in cash, taking Clive by the hand and walking further up the alley. Once they had walked for a few minutes and passed under an archway, Helen grabbed Clive's white linen shirt by the collar and guided him up against a stone wall, pushed his sunglasses up onto his head and kissed him tenderly and enthusiastically. He wrapped his arms around her and she stroked his back and held his buttocks, pulling him towards her. Then she turned them around so that it was her back against the dusty wall, her hands gliding across the front of his shorts before she undid them, lifted her light dress and guided him into her. They could hear people talking a few streets away and smell the sea salt on each other's necks. Insects that neither of them could care to identify made rustling sounds as they scuttled nearby. Somewhere above them a shutter opened.

'Happy honeymoon,' Helen whispered as she pulled Clive towards her one final time.

They just had time to buy ice creams before, the last passengers, they made it back to the ferry.

*

Clive, having eventually breakfasted on painkillers washed down with pints of vitamin C tablets dissolved in water, felt almost normal by eleven. Helen had been out and bought the Sunday papers and was reading them on the sitting-room sofa. The girls were lying on their fronts on beanbags, watching cartoons interspersed with links presented by a frighteningly upbeat pairing of a young man and woman who laughed at each other's jokes and made references to pop culture that flew straight over Clive's head. Katie loved the cartoons and seemed baffled by the two presenters, while Sarah hung off their every word. Clive had climbed up to the attic and got down his old cricket kitbag. He'd bought it before they had children, when he'd genuinely had the time to lose half his weekend to chasing cricket balls all over the lush outfields of the Home Counties. He'd played enough to get quite good at one point, certainly enough to look forward to it. Now the thought made him uneasy. He'd checked that his kit still fitted – which it did, just about – and then writhed around on the floor next to the girls doing some stretches.

'When do you think you last used your hamstrings?' asked Helen.

'I couldn't say. Climbing some stairs? Does that involve hamstrings?'

'It shouldn't stretch them, no. Look, you can stretch as much as you like but you'll still be aching in the morning. Why don't you stretch with the others when you get there?'

'I have a feeling that they'll all be a bit stretchier than me. I'm only doing these stretches so I'm flexible enough to do the stretches that Iain will make us do when I get there. Are you going to come down and watch?'

'Girls?' asked Helen. 'Who wants to go and watch Daddy play cricket?'

Neither of them looked up.

'There's your answer,' she said. 'We'll go out somewhere fun and then we'll come down. Probably have a walk by the river. Walk off all this TV.'

'Great. Then we can all have supper together. I can help the girls with their homework.'

'We've already done it,' said Sarah.

'They did it yesterday afternoon,' explained Helen. 'While you were looking for imaginary truants.'

'More fun than watching *Hamlet*.'

'I don't doubt it.'

Clive got gingerly to his feet. 'Right then, I'd better head over to the pitches. I'll see you all later.'

'Come on, you two,' said Helen, grabbing the remote control and turning off the television. 'Let's go out for a walk.'

The girls obediently leapt up. Katie came over and put her arms around Clive's waist. He rested a hand on her head.

'I wish you could come, Daddy.'

'I do too, darling. But nasty men have made me play cricket. You'll come and see a bit of it, won't you? Please?'

'Are you good at cricket, Daddy?'

'Not really, no.'

'So we should come and rescue you then?'

'Yes please,' said Clive.

8

When Clive arrived at the school sports pavilion Iain Dixon was already changed and waiting for him, a thin roll-up cigarette on the go. The opposition were out on the pitch, limbering up and chucking balls to one another. Iain had hardly talked them up but they looked to Clive as if they knew what they were doing.

'Clive! Great that you're here. The lovely Helen coming along?'

'She'll be along later, possibly. She and the girls are going out first.'

'She didn't mind you giving up your Sunday, then?'

'You can ask her when she arrives. Where do we change?'

'Upstairs, first on the right. Mark's already up there. And Frank.'

'Frank?'

'Harper.'

'Oh good,' said Clive and wandered off in the direction of the pavilion.

Clive climbed the stairs and pushed open a dressing-room door. Mark was lying flat on his back on one of the benches, in a tracksuit. Next to him stood Frank Harper, a drama teacher.

'Hear you two boys were out last night,' said Harper.

'Well, briefly. I had to go to Stratford yesterday. You should have gone.'

'Stratford? What for?'

'*Hamlet*. I had to take some of the A level English lot because of Elizabeth Jones.'

'No one asked me. I'd have loved to. I was looking after a tennis team.'

'I didn't know we had a tennis team,' said Mark, his eyes closed.

'Oh yes,' said Harper. 'They're quite good actually. Not my thing at all, mind. Stupid southern game, tennis. More your thing, Clive.'

This sort of remark was typical of Harper, who spent a great deal of time and effort cultivating a hardy, northern persona and affecting that Frampton's rarefied surroundings were a world apart from the life that he came from. 'The thing about public schoolboys like you . . .' he could often be heard to say in the staffroom. He always described himself as a 'plain old grammar school boy'. The truth was that the school he went to had been a grammar school once upon a time, but by the time Harper got there it was an independent, fee-paying school, and his claims were as disingenuous as his Lancastrian burr, which had only surfaced – people who had known him for a long time claimed – when he commenced teacher training. His wife, tellingly, called him 'Francis'.

Clive tended to ignore Harper. Anyone who criticised other people for having been sent to public school despite actively choosing to teach at one was hardly worth engaging with. As Clive put his kitbag down on the floor, Harper started to strip off to change into his own kit. Mark looked almost fast asleep.

'How are you, Mark?'

'OK, I think. All things considered.' Still his eyes remained closed. 'Went for a bit of a run this morning. Took chapel.'

'Did you preach?' asked Frank.

'I did. Quite badly. It was short though.'

'What did you tell them about?' asked Clive, kicking off his shoes and pulling his kit out of the bag.

'Oh, the usual. Try to be nice. Try not to be nasty. I have a drawer full of sermons in my filing cabinet. If I've not had time to write a new one – if, for instance, some waif has come knocking on my door the night before demanding that I come out and drink – then I pull one out at random and deliver that. Technically they're meant to tie in with that day's gospel, but you can usually fudge it a bit. Today's turned out to have a couple of advent references in it but I managed to skim over them. That's why it was so short. What time is it now?'

'Quarter to,' said Harper. 'We're meant to be starting soon, aren't we?'

He lay down on his back on the floor and began to perform a series of increasingly elaborate stretches, pulling his knees up tight to his chest, then straightening each leg in turn and pulling it back over his shoulders. Each movement was accompanied by an elongated grunt, like a dying harmonium.

'Do you mind?' asked Mark.

'You've got . . . to keep . . . loose,' said Harper, straining away. 'You boys not stretching?'

Mark stood up and gently touched his toes, then held his hands behind his back and pushed his arms out straight until there was a quiet cracking sound.

'Done,' he said.

Outside they could suddenly hear trampling on the wooden steps. The door opened and Iain stood there. Behind him the opposition were trundling past in the direction of their dressing room.

'Right. We're batting.'

'Has no one else arrived?' asked Clive, panicked.

'Not yet. That's why I chose to bat. Very impressive, Frank. You two stretched?'

'I did some stretches at home,' said Clive. 'Not quite like these though.'

'Well, Frank's a very flexible man.'

Harper, still lying prone, lifted both legs in the air and slowly lowered them over his shoulders and then, with his arse improbably high in the air, let out another grunt and made contact with the floor.

'Grotesque,' said Clive.

'Just sensible,' said Harper, getting to his feet. 'I don't want to get injured.'

'Clive would probably get injured just by stretching,' said Iain.

'Is there a batting order?' asked Mark.

'Yes, I thought you and I should open. You can come in next, Frank. And then you, Clive. Unless anybody else turns up first. Then you should probably let them have a go.'

*

Mark and Iain looked every inch the part as the opening pair, scoring runs with ease and apparently having an unofficial contest as to who could look most languid at the crease. From where Clive sat, on a bench outside the front of the pavilion, the bowlers looked pretty quick. Robert Icke was the next colleague to arrive. He galloped upstairs to change and emerged in a shirt that positively dazzled and trousers that he'd ironed a crease into. He'd also slicked back his hair, and so he looked like someone who played the game half a century ago.

'Is there a batting order?' he asked.

'I'm next,' said Harper.

'You could go in after him if you like,' said Clive.

'I've not really played for a while,' said Icke. 'It would be quite useful to sit here and watch for a bit longer. Get my eye in.'

'I haven't played for ages,' countered Clive. 'So I'm in the same position, really. Iain said whoever turned up next should go ahead of me.'

'Well, no one else is here yet, so one of you will have to do it,' said Harper.

'I think Clive should,' said Icke. 'Speaking as his head of department.'

Harper and Icke laughed.

'That settles it then,' said Clive. 'You can definitely go in next if you're going to pull rank.'

Icke continued to laugh. 'Fair enough,' he said.

'Did I have to go to Stratford yesterday because of you?' added Clive.

Icke stopped laughing. 'I don't know what you mean,' he said.

'Instead of Elizabeth Jones. Crouch intimated that you volunteered me.'

'I honestly don't know what you're talking about.'

'Of course you don't.'

'I don't!'

Harper looked as if he was about to make a joke, but then eyed the pair of them warily. Something departmental appeared to be bubbling beneath the surface and he knew better than to get involved in it. So the three men sat on the bench together and said nothing. Out in the middle, Iain and Mark were putting on the accelerator, although from time to time Iain would glance back at them anxiously to check if any more players had turned up. Icke went upstairs to get some pads on and Harper turned to Clive.

'Everything all right between you two?' he asked.

'Oh yes.'

'Iain says that you two sometimes don't see eye to eye.'

'Well, Iain is a gossip. We're fine, me and Icke. We just like to spar a little, that's all. That's what we're always like really.'

'*Did* he suggest that you went to Stratford?'

'Well. That's what Crouch was intimating. Reading between the lines.'

'Perhaps you're paranoid,' said Harper. Helen sometimes called him that.

But Harper could see that Clive didn't want to discuss it any further and allowed the moment to pass. He was always a much easier person to get on with one to one. In a group he had a tendency to overcompensate, to bray a little. On his own he tended to take the armour off and be a little more sympathetic. He didn't do all that class stuff either.

'Oh look,' Harper said. 'Iain's left his tobacco here. How very careless. Shall we?'

'I think we ought, don't you? Little treat for giving up our Sunday?'

Harper passed the little leather pouch to Clive, who un-zipped it and opened it up. Alongside the dark, rich-smelling tobacco there was a plastic lighter, some liquorice-flavoured papers and some orange peel. No filters.

'What's he put peel in there for?' Clive asked.

'Orange peel? Stops the tobacco drying out.'

'Does it?'

'He says so.'

Clive slowly rolled himself a cigarette, tearing off a little edge of some thin card he'd found in the pouch as a make-shift filter, and then passed the pouch back to Harper, who went to work on a roll-up of his own. He was about to light up when there came a tremendous shout from the middle.

'HEADS!'

Iain had connected with a wild swing and the ball was high in the air and coming in their direction. The two men ducked and it flew over their heads, clattering into the pavilion steps behind them.

'Bloody hell,' said Harper. 'That could have hit us.' He got up to pick the ball off the floor and lobbed it back over the bench to Clive, who was taken aback by the sheer hardness of the thing. It must have been ages since he'd last handled a cricket ball. The leather was smooth but rock hard, and the stitches that ran around the ball felt sharp against his skin. He took a few steps towards the boundary rope and flung the ball back in the vague direction of the opposition bowler. It bounced two or three times and came to rest near a different player altogether, who picked it up and shined it against the back of his thigh.

Up to that moment Clive had almost started to enjoy himself, but a pang of anxiety was now rising within him. He could still feel the ball's imprint on his palm. Harper could only have tossed it seven or eight feet to him but his hand was stinging. He had forgotten this aspect of cricket: all the incidental pain. He shuddered at the prospect of the potential for disaster that lay in the afternoon ahead and returned to the bench to look for the roll-up he had dropped when the shout had come. Icke came back out from the pavilion with some pads on, carrying Clive's bat.

'This anybody's?' he asked.

'It's mine. It's fine.'

'Thanks, Clive.'

He came and sat down on the bench next to the two of them just in time to see Iain take another wild swipe and see his stumps wrecked.

'Oh bugger,' said Harper, giving up on his roll-up for the second time and gathering up his batting gloves.

'Good luck,' said Icke.

'Absolutely,' said Clive.

As Harper strode out to the middle Icke turned to Clive. 'Clive. I owe you an apology. I did mention your name to Crouch. Not only your name, I hasten to add. But I mentioned a few names of people that I believed to be free and yours was one of them. I'm sorry if it caused you any inconvenience.'

'I had to drive to Stratford and back, if that counts as inconvenience. And watch half of *Hamlet*.'

'Half of it?'

'That's right. So not as inconvenient as having to see the whole thing.'

'I see. Well, I'm sorry. And I don't want it to spoil today. Let's just put it behind us, shall we? Poor Frank. Looked very embarrassed by our squabbling.'

Clive looked at Icke but said nothing more. Anything he did say would only come back to bite him during the week ahead anyway. Clive briefly considered returning to the subject, but instead he lit the roll-up that he had made and took a long, deep drag on it. He coughed a little, but that was probably just the lack of a filter. Still, pretty heavy and pungent stuff. Iain probably bought his tobacco from some ludicrously sophisticated little emporium somewhere, perhaps in the City of London. An elderly gentleman would have been hunched over a counter with an array of jars behind him containing exotic and fabulous blends.

He took another drag and exhaled. That was better. It was smoother second time around. Icke eyed him suspiciously.

'What?' asked Clive.

A raised eyebrow.

'Don't you ever smoke, Robert?'

'No.'

'Not even at weekends?'

'No.'

'The odd one ever, when you were growing up?'

'Perhaps at university. And only ever once.'

'So not "perhaps" then. Definitely.'

'All right. But once. Only once. And certainly not on school premises.'

'I think it's fine. There are no pupils about. They're probably up to no good themselves somewhere.'

'Well. Even so.'

Clive took another drag as he watched Harper taking guard out in the middle. Clive had no idea if Harper was any good but he certainly looked the part. He walked up the pitch a little and prodded at the wicket with his bat, and then had a little look around the field before settling over his bat to face his first ball. It hit him on the pad and bounced away a few yards but Mark called him through for a run anyway. Mark, of course, was nimble and his running looked effortless. Harper's sprinting hinted at rather more effort. Just shy of the other end he suddenly pulled up, then dropped down on all fours. Iain, still padded up, was watching from a way further along the boundary rope as Harper rolled over onto his back and started rubbing the back of his right leg.

'Looks like he's done a hamstring' he called. 'So much for all that stretching. Who's in next?'

'I am,' said Icke.

'Well, you'd better be ready and alert. He might be coming off.'

But Harper stood up again, with the assistance of Mark and one or two of the opposition players.

'You all right, Frank?' Iain called.

'Cramp,' bellowed back Harper. 'I'll be OK.'

'What a hero,' said Iain. 'Ah, here they are.'

The rest of the team had arrived, all having apparently been given a lift from the other side of town in Michael Timpson's people carrier. Timpson was a maths teacher, and a devout Catholic, hence his need for such a vehicle: he was a father of six. Iain followed them all up to the changing room, leaving Clive smoking and Icke peering at him uneasily. The headache that Clive thought he'd successfully fought for much of the morning seemed to be returning. His mouth felt dry again, and a certain wooziness was welling up inside him. He took a few more big drags on the cigarette and then ground it out on the floor with his heel.

'He's still limping out there,' said Icke.

'He'll be fine,' said Clive. 'Even if he's in agony, he won't give up.'

'Tough northerner, you think? Or perhaps . . .' Here Icke gave a conspiratorial look. '. . . *perhaps* it was all just histrionics?'

'Yes, it could have been, I suppose. A chance for him to indulge his dramatic instincts. He probably wants us to think that he's in agony and is playing on regardless in order to win our praise and admiration. Quite a narrative he's carving for himself out there. I don't mind though. I'd rather watch him pretending to bravely battle it out than watch Hamlet banging on about his woes all afternoon.'

'Was it dreadful?'

'The boys seemed to like it. They were quite enthused.'

'Word is there was some sort of mix-up.'

'Really?'

'Oh yes. Someone said you ended up phoning in a missing persons report.'

'God, people talk round here, don't they?'

'They do. They do.' Icke stood up and performed a few extravagant swings with the bat. 'Right. I think I'll take a walk around the boundary. I'm getting nervous just sitting here. How do you feel?'

'The same, I think. Bit weird, actually.'

Icke gave him another of his looks and then set off, looking gloomy. Clive watched him go, relieved that someone else was sharing his sense of dread at playing in this ghastly game. It was such a silly use of the day. He could have been at home now, playing with the girls. Or reading the paper. They could have all gone for a nice pub lunch. A walk. That's what Wally would be doing now. Sitting in a country pub with his dogs at his feet, about to indulge in a vast roast before heading out into the wilds. He didn't envy Wally often but he did now. Iain had only taken twenty or so steps when there was another shout from the middle. Clive didn't know what had happened but the opposition were gathering in a huddle. Frank was walking back towards him. Iain was back too, divested of his pads and gloves.

'Oh, Frank's gone. Did you see how?' he asked.

'No.'

'You seen my tobacco anywhere?'

Clive held up the leather pouch.

'It's here. We helped ourselves to some. Hope you don't mind.'

'No, no, that's fine. Oh no, hang on, that's not the one I'm looking for. That's my . . . I've got another one. A green one. God, did I leave that out here? Bloody hell.'

Iain swiped the pouch from Clive's grasp and pocketed it, then sat down next to Clive and looked at him for a moment. 'Is this the one you helped yourself to?'

'That's right. Frank and I made roll-ups.'

'And did you smoke them?'

'Well, yes. I did. I don't think Frank had time.'

'Oh God.'

Harper walked past them, shaking his head and muttering something about the bounce.

'Not much you could do about that,' said Iain.

'Unplayable,' said Clive.

Once Harper was out of earshot, Iain glanced around and then leant in close to Clive's ear. 'There's cannabis in that pouch.'

Clive wasn't altogether surprised. 'Well, I didn't see it. Resin, is it? Don't worry, we didn't touch it.'

'It's grass. And it's all mixed in. I do it in advance. Then I can roll up anywhere and it's more discreet looking. And I don't have to faff about when I'm driving.'

'When you're *driving*?' said Clive, loudly.

'Shh. Yes. I don't smoke when I'm driving. But sometimes I roll one, so that I can light it as soon as I get out of the car at home.'

'Have you had any today?'

'Of course I haven't. Not before a bloody cricket match. I'd be mad. How are you feeling? Did you smoke the whole thing?'

How am I feeling? thought Clive. Really not great, suddenly. He had felt OK when he was smoking it. Not good, but OK. But the knowledge of what it was that he had smoked suddenly made all the difference. It hit him like the fresh air hitting a drunk man when he takes that first step out of the pub. Oh God. He was actually quite stoned, and he didn't like it. He stood up, didn't like that either, and sat down again.

'It's pretty strong stuff,' said Iain.

'Well, yes. I can feel it. No wonder Icke was looking at me funnily.'

'You smoked it next to Icke?'

'Yes.'

'Oh Jesus Christ. Do you think he realised?'

'I think he did, in retrospect. I thought he was just being sanctimonious.'

'No, no. It'll be all right. I'll just casually mention that it's some herbal stuff I've started smoking to wean myself off tobacco. He's such a square, I'm sure he'll buy that. Do you need some water or something?'

Yes. Clive suddenly did need some water. A lot of it. He

hadn't smoked a joint for years. The more he thought about it, the more terrified he became. He'd never had much tolerance for the stuff. He nodded, dry-mouthed.

'I'll go and get you some. Don't mention this to anyone. Not even Mark. We'll sort this. And I'll see if anyone else is ready to go in next.' And off he went to the pavilion.

Oh God, thought Clive. I've never seen Iain panic before. I'm in next. I'm in next and I can hardly bloody stand. He looked out at the pitch where Mark and Icke were scurrying back and forth. They might as well have been playing kabaddi. And they looked so far away. Clive could feel his heart beginning to race. He put his hand over his chest and could feel it pounding. He felt hot. And then he felt cold. He looked down at his feet and tried taking some long, slow breaths. He'd read that if you could control your breathing you could control your fears. But it turned out that he couldn't control his breathing. He was panting like a dog – like one of Wally's big beasts running about after a filthy ball. Iain, you bloody bastard. What have you done to me? Where's that sodding water?

Again there was a shout from the middle. Icke was on his way back now. Clive looked around. Iain hadn't returned from the pavilion and still no other members of the team had reappeared. There was nothing for it. He had to go out there. He picked up his gloves and started walking out towards the middle of the pitch. Thirty yards from the rope he crossed with Icke.

'I warn you,' Icke said, handing over the bat, 'he's bloody quick. Mark's making it look easy, but it's not.'

'Wonderful' said Clive, and carried on his way. Beyond the pitch that he was walking onto, all of Wiltshire suddenly seemed to spread before him. Rolling hills and woodlands. This little pitch with white human specks on it was but nothing compared to the vastness of their surroundings.

How insignificant this all is, thought Clive. We are but nothing.

'You all right?' asked Mark.

Clive was rather surprised to realise that he had now made it all the way out to the middle. Already he couldn't really remember the walk there.

'Oh yes,' said Clive. 'Absolutely fine. Tell me. Is everything moving very fast?'

'The bowling, you mean? It's quickish. You'll be fine though. Just stick around with me and we'll have some fun.'

'Oh yes,' said Clive. 'Fun. I like fun.'

The bowler and the fielders were already in position so Clive made his way to the end recently vacated by Icke and adopted what he thought was a reasonable stance. No one moved.

'Do you want to take a guard?' asked the umpire.

'Er, no thanks,' said Clive. 'No, I think I'll just see how it goes.'

Once again he settled over his bat.

'Do you want to put your gloves on?' asked the umpire.

Clive looked down. He was holding his gloves tightly between his right hand and the bat handle. 'Oh yes,' he said, and then dropped them. He put the bat down flat on the floor next to him, then picked up one of the gloves and put his left hand into it. Something didn't feel quite right.

'I think that's the wrong glove,' said a nearby fielder.

'Oh yes,' said Clive, and put the glove down on the floor. He picked up the other one and tried to put it on his right hand.

'Do you mind if I . . . ?' said the fielder, and helped Clive to put the gloves onto the correct hands.

'Thank you,' said Clive.

The fielder moved back to his position and Clive looked back at the umpire and at Mark.

'All good now,' he said. He took a couple of deep breaths to try and calm himself down and then waited for the bowler to commence his run-up. Still no one moved.

'Your bat, Clive,' said Mark quietly. 'You need to pick up your bat.'

As Clive bent down to pick it up he could hear the opposition beginning to snigger. So, having stood up again, he took a little walk down the pitch as he'd seen Harper do, patting down imaginary bumps in the turf. Then he took a long, lingering look at where all the fielders were stood and finally settled over his bat.

'Right arm over, four to come,' said the umpire. 'Play.'

*

The ambulance had come very quickly, apparently. But Iain had known something was up the moment that Clive hit the ground and had called the emergency services immediately from the pavilion payphone. Clive had come round quickly, but the paramedics had thought it best to take him straight to hospital for a check-up.

'It's your head,' one told him. 'You have to take it seriously.'

'I think we should play on,' said Clive. 'I'll be fine.'

They stood him up and walked him to the ambulance. Iain was standing by the open doors as they strapped Clive to a stretcher.

'You're going to be all right,' he said, and gave Clive a discreet wink.

Clive gave him a thumbs up as the doors were closed behind him.

The doctors in Newbury explained to him that he had concussion but no lasting damage. He just needed a few days off work and to take things easy. He was already sitting out in the waiting room again by the time Helen and the girls turned up.

'Well,' said Helen, 'at least you'll be home earlier than if you'd played the rest of the match.'

'Well, that's something.'

'But really, Clive. I mean, *really*. What a bloody stupid thing to do.'

'I'm going to get some time off,' said Clive.

'Yes, but it's not useful time off, is it? You've got to have time off because your head's not working properly. I used to think it was just me who thought that. Now it's been confirmed by a doctor.'

*

Mark rang the doorbell at eight o'clock.

'Oh hello, Mark,' said Helen. 'I'm just helping the girls get ready for tomorrow. Clive's in bed. But he might be awake. Try him.'

Clive was indeed awake when Mark knocked. He was sitting up against a makeshift mountain of cushions and pillows, staring at a wall and thinking very slowly about life.

'Come in,' called Clive. 'Oh, it's you. I was waiting for a cup of tea.'

'I'll make you a cup of tea if that's what you'd like.'

'Don't bother.'

'How are you feeling?'

Mark sat down on the edge of bed, then felt self-conscious about it and stood up again.

'It's OK,' said Clive. 'You can sit there.'

'Really, it's fine. Anyway, you're feeling . . . ?'

'I just ache, really. And I feel a bit . . . slow. Did we win?'

'We did. With ten men. How many days does it take a concussion to wear off?'

'Loads, I hope. I could do with quite a few days away from the sodding place. Not that anyone will notice.'

'We will. We'll suddenly realise that we have to do breakfast duty and take people to the theatre. Maybe we'll notice that no one else is doing anything. Still, half-term soon.'

'Mmm.'

'Have you plans?'

'No.'

'Right, well, I just wanted to check that you're doing all right. I'd better get back to the pub to celebrate with the others. Iain's pretty shaken up by your accident, by the way. He asked me to check on you. Said to tell you everything was fine. Said you'd understand.'

'I'm never going to play for his fucking team again. Even if he has got me some days off. Was it very fast, the ball that hit me? I can't remember it at all.'

'What?'

'The ball that hit me. Was it very fast?'

'You didn't get hit by a ball.'

'No?'

'No. You . . .' Mark stopped and smiled at the memory. 'I'm sorry. It's just that you . . .' Mark started laughing. 'No. What happened was that you . . .' Mark was screeching hysterically now. He looked down at the floor and gathered his composure. 'You came in looking *unbelievably* nervous.'

'I was nervous.'

'Yes, but this was just . . . wild-eyed panic. You couldn't get your kit on properly. You faffed about for ages. People had to help you.'

'I remember that bit,' said Clive, slowly but testily.

'And then eventually the bowler ran in to bowl and you took quite the wildest swing at it, long after it had gone past you. You completely lost your balance, staggered about for a bit and then fell directly on top of the stumps. That's the mark you can see on your forehead. Your full weight landed on it.'

'What?' said Clive. 'So I was out?'

'Yes!' laughed Mark. 'Spectacularly. And painfully. Horrible to watch, actually. But all right to laugh at, now that you're OK. Well, sort of.'

'Bloody hell,' said Clive, rearranging his pillows so that he could lie down. He pulled the duvet up over his head. 'Turn the light out, will you?'

9

Clive couldn't remember the last time that he'd had a lie-in during term time. Perhaps it had never happened. It was blissful. Admittedly, he felt incredibly groggy, but he had the place to himself and it was all beautifully quiet. Helen had even changed the sheets that morning, before taking the girls to school. It felt like being in a hotel. It was Helen who had phoned Icke last night and told him that Clive would be off work for a few days. Icke, who had witnessed the accident in the flesh, said that he was not at all surprised. Once the others had left, Clive lay in bed just staring at the ceiling for an hour. Or maybe it was two. He was drifting in and out of sleep but had no idea how long he was out for each time. Sometime late in the morning he got up to use the loo and take a couple of painkillers, pausing to inspect the bruise on his forehead in the bathroom mirror. It really was quite spectacular, spreading to cover his right eye and showing at least six different shades of purple. He put on his dressing gown and went downstairs to make a pot of tea and some toast. On his way to the kitchen he had picked up the post and the newspaper from the front doormat, and now he spread them out in front of him on the kitchen table alongside his breakfast. He read, in their entirety, the first ten pages of the broadsheet, and then spent a few minutes on the sports pages. It was heavenly really, Clive thought. Some of what he was reading wasn't really sinking in, and sometimes his concussion meant that he had to go back to the start of a paragraph several times over, but at least he wasn't at work. Perhaps, thought Clive, it would be possible to eke out his concussion symptoms so that they could last the whole week. Then it would be the half-term holiday and all together he wouldn't have to set foot in a classroom for nearly another three whole weeks. He opened the post. Everyone wanted money. There were bills from two energy companies he was reasonably convinced weren't his suppliers and a begging letter from his university. All of the letters were torn in half and placed to one side. Two copies of the free local paper had come through the door, so one of those got torn in half too. The other he idly flicked through. There wasn't much by way of local news. The county council were still in deep and unresolved discussions about what form Frampton's memorial to the Princess of Wales should take. There seemed to be a fifty-fifty divide between those who wanted a fountain and those who were keen for a bandstand. There was also a two-page spread about a recent charity duck race. The rest of it was adverts for local businesses and most of the shops on the high street.

'Half-term holidays not sorted yet? No problem!' said one, above a black-and-white photograph of three members of staff at a local travel agent. 'Why not pop in for a face-to-face consultation?' Clive was mulling over whether he would want to leave his holiday plans in the hands of these people when the phone rang out in the hall. It wouldn't be Helen, because she had specifically told him to get some rest and not answer the phone. Clive let it ring twelve times and then went out to listen to the answerphone machine.

'Hello, Clive, it's Linda here, from the headmaster's office. I hope you had a nice weekend and the trip went well. If you have a chance to run the keys over today, I'd be very grateful. Thank you.'

I won't, thought Clive, and went back to bed.

*

He spent the rest of the day and most of Tuesday and Wednesday in bed too. He could feel the concussion lifting but was still happy to milk his condition for all it was worth. It was good being home already when the girls got back from school. He came downstairs for supper and then returned to bed, and Katie would come to him when she wanted her bedtime story. On Monday, Tuesday and Wednesday, Helen took great pleasure in calling Icke in the evenings and letting him know that Clive showed no sign of improvement, even though on the last of those evenings he felt well enough to come down to the kitchen for a glass of wine.

'Do you think I should go back?' he asked her.

'No,' said Helen. 'I think you should stay at home. When you're not there they will realise just what it is that you do. What you're capable of. That they undervalue you. Stay at home until half-term. Which we still need to plan for.'

'I'll deal with it,' said Clive. 'I've got a plan.'

He meant it. On Thursday he waited until a point in the morning when lessons would be well underway and no one from the school would be out in the town, and then he got dressed and made his way to the high street and the travel agent.

A young man with spikily gelled hair beckoned him to take a seat opposite and asked how he could help.

'It's about half-term. I thought perhaps I might be able to book something.'

'Half-term? Cutting it a bit fine, aren't you?'

'Well, yes. I saw your advert in this week's . . .'

Clive suddenly couldn't remember the name of the local paper. The *Gazette*? The *Argos*?

'You know, the local paper. The free one.'

'The *Advertiser*?'

'That's it. I saw your advert in the *Advertiser*.' Just saying that sentence made Clive feel drunk. Maybe he wasn't feeling as well as he thought. Was it called the *Advertiser*? 'It said that you could sort half-term things, so I just assumed that . . .'

'We've been running that ad for four weeks, to be honest. But I'm sure we can do something. Flying could be tricky.'

'Just abroad, really. Somewhere quiet. A holiday let maybe? Somewhere we could drive to.'

'How long do you want to drive for? A couple of days?'

'Oh no. As little as possible, really. I mean, I'd be happy to get to France and then just stop, I suppose. Something in a village, perhaps. Little house. Bit of garden. Some sun.'

'We can't sort the weather for you, but everything else should be OK. We can arrange the house, ferry tickets, travel insurance. Like I say, it's tight. But leave me your details and I'll give you a call later with a couple of options.'

'Wonderful.'

'And can I ask what your budget is?'

Clive named a figure off the top of his addled head and then, unsure how the transaction was supposed to end, shook the man's hand and left the shop.

As he walked back towards the house he was feeling rather pleased with himself for having done something. Now that the concussion was lifting, thoughts that had been developing and building up for days, weeks and months, travelling slowly and opaquely through the mists of his mind, appeared fully formed. Getting hit must have unblocked something.

One of the most clear-cut of the thoughts that he had had this week was the sudden realisation that his and Helen's marriage, if he wasn't careful, was on the verge of trouble. They had got out of sync. Not massively, but just slightly. In a way, that was more damaging. A train that is missed by seconds is more frustrating than one that is missed by minutes. There was a time when he and Helen had finished each other's sentences. Now they trod all over what the other was saying, cutting one another off at just the wrong moment, muffling vital sounds. Their conversations resembled a series of collisions. And it had been like this for too long. He was almost embarrassed by how slow he had been to address this. Did Helen realise? She must do. Did he love her more than she loved him, or did he simply hate her less?

The sudden realisation should have made him feel gloomy but he actually felt upbeat. Because now that he could be honest with himself that there was a problem, he could do something about it. If he wanted to. And he did, he felt. But what? It was the job. He was sure of it. That was the cause of all their problems.

What Helen didn't like about Clive was what his job had done to him. And that he wasn't better at it. Clive's attitude to his job had been one of resistance. And it had failed. He would have to change tack completely. He had to play the game. Buy in. Be a believer. Show real willing. Even – *Christ* – support the headmaster. But if he could do these things, he could progress. And if he was progressing, he might become happy rather than miserable. And if he was progressing, then Helen would certainly be happy.

If he achieved success at school, he would put himself in a position to control his own destiny more. He could end up in charge of something. He could delegate. He could actually be at home more, spend more time with the girls. Accept or change, someone had once told him. But who? A self-help book? Was it someone who'd come to the school to speak? Anyway. They were wrong. You need to accept *and* change. Clive had to accept the realities of his situation and then change himself to fit them. From the start of next half-term he would be a new Mr Hapgood. A better teacher. A better colleague. And on this holiday, if it happened, he would be a new Clive. A new Daddy. He would be happy. He would be fun. They would all have fun. Together. Clive was going to prove to his wife that he could do this. Because if he couldn't, then the consequences were unthinkable.

10

The third-form boys were already at their desks when Clive came in, and he walked to the front and picked up a marker pen.

'Morning, boys,' he said. He was curiously relaxed about the whole thing.

It was Friday morning and he'd had a call from Icke asking him to cover for someone who was considered even more ill than he was. If he hadn't just had a call from the travel agent telling him that everything was all sorted, he would probably have said no. But as it was, he was in high spirits and felt that one quick lesson would be manageable. His concussion, if he was honest with himself, was largely gone.

'You're late, Sir,' said a strangled voice.

Clive turned round and eyed the class. Jonathan Findlay was the only one among them he knew.

'I'm not late,' said Clive. 'It's exactly five past eleven now. That's the time this lesson starts, isn't it? I'm ready if you are. OK?

'So then. The Tudors. You've learnt all about them, I'm told, so I thought it might be fun to have a little quiz. I'll just make a note of the questions, you can write down your answers and then mark each other's work. Let's start at the beginning. What year was the Battle of Bosworth? Bonus point if you know the month.'

He took the top off the marker he held in his hand and turned back to write on the board. The pen's tip was mere millimetres from the board when a different but still strangled voice said, 'Sir was late.'

Clive turned around again. Who had it been this time? They were a sea of identical blank expressions.

'Did someone say something? No? Then we'll carry on.'

Clive turned around to write but another voice started up.

'Late, late, late.'

Clive spun around again. The faces were no longer blank – they were nearly all smirking. Even Findlay was looking mischievous.

'Look,' said Clive. 'I wasn't late. I just wasn't as early as you. An important difference. It's half-term tomorrow. You'll all be at home very soon. Would it be so hard to wait another day to play some silly games?'

Nobody answered.

'Fine. Let me answer for you. "No, Sir. It wouldn't." Right answer? Well, don't just nod at me. Speak. Can you manage one more day?'

'Yes, Sir,' they all said in unison.

'Good. Thank you.'

Clive had only been back in a classroom for a few minutes and already he felt nauseated. He just wanted to get through it. He turned around to write on the board but a voice called out sarcastically, 'Good. Thank you.' Clive was too quick this time. The culprit was a red-headed boy sitting at the back in the corner.

'Problem?' Clive asked.

'No, Sir.'

'So why the silly voices?'

The boy looked sheepishly back at Clive. He seemed more humiliated by the glances he was getting from his fellow pupils for getting caught than he was by the fact he'd been caught in the first place.

'It's not just me, Sir.'

'Oh really? Who else was making stupid noises?'

'Well . . .' said the boy, looking down at his desk rather than at the boys along the row all glaring at him.

'It's all right. They can tell me themselves.'

Nobody said anything and so Clive resumed. 'Fine,' he said. 'You can keep quiet. But you'd better stay quiet when I've got my back to you too. Right. Question one. Come on. Pens out. The Battle of Bosworth. Year. Month if you know it.'

Clive swivelled around and started to write. Or tried to. But the pen left no mark on the board. It just gave a dry squeak. There were some chuckles from behind him. Clive sighed and looked around for another board marker, but there was nothing else there. He opened his desk drawer and had a look there too, but to no avail. The boys were sniggering openly now. Clive knew that there were always spare pens in there. This prank wasn't opportunistic. It was planned. 'No trouble,' that's what Icke had said. 'It can be in your own classroom, it'll be fine.'

'OK,' Clive began. 'You've been in my drawer and taken my pens. Great. Very funny. But if I don't have any pens, then I can't write anything on the board. And if I can't write on the board, then I can't note down what the questions are. So none of you can get any marks. It makes it harder for you to learn and harder for me to teach.'

'I thought you always found it hard to teach, Sir.'

This came from a boy at the front. Floppy black curtains of hair.

'Would you care to expand on that?'

'I meant that teaching is a very difficult job.'

It can be, thought Clive, now cursing himself for agreeing to take this class. If only Helen had been at home and picked up the phone.

'Right, where are the pens?' he said. 'Anyone?'

Nothing.

'Fine then. So I can't teach.'

'I always thought that, actually,' said a voice.

This time it was a voice he recognised. Clive actually felt genuinely hurt. He would make an example of him.

'Findlay,' said Clive. 'Get out.'

'I was only joking, Sir.'

'Just go.'

Findlay looked imploringly at the other pupils. They looked away.

'I don't really think that I deserve to be spoken to like that by you,' said Clive. 'Out.'

Findlay started towards the door.

'Your things, Findlay. Don't leave them in here. You're not coming back.'

But Findlay was already making for the corridor. As he opened the door, Clive dashed forward and scooped up the boy's things – a heavy lever-arch file and a couple of text-books – from the bank of desks and ran back towards the door with them. Findlay was standing out in the corridor with his back to the classroom.

'I said, "Take your things,"' called Clive, and then flung the boy's possessions in his general direction before marching back into the classroom to address the others.

'Anyone else want to misbehave?'

The rest of the class muttered a few 'No, Sir's.

'Right then. Someone tell me where my board markers are and we can get on with this.'

Problem solved. Someone pointed towards the bin in the corner and Clive walked over and removed the pens from it.

'Right then,' he said, beginning to write on the white-board. 'Bosworth. Year and month.'

*

Clive didn't even stop by the history staffroom once the lesson was over. He walked over to the council office to tell Helen the good news.

'What are you doing here?' she asked, as Clive entered her office without knocking.

'I've just come to tell you that we're going to France tomorrow. For a whole fortnight.'

Helen was so pleased with this news that she gave Clive a kiss on each cheek and then one on the mouth. Clive, for his part, actually felt proud.

*

'You wanted to see me, Headmaster?'

It had been quarter to eight when the phone rang downstairs, just as Clive was reading to Katie. Helen had appeared at the door and said that she had better take over as Crouch was on the phone. Clive apologised to Katie. 'Still,' he said. 'France tomorrow!' Sarah called goodnight to him without looking up from her book.

'Hello?'

'It's Julian Crouch here, Clive. Sorry to call you at home so late. I wonder if you might come over for a short chat?'

'Now, Headmaster?'

'Yes, I think that would be for the best.'

'I'd better just tell Helen. Are you in your office?'

'I'm at home, Clive. Arabella and I were rather hoping to watch some television this evening but something's come up.'

The home he referred to was on the edge of the school grounds and could only be accessed by a sweeping drive that led from the road on the opposite side of the grounds to where Clive lived. It was one of the oldest buildings in Frampton, predating the school and having once housed it in its entirety. The years had not been kind to the house, however. Or perhaps it was fairer to say that they had been too generous. Successive extensions had been lavished on it in a number of styles that refused to overlap aesthetically. The façade alone managed to be both Italianate and mock-Tudor.

It was half past eight by the time Clive had ground out a cigarette on the drive and then walked up it to ring the brass bell on one side of the brick porch. It was Arabella who answered.

'Hello, Clive,' she said, proffering a cheek for Clive to kiss.

'Arabella, how nice to see you. And the house. I don't think I can have been here for ages.'

'Yes, the big garden party was two summers ago already. We must have another one. It's been entirely redecorated since then,' she said, as she led him into the hallway.

'So it has,' said Clive, attempting to take it all in in one look, an almost impossible task given how ornate a job had been done. The double-height hall had burgundy patterned paper on the walls, and in gold frames there hung photographs of the Crouches and their children at various graduations and reunion dinners.

'I chose it all myself,' said Arabella, who was wearing a lavender-coloured turtleneck jumper with a thick, gilded necklace of links over it.

'Did you really?' said Clive. 'Well, it looks absolutely lovely.'

Clive didn't hold particularly strong views on interior decor, but never in his life had he ever fought so hard not to shout the words 'what horrific cushions'.

'Julian's in his study. I'll see you on your way out.'

Clive knocked tentatively on the study door.

'Hello?' called Crouch.

'It's Clive. Clive Hapgood.'

'Do come in.'

Crouch was sitting behind his desk and he too was wearing lavender, a V-neck in his case. Clive wondered if Crouch and Arabella hadn't seen each other this evening or if this coordination was deliberate.

'Headmaster.'

'Would you mind shutting the door? Have a seat.'

Clive obeyed.

'So,' said Crouch.

'You wanted to see me, Headmaster.'

'I did, Clive. I did. A little problem has popped up. At least, I hope it's a little problem. I've had a phone conversation with Jonathan Findlay's mother this evening.'

'I see.'

'Do you know what that conversation will have been about?'

'If it's about me sending him out of a lesson, she really needn't worry. I don't think it was characteristic behaviour. He's generally pretty well-behaved, I'd have thought.'

'It's about rather more than you sending him out of a lesson, Clive. It's about you assaulting him.'

Somewhere deep in Clive's stomach a knot formed. 'Assaulting him? That's completely ridiculous.'

'Apparently you threw something at him, and it hit him. Cut him. That counts as assault, don't you think?'

Clive swallowed hard and tried to recall the events of the morning.

'Is that what happened, Clive?'

'I don't know, Headmaster.'

'You don't know?'

Crouch was wearing a pair of thick-rimmed reading glasses, and he was now peering sceptically at Clive over the top of them.

'He didn't pick up his things when he left the classroom and so I ran – I *went* – after him and I threw them into the corridor. I don't know that they hit him. I certainly didn't see them hit him.'

'So you don't know for sure that they *didn't* hit him?'

'Well, I don't know if they did or didn't. I threw the things into the corridor and then went back into the classroom and tried to teach. They were being very difficult.'

'They? Or just him?'

'Well, all of them. They had taken my pens and they were making noises and . . .'

'So why was poor Jonathan Findlay singled out?' asked Crouch.

'I had to make an example of someone.'

Crouch now took off the reading glasses and folded them carefully before placing them down on the desk in front of him. 'When I spoke to Mrs Findlay she said that Jonathan felt that he had been singled out unfairly. Do you understand why he might feel like that?'

'Well, he was the only one that got sent out, yes. It meant that the others settled down.'

'So you were singling him out?'

Clive couldn't tell if the room was incredibly cold or incredibly hot. 'Look, Headmaster. The boy was being rude. I took action.'

'Yes,' said Crouch. 'I see. OK. Well, there we are.' He sat back in his chair and folded his arms. 'I must say, Clive, that I was very concerned by what Mrs Findlay had said. And so I thought it was important to get the facts straight. I spoke to Jonathan's housemaster and he interviewed the boy. He says that Jonathan definitely maintains that you threw something at him and that it hit him. He was shown the cut. And then I asked Jonathan's housemaster to speak to some of the other boys in the class.'

'Well, they won't have seen anything. If he was hit, it was outside the classroom.'

'It was more about whether or not young Jonathan being asked to leave the classroom was fair or not. Given how everyone was behaving. Now I'm not suggesting that they weren't being tricky. And we all have limited patience. But a straw poll of some of the boys in the class suggests that the way you treated him was unfair.'

'Is there anyone else you spoke to about this before speaking to me?' Clive asked.

'I wanted to get the facts straight before I spoke to you.'

'The facts? A lot of people have been spoken to who can't possibly have seen some of what has been claimed. These people don't know the facts. I know the facts.'

'And what are they, Clive? Did you throw something at the boy and did it hit him?'

'I don't know.'

'These don't sound very much like facts to me, Clive.'

Clive looked despairingly at Crouch, and then above the headmaster's head at the picture on the wall behind him. It was an oil painting of Crouch in full academic dress, standing on the lawn in an otherwise empty quad. It made him look like a television detective.

'Let me put it this way, Clive. Do you refute Jonathan Findlay's version of events?'

'Yes,' said Clive. 'I do.'

'Right. Thank you.' Crouch stood up and gestured for Clive to do the same. 'I'm sure you understand that we will have to investigate this further, Clive.'

'Yes, Headmaster.'

'But there's nothing more that can be done this evening. We'll have to have a look at it after the half-term holiday. That may give things a chance to simmer down a little.

'I hope so.'

'It's not been an easy time for the Findlay family, of course. The parents divorced last year. Did you know that?'

'I didn't, no.'

'Well. We shall discuss this again in the future. After the holiday. Any plans?'

'We're going to France.'

'Oh, how splendid. We adore France.'

It had always been hard, Clive thought as he walked slowly back to his own home, to gauge the seriousness of what the headmaster was saying. It was his actions that told the true story. Why hadn't he mentioned the concussion? Surely, whatever the truth of what had happened in the corridor, the concussion was a mitigating factor. He honestly had no recollection of Findlay having been hurt. Was that because he hadn't hurt him or because some remnants of his concussion were clouding his memory? The headmaster had seemed calm and controlled, but that didn't necessarily mean that there would be no further trouble; it could just as easily mean that a long-held plan to get rid of Clive was now in motion. It was hard for Clive to be objective, but it wasn't completely impossible that he could be sacked. Thoughts like that had to be dismissed from his mind before the family went off on holiday. He quickened his pace, and when he got home he told Helen that it had been just an informal chat about how Flora was settling in. 'I really don't know why it couldn't have waited. Can I help you pack?'

PART TWO

June 1998

11

Katie and Sarah had both been sick by the time the car finally reached Newhaven. It was Katie who went first, having complained of sickness on their slow journey around the south-western leg of the M25.

'Can you just hold on?' said Clive

'I feel really sick,' pleaded Katie.

'We don't have time to stop,' said Helen.

'I mean *really* sick,' said Katie.

'Can you hold on for a little bit?' said Clive.

'I don't think I can,' said Katie and emitted a guttural noise that was part stifled burp and part lament.

'What if we open all the windows?' asked Helen.

They wound down their windows, and then Helen turned up the cassette player, which was playing a tape of *Paddington* that they had all heard many times.

'That's really loud,' yelled Sarah.

'It has to be loud,' shouted Helen, 'because the windows are down.'

'WHAT?' called Sarah.

'Turn it off,' snapped Clive.

Helen ignored him, so Clive leant over and did it himself.

'We were all listening to that,' said Helen.

'It was too loud. We know what happens next. Paddington floats out to sea in a bucket.'

'This is supposed to be a holiday, Clive. Just calm down, will you?'

'We're not on holiday yet, we're on the M25. Oh, for God's sake.'

As they rounded a curve they could now see hundreds of brake lights stretching into the far distance.

'What time's the ferry?' said Helen.

'It's at five something.'

'Five what?'

'It's on the piece of paper,' said Clive.

'And where's the piece of paper?'

'Glovebox?'

Helen tried the glovebox. 'Any other suggestions?'

'Not in the glovebox?'

'No, Clive. It was in the glovebox but I just want other suggestions for fun.'

'All right. Under the seat? The boot?'

'The kitchen table?' suggested Helen.

'Oh God. Yes, probably.'

'Well, don't say it so calmly.'

'You were asking me to be more calm a minute ago.'

Clive brought the car to a sudden stop as they reached the traffic jam.

'When I was asking you to be calmer,' said Helen, 'I didn't realise that you'd left all of our tickets on the kitchen table.'

'The piece of paper is not the same as the tickets. The tickets are in the bag at your feet. With the passports. Or should be.'

'Shall I check?'

'Please.'

Helen unzipped the bag and had a rummage around, before zipping it up.

'Well?' said Clive

'Well what?'

'Are the bloody tickets in there or not?'

'Yes.'

'Passports?'

'Passports.'

'And what time is the ferry?'

'I don't know,' said Helen.

'It'll be on the tickets.'

'I thought it was on the piece of paper.'

'It's on both.'

'What is this piece of paper then?'

'It's a sort of itinerary with directions,' said Clive.

'And it's on the kitchen table?'

'I don't think I can hold on any longer,' called Katie.

'Just try,' said Helen. 'Clive, can you get there without the directions? Because I haven't looked at a map. I had to go to Swindon this morning.'

Helen had gone to Swindon to buy some new suitcases, because when Clive had got their old ones down from the loft the night before, he had found they'd been torn to shreds by mice. The mice had been dealt with over two years ago, and they hadn't had need of their suitcases in all that time. So Helen had gone to an absolutely heaving shopping centre in Swindon to buy two eye-wateringly expensive suit-cases. Clive had been tasked with preparing lunch and had served leftovers.

'I think,' said Clive, 'that it's M4, M25, M3, A23 and then left a bit before we get to Brighton.'

'Well, I hope there are signs.'

'For Brighton?'

'For Newhaven Ferry Port.'

'Of course there'll be signs for Newhaven Ferry Port. What else will they have signs for in Newhaven? Lord Lucan?'

'Why Lord Lucan?'

'Because that's where he left his car before he disap-peared,' said Clive, trying to change the subject.

'I think if there were signs they'd have found him by now, don't you?'

'Maybe I'll disappear when we get to Newhaven too.'

'Maybe I will,' said Helen.

'Good,' said Clive.

It was at this point that Katie broke the tension by being very violently and noisily sick. Sarah helpfully described the scene in case her parents missed any of the graphic detail.

'Katie's being sick!' shouted Sarah. 'She's being sick everywhere. It's on her dress. It's on the seat. It's on her shoes. It's on me.'

'Clive, find somewhere to pull over.'

'We're in a traffic jam on the M25. Where would you suggest?'

'The hard shoulder.'

'Really?'

'Just do it. Stick your hazards on and pull over.'

Clive did as he was told and was rewarded with some aggressive honks from drivers who thought he was trying to undertake. Helen got out and opened Katie's door. It really had gone everywhere. Clive inched his way around to the boot. They hadn't anything as practical as kitchen towel with them, so they would have to use real towels. He passed Helen clean clothes for Katie and then began the task of wiping down the seats. Then he got out more towels to put over the seats so that they would be dry enough to sit on. Helen recovered a plastic bag from the verge to put the sick-covered clothes and towels in and put it in the boot.

The girls and Helen strapped themselves in, but as the traffic was now moving again it was a little more difficult for Clive to get into the driver's seat. A singular lack of compassion in the left-hand lane left him sitting there with the indicators on for a good while before he could edge out into the traffic.

'It really smells,' said Sarah.

'We know,' said Helen. 'We can all smell it.'

'But I'm the closest to it.'

'*I'm* the closest to it,' said Katie.

'Can everybody please calm down?' said Clive. 'Would anybody like to listen to *Paddington* again?'

'Or we could just have a conversation?' said Helen. 'We'll have to get used to talking to each other if we're going on holiday, don't you think?'

'Can we have a conversation about how much it smells?' said Sarah.

'No,' said Clive.

'But it really smells.'

'Let's just sit tight, shall we?' said Clive.

Helen leant forward and turned the cassette player on.

'I feel sick,' said Sarah.

'Please don't be sick,' said Clive.

'I can't control when I'm sick,' said Sarah.

And as if to underline this point, she too was violently and noisily sick.

'Please can you turn *Paddington* off?' said Clive.

*

In the event, they found a turn-off that took them towards Worthing. The windows remained down, *Paddington* remained off, and Clive repeated the phrase 'everybody hold tight' just often enough to render it utterly absent of meaning. They pulled up outside a branch of Spar in a small village and Clive helped both girls out while Helen ran into the shop, in which, moments before, the lady behind the counter had taken a sizeable bite of an incredibly flaky Danish pastry.

'Oh, excuse me,' said the lady eventually, once she had had chewed and swallowed enough of the bite – all the while gesturing contritely and fanning her mouth – to enable her to enunciate. 'I'm just having a bit of a late breakfast. Or is it an early lunch?'

'I think it might even be a late lunch,' said Helen.

'I think I've overdone it in the microwave. It's scorching. Can I help you?'

Helen, momentarily distracted by the idea of somebody putting a Danish pastry in a microwave, eventually said, 'Kitchen roll,' and 'We're trying to catch a ferry.'

'Excuse me?' said the lady. She put the Danish pastry down on the counter on top of a paper bag. Helen could see that it was steaming a great deal.

'Or wet wipes? My daughters have been sick in the car.'

'Oh dear,' said the lady, now straightening her name badge. 'Carol,' it said. 'Happy to help.'

'We're in a bit of hurry.'

'Yes, I bet you are. It's always hard to leave yourself enough time on long journeys when you've got children, isn't it? We had three. All grown-up now, but they used to get car sick.'

'If you could just tell me where I might find them?' said Helen.

'Wet wipes or kitchen roll?'

'Either.'

'They're both on the same aisle, luckily. Aisle Two. Well, we've only got two aisles. It's the one on the right.'

Carol had only been in Helen's life for under a minute and, being someone who always saw the best in everyone, would have struggled to understand just how much Helen already hated her.

'Thank you,' said Helen.

An elderly gentleman in a Spar uniform was crouching down in the entrance of the narrow aisle.

'Excuse me,' said Helen. 'Can I just squeeze past?'

He stood up, holding a clipboard, and smiled warmly at Helen, who grimaced back as she squeezed by. There wasn't space for people to pass, especially if one of them was holding a clipboard perpendicular to his body. Ideally, he'd have stepped out of the way, but he was either entranced by Helen's charms or impractical. Instead he grinned while Helen contorted. Then she scanned the shelves. Kitchen roll should be easy to spot, surely. She looked all the way up and down the aisle without success before the man with the grin said, 'Can I help you?'

It said 'Roger' on his name badge.

'Kitchen towels,' said Helen. 'And wet wipes.'

'The other aisle,' said the man possibly called Roger.

'Is this Aisle Two?'

'It is . . .'

'Right. So the kitchen towels and wet wipes are in Aisle One, are they?'

'Always have been. Well, since I've worked here.'

'Great,' said Helen. 'Can I get round at the other end?'

'It's blocked off. I'm doing a stocktake, you see. There's things on the floor.'

'Well, if I could just get past you again . . .' said Helen and steered Roger out of the aisle.

'Found everything you need?' asked Carol, as the pair passed her.

'Not quite,' said Helen. 'I think I must have been looking in the wrong aisle.'

'Aisle Two for kitchen roll,' said Carol.

'Aisle One, Carol,' said Roger. 'Certainly since I've worked here.'

'Oh,' said Carol. 'Well, maybe try that one then . . . And Ken,' she added, 'you've got Roger's badge on again.'

'I know. I forgot mine. But Roger's was in the staffroom. It's more important that people know that I'm happy to help than that I'm called Ken.'

'By the way,' said Carol, 'I'd avoid the microwave in there. It's incredibly hot.'

'What, all the time?'

'Just when you use it.'

'Thank you, Carol. Noted.'

Ken returned to his spot in Aisle Two to recommence what Helen presumed to be Britain's slowest ever stocktake just as she arrived at the counter with kitchen roll and wet wipes.

'I'm going to have to leave that for a bit, I reckon,' said Carol, casting a despairing glance at the smouldering Danish pastry.

'Good idea,' said Helen. 'How much do I owe you?'

'Is it very smelly?' asked Carol.

'Your pastry?'

'The sick.'

'Yes,' said Helen, amazed at what some people seemed to be interested in.

'Bit of advice. Baking powder. Gets rid of the smell.'

'Really?'

'We used to absolutely cover our upholstery with it. Well, the bits that had sick on.'

Helen wasn't sure about taking advice from someone who failed to grasp the sole purpose of a microwave. 'Have you got any?'

'Now that I don't know,' Carol said as she scanned the kitchen rolls. 'Ken?'

Ken slowly stood up and removed the biro from his mouth. 'Carol?'

'Baking powder?'

'Yes?'

'Have we got any?'

'Now that,' said Ken, 'I don't know. Is it the same as bicarbonate of soda?'

'I don't . . .' began Carol.

'Yes,' said Helen. 'Just point me to the aisle.'

'It's probably quicker if I get it for you' said Ken. 'If we've got any.'

After forty-five agonising seconds had passed, Helen looking at her watch and Carol blowing on her pastry, Ken said, 'Aha!' and came back down the aisle to present a small pot of the stuff to Helen with a grin that would not have been out of place on the face of a restaurant troubadour handing a lady a plastic rose.

'Thank you,' said Helen. Just as Carol scanned it through, Helen remembered that her purse was in the car.

Clive had helped both girls change into fresh clothes – a second set for Katie – and was now trying to force more dirty clothes into the plastic bag from the hard shoulder.

'What have you been doing in there?' he asked.

'Care work,' she replied. 'Money?'

'I hope you're being polite to them.'

'They're idiots.'

'You shouldn't be rude to people who work in shops.'

'I'm not. I'm being rude *about* them. Honestly, Clive, what is this? I'm trying to be quick. Because you can't remember when the ferry is.'

'It's on the tickets.'

She held out a hand. Clive flinched.

'The money, Clive. Give me some money.'

Clive fished in the pocket of his holiday jeans and pulled out a ten-pound note. She snatched it from him and ran back into the shop. Carol, in the meantime, had dared to take another bite of her pastry and was now dealing with the consequences. Helen put the note down on the counter and Carol held it up to the light.

'We have to check for fakes,' she said. 'Although I don't really know how you're supposed to be able to tell.'

Outside, Helen and Clive set to with the kitchen rolls and wet wipes, and then Helen began to sprinkle the baking powder all over the seats.

'What are you doing?' said Clive.

'Baking powder. Gets rid of the smell.'

'Really?'

'Apparently. It just means we have to go through customs with white powder all over the seats.'

They all climbed into the car and sped on their way to the ferry terminal at which, it transpired, they had arrived an hour earlier than they needed to.

*

'The girls don't normally get car sick,' said Helen. 'I think it was the leftovers.'

'Do you have to talk about it?' shouted Sarah from the back.

'No,' said Clive. 'We don't.' Then he added, 'If it was the food, then we'd have been sick too.'

'Not necessarily.'

'Please can you stop talking about it?' asked Sarah.

Clive looked out at all the other cars, which all seemed to be much fuller than theirs, rammed with suitcases and toys and duvets and sports equipment. Some had bike racks on. Why didn't they have a bike rack? Because they never went anywhere. Not like they used to. These people probably went on holiday all the time. Clive felt a pang of envy as he glanced around at all the packed estates. Confident-looking mums and dads got out of their cars and strolled up and down, chatting freely. Up ahead, men in high-vis jackets had appeared and started signalling to the cars to start snaking forward in the direction of passport control.

'It wasn't the food,' Clive said quietly, as the engine started.

Helen said nothing. And nor did she need to, because a few hours later, at a point in the Channel equidistant between Newhaven and Dieppe, she and Clive both began to feel sick too. Helen made it to a toilet cubicle. Clive only had time to dash out onto the deck and disgorge the contents of his stomach over the side. His vomit, despite the wind, hit the water three floors below him, and he watched its flecks mingling with the foam and then disappearing into the water as he leant out over the rail, contemplating another argument lost and another hour of his life slowly passing by.

12

The key to the gîte was in a metal box fixed to the trunk of one of the pine trees that lined the narrow drive along one side of the building. Helen had to scrabble around in the dark while Clive manoeuvred the car about in an attempt to throw light from the headlamps onto the different trees. The girls had fallen asleep on the ferry and then been carried down the stairs to the car deck and gently strapped in, before waking with starts when the car clanged violently off the ferry ramp.

'Where are we?' said Katie.

'France,' said Sarah.

'A place called Dieppe,' said Clive. 'Oscar Wilde used to come here for his holidays.'

They negotiated their way out of town, eventually taking a long, straight road through an industrial area, and by the time they reached the outskirts the girls had both fallen asleep again. Forty minutes later they had arrived in the village of Monvachel, found the key and, with the girls still in the car, they let themselves in to the property. The smell that hit their noses was unmistakeable.

'Touch of damp?' said Helen.

'Probably been no one here for a while,' said Clive. 'Let's open all the windows.'

They went around the house opening the windows and exploring. It was a two-storey stone barn with a big open kitchen and sitting room on the ground floor with two bedrooms off it. At one end of the sitting room was a large wood-burning stove in a fireplace. A staircase curled behind the broad chimney stack, leading to two much bigger bedrooms and a bathroom in the eaves. One room had a wooden balcony, and with some difficulty they unlocked the glass door and stepped out into the night. They stood there for a moment, just breathing in the still, mild air. Clive let out a long, slow breath and felt something inside him uncurl slightly in the vast darkness. He held out his hand and Helen took it, then rested her head on his shoulder. He leant his head against hers and a full, blissful minute passed. Then Helen extracted herself, kissed him on the cheek and said, 'Let's unpack the car.'

Helen and Clive took the duvets off the single beds and shook them out on the balcony. There was a layer of something on everything, thin but nevertheless discernible. Everything needed to be encouraged somehow, cushions to be plumped, taps to be forced. Door catches needed to be turned, drawers to be slid open, switches to be pressed and lights to flicker slowly into life. Then they carried the girls up to their room.

'Teeth?' said Clive.

'We can't wake them again.'

They closed the door and tiptoed downstairs, then sat down on a sofa with a glass of tap water each.

'I think we ought to get some bottled water tomorrow,' said Helen, after a sip.

'Shall we go to bed?' said Clive.

'I'm going to have a bath.'

Clive didn't know why he thought that Helen would want to make love with him after a journey like that, but he had it in his mind that she might.

'A long one?'

'Yes, I think so.'

'I think if you try to have a bath and there's no hot water it'd be so annoying that it just isn't worth it. I'd certainly be annoyed if it was me.'

'Yes. But I'm not like you, Clive.'

And there was hot water. Lots of it. As the bath ran, Clive and Helen shook out their own duvet in the other upstairs room and by the time Helen was lowering herself into the bath, Clive was already fast asleep.

*

They didn't sleep for long, but it was deep. They had left the shutters open, and not long after six the room was filled with light. Helen got out of bed and stood stretching by the window. Clive watched the light falling on her bare breasts.

'You're very beautiful, you know,' he said.

'I'd like a tan,' she said.

'What's out there? Other houses?'

'Outbuildings. Looks like there might be firewood.'

'We won't need to light the stove, will we?'

'Something nice to sit in front of in the evening. Drink wine in front of.'

Clive looked at her body again. When he looked up at her face, he saw she was looking straight at him.

'Would you like to . . . come back to bed?'

'Teeth.'

'Of course.' Even as he was moving towards the door, Clive was slightly embarrassed by the alacrity with which he was scampering off to get ready. He moved the brush around his mouth and had a quick wash in the basin, followed by a squirt of aftershave. When he returned to the room Helen was still at the window.

Clive stood behind her and put an arm around her midriff.

'Ooh,' she said. 'Aftershave. Very nice.'

He attempted to lead her to the bed, but without success.

'I have to brush my teeth,' she said.

'I don't mind.'

'You should. I won't be long.'

Clive fetched a condom from his suitcase and popped it under the pillow. He could not believe quite how excited he was. It was like being nineteen. He climbed back onto the bed and experimented with a variety of postures, settling eventually for propping himself up on one elbow with a fist against his temple.

Helen laughed when she saw him. 'That looks uncomfortable.'

'Are you going to take your knickers off?'

'Knickers is such an unsexy word.'

She climbed into bed beside him. Clive lay on his back and she put her head on his chest. He kissed the top of her head and held her close. Then she kissed him on the lips before rolling over onto her back. Clive rolled over too and they began to kiss more urgently. She ran her hands over his back as he kissed her chest.

'I like being on holiday,' he whispered to her.

'Take these off,' she said, tugging at the waistband of his boxer shorts.

He did as she asked with more urgency than grace, kneeing Helen in the thigh as he did so.

'Sorry.'

He knelt over her now, and she lifted her hips and removed her own underwear in one fluid motion. They kissed each other's necks and their fingers intertwined.

'Condom?' she said.

Clive pulled it from under the pillow and knelt to remove it from the packet and put it on. Helen watched the look of absorption on his face. They began slowly. It had been a while, and their rhythms were, at first, tentative. But gradually, like a hesitant organist and church congregation, they settled into a shared tempo.

'Don't scrunch up your face,' she said. 'You look like you're in pain.'

Clive was wearing the expression of a man who knows he's had one too many concentrating behind the wheel of a car. He seemed unable to relax his facial muscles without slowing down to the point where Helen could barely register his efforts.

'Why have you stopped?' she asked. 'You've not finished, have you?'

'I'm just trying not to screw up my face.'

'Can you do that without grinding to a complete halt?'

'Look, it'll take us a few days to get back into the swing of things,' Clive said.

'It'll take me a few days to climax at this rate.'

This stung Clive, who immediately began to thrust faster.

'Seeing as we're allowed to give feedback, you might think about using a more encouraging tone,' he said in bursts.

'That's better,' she said. 'Although you're doing that face thing again.'

Clive said, 'Maybe this is why some people wear blind-folds.'

Helen laughed and pulled Clive's head towards hers. They could whisper straight into each other's ears now.

'Happy now?' Clive asked.

'Yes,' moaned Helen. 'I can't see your face.'

Helen's mockery was just the motivation he needed, it transpired. It had been so long since they had achieved this level of intimacy that Clive had almost forgotten how Helen behaved during sex. Suddenly she let out a loud, exclamatory squeal. Clive took the full force of this delighted cry directly into his ear and reeled slightly. He too let out a cry, but one symptomatic of agony rather than ecstasy.

'What is it?' Helen asked.

'I think my ear's popped.'

'Don't stop.'

Clive raised himself up on his elbows now, more out of a sense of self-preservation than a desire to experiment. Helen looked deep into his eyes and smiled.

'Happy?' she said.

'Very,' he said, although his ear really was ringing from the force of her cry.

Still, he felt a certain smugness as he proceeded. It wasn't inconceivable that they had been at it for as many as eight or nine minutes. Helen, despite her teasing, did seem to be enjoying herself. Clearly they had just needed to be reawakened like the house, to undergo the sexual equivalent of plumping up their cushions. Now it was just a matter of not getting overexcited. Helen moaned again and Clive was reminded of the first retching noises that she had made on the ferry yesterday before she bolted so desperately for the loo. This certainly helped him keep a lid on his excitement. As Helen pushed him over and then rolled on top of him, he felt momentarily seasick.

'Are you OK?' she asked.

'Yes,' he said, taking in deep lungfuls of air, just as he had been forced to on the deck of the ferry yesterday. But there was no railing to lean against now, no wind to feel against his face, no bin to lower his head gently onto and mutter the word 'Christ' over and over again.

'You're looking very serious,' said Helen.

'You're looking very beautiful,' he said.

'You're holding something back,' she said. 'I can feel it.'

'I just want to make you happy,' he said.

'You will. You are.'

She put her hands on his shoulders and pushed herself into an upright position. Clive held her by the waist and tried to surrender himself to the moment. I'm allowed to be happy, he realised. I am on holiday, he thought with each thrust. Helen's face and neck were flushed now. Clive, meanwhile, was worried whether his pelvis could cope with this sort of treatment.

How can she give herself so freely? he wondered. What does she think about during sex? *Who* does she think about during sex? Her arms were behind her head now, her back arched. Imagine being able to let yourself go like that, thought Clive. Imagine being able to make that much noise. He'd be terrified of waking the girls.

'Shhh,' he heard himself say.

'What?' said Helen.

'Shh. You're being too loud.'

'We're having sex, Clive. Or at least I am. There's bound to be noise.'

'The girls can be light sleepers.'

'Stop worrying. Please.'

'I'm worried they might hear.'

'They won't.'

Clive had stopped now.

'Please don't stop, Clive.'

'I can't help it. It's the girls. It's making me nervous. You don't know how loud you are.'

'Honestly, Clive.'

The intense look that Helen had been wearing for some time instantly dissolved. Clive felt a sudden coldness as she climbed off him.

'I'm sorry,' he said.

Clive rolled over onto his side and removed the joyless condom from his now flaccid prick. As he did so, he heard the door behind him open slowly.

'Are you OK?' It was Sarah's voice. 'We could hear Mummy shouting.'

'Has Daddy died?' asked Katie.

'No, no,' said Helen. 'He's on surprisingly good form.'

Helen gave Clive a knowing look. Fifteen seconds earlier and they would have been caught like bees in jam.

13

According to a note pinned up in the kitchen, there was a little shop in the village but a proper bakery in the next village, three kilometres south along the valley. Helen suggested they walk. The valley road was narrow, barely wide enough for two cars, and without pavement. But a newly laid cycle path ran fifty metres alongside it, with gleaming tarmac and signposts telling them how far it was to each village and town on a route that went deep into Normandy. North, it would be twelve kilometres back to Dieppe. The village of Ricarmont was the first stop to the south. The sun was already high in the sky, and the girls complained as Helen and Clive rubbed sun cream into them before they left the house.

'I want a suntan,' said Sarah.

'You'll get one,' said Helen.

'The cream will stop it.'

'It won't. It will stop you getting burnt.'

'Why aren't you putting any on then?'

'I want to put it on you first. I'm protecting you.'

In truth, Helen wasn't planning on using much cream. She was so thrilled to be in real sun – real French sun that you could feel through your T-shirt. She wore flip-flops, the shortest shorts she owned and a flimsy olive V-necked T-shirt. Clive, on the other hand, would definitely need cream. He was almost incredibly fair-skinned in all places other than where his skin was chafed or ruddy. He had on an old straw hat with a faded pink polo shirt and linen trousers. His boat shoes were so battered they looked as if they had weathered a storm. He put cream on Katie and then anointed himself.

'Not that much, Clive!'

'I don't want to burn.'

'That's too much. It won't go in. You've put on enough for both of us. Stand still.'

Helen scraped the excess off Clive's neck and arms and covered her own. As she walked along, watching Clive and their daughters up ahead, the heat prickled. Clive liked to stride when he was out in the open air, as if powered by restlessness. The girls swung their arms and almost skipped while Clive stopped and pointed at things that he wrongly imagined they might find interesting.

'Look, girls! Wheat!'

Helen held back to observe the happy scene. This was how she wanted a holiday to feel: sun, open space, the girls larking about and Clive looking relaxed, although each time a lorry heading to or from Dieppe thundered past Clive would jump, and Helen watched the girls tease him for it. The noise shouldn't have been enough to startle a grown man. Perhaps the jumpiness was a measure of how wound up he had been by the school year. At times he had been driven quite mad, lapsing into sullenness or prone to coruscating rants. The way the school treated him had occasionally left him incandescent in the past, but recently it had been worse than ever before. Thank God for his injury, or he might not have booked a proper holiday. They would have just gone on a few day trips to visit parents or castles, and the time off would have been frittered away. Here they could breathe different air, eat different food, inhale different smells. Just seeing road signs written in a foreign language made life seem better somehow.

Helen felt a sudden surge of joy. It was so lovely – and rare – to see her girls and her husband having fun together. How precious the three of them looked. And how happy.

The girls hated Clive having to work the hours he did, and Helen was sick of having to explain to them when he had been called away. But no one could get in the way here. What a difference a little over two hundred miles and a bit of real sunshine could make. Why couldn't life always be like this? Helen only snapped out of her reverie when she heard Clive loudly shouting, 'Look, girls! Corn on the cob!' She laughed at how little interest the girls showed at this excited utterance and broke into a jog to catch up with them.

*

Ricarmont was a big village. It had a square, a civic building, a war memorial and a small children's playground. There was a fishmonger and a petrol station with a little supermarket. The bakery was only large enough for one customer at a time. No one was behind the counter when Helen entered, but when the bell above the door rang there was a shout and movement from behind a sacking curtain. It was flung open by a tiny elderly lady, dusting flour from her hands. She must have been about seventy and looked incredibly strong.

'Madame?'

'Bonjour, madame. Vous avez . . . croissants?'

'Non.'

'Ah.'

'Croissants,' said the old lady, and indicated along the street with a violent jerking of her thumb.

'Ah, merci.'

Some sort of transaction was expected though, so Helen pointed at random at a loaf and said, 'Pain.'

'Deux?' said the old lady.

'Oui,' said Helen.

'They don't do croissants,' she said, handing the two large loaves to Clive outside.

'Look at the size of these! It was you that wanted us to walk. Now I've got to carry these back. They're like water-melons.'

'Someone does croissants further along apparently.'

'Right. Well, you go ahead with the girls and I'll start lugging these. I might have to flag down someone with a van.'

The second bakery was very splendid indeed. The sign had gold lettering against a shiny black backdrop, and crois-sants were just the start of it. In the window there was an array of bright and fabulous cakes, as well as vivid-looking macarons. The smell of crème pâtissière hung in the air. Helen and the girls stood marvelling at the window display.

'Looks a bit pricey,' said Clive.

'We're on holiday,' said Helen. 'Let's have fun.'

'By "fun" do you mean "Let's eat cake for breakfast"?'

'That is exactly what I mean. Come on, you two.'

Helen put an arm round the shoulder of each girl and walked them into the shop.

*

Helen and Clive sat on a bench at the edge of the playground as the girls played noisily, clambering over the wooden climbing frames and taking turns on the lone swing. Two young French boys were also playing and, though the girls and they had little language in common, they developed an instinctive shared understanding, taking turns and laughing at jokes or noises. The boys' mother was watching on from the other side of the playground but did not respond to Clive and Helen's joyous bonjouring. Clive had eaten two crois-sants and drunk a cardboard cup of coffee, and was now watching his wife eat the last of the half-dozen macarons that she had bought to cleanse her palate after eating a slice of extravagant chocolate cake. There would be, Clive knew, no weight gain.

'How much did that all cost?'

'I'm not telling you.'

'Was it as much as the ferry?'

'Not quite.'

Helen popped the last tiny morsel of the macaron into her mouth and then wiped her lips with a paper napkin, which she crumpled into a ball and tossed into the empty paper bag at her feet. She stretched out to her full length along the bench, using Clive's lap as a pillow.

'Are you happy?' she asked him.

'Perfectly,' he said.

*

An hour and half later they arrived back at the gîte, laden down with things from the little supermarket, and went out into the garden. It was a sun trap, surrounded by high trees on three sides but large enough for their shade not to matter. There were dense fig trees, and the terrace that ran the length of the house had a table and some weathered sunloungers. Helen kicked off her flip-flops and found the short grass to be thick and springy, the occasional prickle tickling her bare feet. As the girls climbed trees and played tag, Clive's eye was drawn to an antique stone barbecue at the far end of the house. A search in the undergrowth at its base yielded some large, rusted grill racks that slid haltingly onto brick runners.

'Look at this!' Clive called.

Helen, already reclining on a sunlounger, book in hand and sunglasses perched on her nose, nodded back. 'Wonderful,' she said, as if he was a child showing her a drawing.

'We could clean it up.'

'We?'

'Well, I could. Barbecue one night?'

Helen tried to return to her book but there followed an unpleasant scraping sound and a series of expletives that made it hard to concentrate. Clive, having managed to slide the grills into place, was now having trouble sliding them out again.

'Everything all right?'

'Just rust probably.'

He heaved at them again, giving out a loud grunt, like someone trying to lift a seal out of a bath.

'You'll get a hernia,' called Helen.

'It's coming. Just needs another . . .'

He heaved again before finishing his sentence, and his efforts were accompanied by an even more anguished grunt, as if the seal that he was lifting out of the bath was resisting his efforts, perhaps even holding onto the taps.

'Do you know the French for "hernia"?'

'No,' said Clive, as the first of the grill racks came loose and he held it aloft. 'Look at that,' he grinned.

'Why don't you just relax? Come and read your book.'

'Let me just get the other grill out and I will.'

Helen watched as Clive struggled for nearly fifteen minutes, swearing loudly and continually, to work the second grill loose. When it was finally out he was drenched in sweat.

'That was a bit trickier than I thought it would be,' he said. 'Still, time well spent, I reckon.'

'Really?'

'God, I'm hot. I'm going to get some water.'

Clive bent down to kiss her, before going in to fetch a jug and glasses. Helen wiped his sweat from her forehead, slid further down her lounger and began a fresh chapter.

*

They ate outside, a lunch of cheese, bread and salad with water at one o'clock, and then supper five hours later, identical but for the addition of wine and lemonade. The girls had played all day. Helen, as she took great delight in telling Clive, had read over 300 pages.

'Is all of France like this?' asked Katie during supper.

'No,' said Sarah. 'Some of it is Paris.'

'I like it,' said Katie.

'I love it,' said Sarah.

The conversation stopped and the only sounds were a gentle evening wind breathing through the trees and the slow buzz of becalmed crickets.

'Why are we so tired?' asked Sarah.

'Fresh air,' said Helen.

'Doesn't Frampton have fresh air?'

'Let's not think about Frampton,' said Clive.

Once the girls were in bed, Clive and Helen opened all the windows and then brought in wood and lit the stove. They drank wine and chose one of the slightly dusty videos from the drawer under the television. It was a period drama set in the Raj. Everyone in it was beautiful and pristine, despite spending most of the time asserting their need to get into the hills to escape the dust.

'We should get some roll-ups,' said Helen, who never suggested such a thing unless she was genuinely relaxed. They managed two-thirds of the film.

'Not a bad day,' said Clive as they climbed upstairs.

'No,' said Helen drowsily. 'Not bad at all.'

14

'Is that rain?' Helen asked.

In response Clive made a noise halfway between a grunt and a groan that signalled to his wife that he was alive if not fully conscious, the sort of sound that would have made a member of a search-and-rescue team stop and bid the other searchers be silent for a moment. Helen rolled over to see Clive's eyes flicker but not open. A single fingernail to a love handle was normally enough to rouse him, but this morning it took her four goes of increasing intensity before Clive was awake enough to form words.

'What?' he eventually said, his eyes still closed.

'The noise. On the window. Is it rain? Can you check?'

Clive forced a yawn through a pin-sized opening between his lips, and slowly turned over so that he could look down at his wife through scrunched-up eyes. 'You want me to check if it's raining?'

'Yes,' she said.

'I can't hear a noise.'

'I can. I've been listening to it for ten minutes.'

'It could be branches tapping against the pane. Why don't you check?'

'Because I'll get cold. And then I won't be able to go back to sleep.'

'What time is it?'

'Quarter past six.'

'You've woken me up at a quarter past six to find out if it's raining?'

'You probably need the loo anyway.'

Thinking about it, Clive now realised that this was sadly the case. He swung his legs out and down onto the floor, then levered himself up uncertainly to start tottering towards the door.

'Where are you going?'

'The loo.'

'Go to the window first, can't you?'

'Can't you wait until I've come back?'

He was already desperate but turned on his heels and advanced, in the half-light, towards the window and peeked behind the heavy though translucent curtain. Little spots of rain were indeed hitting the glass. Clive let go of the curtain and made once more for the landing.

'Well?' said Helen.

'You're right,' said Clive.

'Dammit,' said Helen, as the door closed. Then she shouted after him.

'Don't wake the girls!'

His task completed, Clive padded downstairs to fill the kettle. As he waited for it to boil he stood at the kitchen counter and stared out of the window at the dawn sky. There were dark grey clouds as far as the eye could see. He peered down at the flagstones under the window and saw that they were slick with rain. The realisation that it had been going on all night gave him hope that it must surely soon stop. He filled the cafetière with hot water and coffee, gave it a stir and then watched intently as the brown grounds dispersed and flicked about inside the glass vessel, the clear water slowly turning first cloudy and then into a thick chestnut mud, and he became lost in a philosophical reverie. Helen appeared in the kitchen behind him, in a pair of his boxer shorts and one of his T-shirts.

'What are you thinking about?' she asked.

'Hope,' said Clive.

'What about it?'

'It's pointless.'

'Why?'

'It has no bearing on outcomes. I might hope that it stops raining soon, but whether or not it will bears no relation to my hope.'

'You could say the same about worrying.'

'Actually, maybe hope does have a purpose to it. It makes the now more bearable.'

'You've changed your tune. How?'

'Well, let's say you were tied to a tree. Hypothetically.'

'Of course.'

'And I fired an arrow at you.'

'Also hypothetical?'

'For now, yes. As the arrow was coming towards you, if you were thinking, "I hope that arrow doesn't hit me straight between the eyes," that would probably make the situation slightly more bearable than if you were worrying that the arrow was definitely going to hit you between the eyes. Yes? Hope gives more comfort than worry.'

'I'd probably be thinking, "This isn't like Clive."'

'It's hypothetical.'

'Right. But it's actually raining and we'll just have to cope with it. Whether by hoping or worrying. Are you going to plunge that coffee?'

'Why don't you? Then it's a team effort.'

Helen plunged as Clive took the milk from the fridge.

'We'll need more of this,' he said.

The girls were soon downstairs in their pyjamas.

'It's raining,' said Sarah.

'But it will probably stop soon,' said Clive.

'We hope,' said Helen. 'What shall we have for breakfast?'

'Croissants,' said Sarah.

'Yes, croissants,' agreed Katie.

'OK,' said Clive. 'Shall we all get dressed and drive to the bakery?'

Helen and the girls looked at Clive, then out at the rain and then back at him again.

'I'll go and get dressed,' said Clive.

*

The croissants, being eaten further from their source, had less warmth than those eaten yesterday. And being eaten inside on a rainy day, rather than outside on a sunny day, they were less delicious. They definitely cost the same, Clive reminded everybody.

'Is it always like this in France?' said Katie, punctuating a long silence in the kitchen.

'It's like this everywhere sometimes,' said Clive.

'Even in Africa?' asked Sarah.

'It rains in Africa,' said Helen.

'Even in the Sahara?'

'Even in the Sahara.'

'When it rains in the Sahara it's torrential,' said Clive.

'What's "torrential"?' said Katie. 'Is it an animal?'

'This is torrential,' said Helen, pointing out at the garden, which was now being absolutely lashed with rain. '"Torrential" means that it comes down in great amounts. Huge quantities of water. And it comes suddenly too. You could just be standing there, enjoying yourself, when all of a sudden . . . whoosh! Water is pouring from the sky.'

'Wow. Would that be frightening?'

'It could be very frightening. Even when it's not raining the weather there could be frightening. They have hurricanes. And dust devils.'

'Devils?'

'I know what dust devils are,' said Sarah. 'They're like tornadoes. Only with dust.'

'That's right,' said Helen. 'Which is why the likelihood of "just standing there, enjoying yourself" in the Sahara is pretty small.'

She flashed a look at Clive, who was glumly adding more butter to a croissant already dripping with the stuff.

'Or were you talking hypothetically?'

Clive finished slowly chewing a wedge of croissant. 'The prospect of us enjoying ourselves today is pretty hypothetical, I'd have thought.'

He meant it as a joke, but it came out more coldly than he intended. Helen returned to her own croissant.

'Girls,' she said, 'why don't you watch a video? And Clive, why don't you light the stove? I'll clear this up.'

Minutes later, the fire was ablaze and the girls and Helen were snuggled up on the big sofa watching *The Mighty Ducks* with French subtitles. Clive offered to make tea and disappeared into the kitchen area. Moments later he was back, shaking the milk carton.

'This is all gone now.'

'Oh sorry, yes. The girls had some when you were out.'

'And put the carton back in the fridge?'

'I'm sure they were just trying to be helpful.'

'Yes,' said Sarah. 'We were.'

'Well, it's not helpful,' said Clive.

'Sorry, Daddy,' said Sarah.

'It's not their fault that the milk's empty, is it?'

'No. But the carton in the fridge gave me hope.'

'Let's have it black.'

'I don't have to go all the way to Ricarmont. I'll try the shop here.'

'Wait until it's stopped raining. Come and sit down with us.'

Clive looked out of the window at the rain still pouring down. As he went back into the kitchen to collect the two black teas he heard Katie ask, 'Mummy, why is Daddy sad?'

'Daddy's sad about milk.'

'It's the rain!' he shouted through. 'I'm sad about the rain.'

*

It rained for all of *The Mighty Ducks* with French subtitles, and for all of *Mrs Doubtfire*, which didn't have French subtitles but whose picture flickered every fourteen seconds.

'We should do something about lunch,' said Clive as Robin Williams was cheerfully reunited with his children and the credits began to roll.

'If you and Mummy split up,' asked Sarah, 'would you dress up as a woman just so that you could come and see us?'

'He might,' said Helen.

'Mummy and Daddy aren't going to split up,' said Clive.

'But would you though?'

'Of course I would,' said Clive. 'Now, let's turn this off for a bit. Mummy and I will get some lunch out and you two can go and bang on the windows and tell the sky to stop raining.'

The girls carried out this instruction with such relish that after two solid minutes of it Clive and Helen were begging them to stop. Lunch consisted of everything that was left in the fridge.

'Is it too early to open a bottle of wine?' asked Helen as they sat down.

'I think I'll have cider,' said Clive.

'Can we watch another film?' asked Sarah as soon as they'd finished eating.

Helen looked out of the window at the unrelenting Normandy rain. 'You'd better had. But first, we're all going to run around the garden once in the rain.'

'All of us?' asked Clive.

'All of us,' she confirmed. She opened up the double doors out to the garden. 'It really is foul out here,' she said. 'Anyway, let's do it. Then we can put more wood on the fire and make some hot chocolate.'

'There's no milk,' said Clive. 'And there's not much firewood left.'

'Then you and I have some little jobs to do. Everybody ready?'

'Yes,' said Sarah.

'Right then,' said Helen. 'One, two, three . . . Go!'

The four Hapgoods ran out into the rain and sprinted around the garden. Katie slipped as she was turning at the bottom and Clive had to scoop her up and carry her back to the house. The moment they stepped inside Helen slammed shut the doors behind them. The four of them stood there dripping.

'Was that a good idea?' said Clive.

'It was brilliant!' said Katie.

'I'm going to go and bring in some more wood,' said Clive. 'Seeing as I couldn't get any wetter.'

He picked up the large, square wicker basket with rope handles from the hearth. It was heavy even without logs in.

'Take this as well,' said Helen, proffering a grey bin bag from the kitchen.

'What for?'

'Put it over the wood before you take it out into the rain. Stop it getting wet.'

The girls went upstairs to change. Clive stuffed the bin bag into his pocket, then opened the double doors again to lug the basket outside and around the back, across the gravel to the outhouse. There was plenty of firewood in the outhouse, but a number of holes in the rusty roof meant some of it was too wet to use. Clive gradually filled the basket with good-sized dry logs. Then he tried to lift it. So heavy was it that when he squatted down and heaved it hard, one of the rope handles gave way in his hands.

Instead he dragged it towards the entrance. It was fine dragging it slowly across the concrete floor, but once he was outside, the square edges bit and sank into the wet gravel. Any pull on the remaining handle just buried the basket deeper into the muddy stones, so he pulled it back towards the outhouse. Just a few seconds out in the open had already left the wood on top looking wet, and so he took out the bin bag and laid it across the top, tucking it in around the edges. To pick the basket up he pushed it up against the wall and leant into it, slowly working it up between his legs and the wall so that he could get his hands far enough under the edges to take the weight. It was too big for him to be able to reach the middle of the sides, but he could compensate for this by letting the basket tilt back towards him. He moved slowly, with bended knees, and half stomped and waddled. The weight, with his feet on the wet stones, was considerable, and twice he stopped to readjust it and take deep, steadying breaths. The rain slanted from right to left as he moved towards the house, small hailstones hitting him like pinpricks. He could have just carried the logs in two or three loads, but a ludicrous determination urged him on. He wanted that feeling of achieving something, of being a provider, a father figure, a man. He was going to see it through to the bitter end, no matter how literally back-breaking it was. It wasn't even glory he sought, but just to be seen as competent. 'Just keep moving,' he told himself. 'Step by step. Inch by inch.'

He had covered about half of the eighteen feet or so to the end of the house and the tantalising prospect of a flagstone path when a gust of wind buffeted him to his left and picked up the bin bag with it. As it blew away from him, Clive instinctively stuck out his left leg and tried to trap it. This he briefly managed, but his foot slipped straight across the wet bag. Knowing that he was dropping the basket, he tried to push it away but only managed, as he fell sideways, to push it above him. Mere nanoseconds after he hit the gravel, the basket landed flush on him, an edge winding him and its heavy contents spilling out onto his head and shoulders. His first instinct was to just lie there, his second (prompted by the cold rain soaking through his shirt) was to get up, and his third (prompted by a numbness in his right shoulder) was that he couldn't. Instead he closed his eyes to the rain and cumbersomely rolled backwards and onto his left side. From there he could lever himself into a standing position. He could still move his elbow and fingers, but he was sore and wet and the job was still unfinished. He filled the basket a third full and was just able to drag it to the double doors. He opened them and began to stack the wood inside.

'Everything all right?' Helen called.

'Basket handles snapped. Just going to bring it in in stages.'

He waited for a sympathetic response but none came, so he returned to fill the basket a second time.

'Do you think you can shut the doors?' he was asked. 'You're letting a lot of cold in.'

'Fine,' he said, and closed them behind him before fetching what remained of the spilled wood and letting himself back into the house. He shut the doors once more and conveyed the logs to the side of the stove.

'I'm just going to nip upstairs and change,' he said. 'Maybe have a quick shower.'

'Why not? We're just watching *My Girl*.'

'Super!' he said.

No one looked up at him from the cushion-strewn sofa. Had they done so, they would have seen him soaked and dirty, and the grimace on his face as he rubbed his sore shoulder. And they would have seen the wet footprints he left on the stairs as he squelched sadly up them, in search of comfort of any sort.

*

The ending of *My Girl* didn't leave Clive in the same emotional state as the rest of his family. He was moved more by the signs that the rain was finally abating. He tried to turn off the television before the credits had finished rolling but was loudly shouted down by the sofa's teary inhabitants.

'We want to hear the music!' shouted Katie.

'I want to read all the names!' shouted Sarah.

'I want to see if any animals were harmed during the making!' called Helen.

'Perhaps some were trampled to death by hordes of people fleeing cinemas?' offered Clive.

He waited until the end of the credits and said, 'Shall we all go out for a walk? See some natural light?'

'It's still raining,' Helen said.

'Hardly. We can wear our raincoats.'

Clive saw a look flash across Helen's face.

'You didn't . . . ?'

'Nope. You?'

'I packed one for myself,' said Clive. 'You didn't?'

'I was probably distracted by packing all the T-shirts and shorts and swimming costumes and sun cream that you kept telling us we'd definitely need.'

'Can Katie and I watch another film while you two argue?' asked Sarah.

'No!' said Clive.

'Yes!' said Helen.

'Right,' said Clive. 'Seeing as I'm the only person who's brought a raincoat with them, it looks like I'm the only person that can go out for a walk, doesn't it?'

'Where will you go?'

'To the shop. Get some milk. Something for supper.'

'And wine?'

'Definitely.'

The girls had already chosen another video and were inserting it into the player.

15

By the time Clive had found his raincoat the rain had stopped. But water still dripped from the trees and ran down the wide gutters as he walked down the steep road towards the centre of the village. If they had all brought raincoats, Clive thought, then he wouldn't be out walking on his own, which was actually exactly what he needed. The business with Findlay had started to occupy his thoughts and he hoped to mull it over and put it to rest.

At a crossroads further down the hill, the view suddenly opened out as if emerging from a tunnel. Away to the south he could see that rain was still falling. Ahead of him the clouds where still white but thinning out, and to the north the sun had broken through, scattering patches of golden light across the wheat fields that lay along the valley. If he carried straight on, he would descend down to the bottom of the valley and the old train line. If he turned right, the road would curve around and down to the little town square and the shop. The shop can wait, he thought.

He waited for a pair of lorries to pass and then crossed over and resumed his descent. The smell, away from the main road, grew lighter and more refreshing. The wet conifers had been giving off a claustrophobic, treacly aroma, but here it was different. Clive liked the scent in the air after rain had fallen; a feeling both new and familiar at the same time. There were a few bungalows dotted along the road. Outside one, an older lady was brushing her front step with a stiff broom. Clive offered a cheery 'bonjour' and she replied with a smile of the eyes. Further down the hill a man in an old boiler suit was poking out from under the chassis of a battered red Datsun. He uttered a succession of oaths as he hammered at the underside, then looked up at Clive, grunted something indistinguishable, and carried on. Clive empathised with the man's hopeless fury but envied him for being capable of mending a car.

He crossed over the abandoned railway path that they'd walked along yesterday. In the distance he could see a little convoy of cyclists, not much more that dots really, but unmistakable in their shapes, like upturned ants. He soon reached the valley's floor. For a valley that size the river piddling through it seemed insubstantial, even after all that rain. It did look like it widened to the south, but where it passed through the village it was less than fifteen feet across. Clive fancied that he could wade it easily. The bridge across it was wide enough only for only one car at a time, but there was no sign up to show who had priority. Maybe no one was ever in a hurry. Instead of turning back, he crossed the bridge and stepped off the road to make his way along the riverbank. A wooden platform jutted out into the river, not in the best structural health and slippery after the rain. Clive gingerly tested his weight on it and it seemed solid enough. He took off his raincoat to sit on, removed his shoes and socks and rolled up the legs of his trousers. He lowered his feet into the water and found it to be cold, bracing even. If he could just become accustomed to the chill, then it would be calming. He shut his eyes and just thought about the water flowing around his feet, concentrating on the feelings and the sensations. It was like the relaxation tape he had once bought to help him sleep after Sarah was born. Even when she was quiet he had lain awake at night, terrified about how he was ever going to pay for everything.

Birds sang an unidentifiable tune in the trees overhead. Wind gently rustled through the bulrushes. He heard a hollering and opened his eyes. The convoy of cyclists that had been tiny dots minutes ago were now life-sized and speeding along the path opposite him. He watched them for as long as he could before they disappeared into the trees and the valley was once more silent of all human noise. He couldn't actually see the gîte from where he sat, but he could pinpoint the place where it would be and thought of Helen and the girls. He stretched his back, then put his hands behind his head and leant back on them. He closed his eyes and waited for calm to envelop him.

Then a fish touched his foot and he found it absolutely disgusting.

*

It took only a few minutes for Clive to walk back from the fishing deck and over the bridge towards the town square and the little shop. It was, he now saw, not one little shop but three that must gradually have conjoined over time. There was a grocery section, a *tabac* in the middle selling some hot meals and drinks, and then a third section – a less natural transition, this – that sold bicycles. Either one family had slowly bought them all up over time or there'd been a succession of hostile takeovers, and a bike salesman and grocer were brutally chased out of town. One portly and tired-looking man (perhaps exhausted from the hostile takeovers) made his way from room to room, each with its own till, serving customers wherever they were to be found. Clive only understood this system when he walked into the *tabac* holding some milk and cocoa powder and was shooed back into the grocer's.

'Pardon,' said Clive.

'Is not problem,' said the man, 'is just all different.' He indicated the different tills and then tapped his temple. 'You know?'

'Je comprends,' said Clive, who didn't. He placed the milk and cocoa on the counter, and then looked around for wine. 'Du vin?' he asked.

'Is next door. Au tabac.' The man indicated the door through which he had just urged Clive. 'You pay here for this and then there for that. Oui?'

'Oui,' said Clive.

The man smiled at him, and shrugged, as if the shop's workings were completely beyond his control. Maybe they were.

'C'est ton magasin?' asked Clive.

'Oui. And my wife. I have son too, but he doesn't work. He sleep.'

'Il est un petit bébé?'

'Non. Il est paresseux.'

Clive thought that this must mean depressed. 'Ah,' he said sympathetically. 'Je suis désolé.'

'You know "parasseux"?

'Oh yes.'

'Is "lazy".'

'Bon. Je comprends.'

The man chuckled. 'We would all like to be lazy, yes? But there is always the work, yes?'

'Oui,' said Clive. 'Always.'

Clive paid for the groceries and then followed the man through to the *tabac*. There was a glass counter here containing some hams and cheeses, and bottles of wine and cider. There was a handful of tables with menus on too. Clive selected a couple of bottles of wine.

'And something for now?' asked the man, indicating a couple of draught pumps on top of the counter. 'Is beer.

Good beer? And is sunny now. You can sit outside, and drink beer and not worry?'

Clive, yet to respond, watched the man reach for a glass and begin to fill it. Clive carried his shopping out to the square in a blue plastic bag, which he set down next to one of the small metal tables. The man followed him out carrying the beer and a cloth to dry Clive's chair. Clive sat and took a first tentative sip of beer. It was cold and frothy and, Clive could instinctively feel, the sort of thing that one could drink all afternoon and evening with very little consequence.

'Is good, yes?' said the man. He was now working his way around all the tables and chairs, drying them and laying out menus.

'C'est bon,' said Clive. 'Maintenant je suis paresseux!'

'Exactly,' said the man, scurrying inside. 'Is your turn!'

A phone was ringing from somewhere within the building. Clive heard the sound of a receiver being picked up from a cradle, and the man say one or two words and then howl with laughter for an incredibly long time. The receiver was then replaced without any further words, and then the man was outside again with a roll of blue kitchen towels to try and dry the tables and chairs. Clive was already halfway through his beer.

'You want parasol? I get you parasol.'

'C'est d'accord.'

Clive's protests were ignored and a parasol dragged over and placed next to his chair. The man pulled on a rope and its canopy sprang open. A healthy dose of the day's rainfall now flowed down over the taught fabric and cascaded in a neat circle all around Clive. The man, however, took a sharp soaking and muttered to himself, presumably about failing to learn lessons from history, before using the blue kitchen towel to wipe his clothes and big bald head. Clive had wanted to feel the sun's long-wished-for glare on his skin but did not now feel that he could move from underneath the parasol on account of the sacrifices the device's owner had undergone in order to bring him shade. Instead he continued to sip his beer.

A man in overalls was approaching the grocery and Clive's damp friend hurried off to serve him. Clive sat back and stretched out. It was a pretty little spot, the square. It was flanked by tall, slightly crumbling stone houses, each bearing a few remaining vestiges of crumbling white paint. To his left was a large church, built from a much darker stone than the houses nearby, and with a steeple so tall that Clive had to lean right back to see the golden cross that adorned it. In the middle of the row of houses to his right was one immaculate building with a French flag above its entrance and an array of hanging baskets, rich with red, white and blue flowers. A lady came out from it clutching a folder and locked the heavy wooden door behind her before climbing into a 2CV, which started noisily and drove slowly past where Clive sat. A 'mayorie'? Was that the word? Three storeys up, beneath the sharply pitched roof, the words '*Liberté*', '*Egalité*' and '*Fraternité*' were carved into the stone. How splendid this was, Clive thought. Its English equivalent would be built from modern red brick. Or an old building butchered with modern signage in the local council's arbitrarily chosen colour scheme. Certainly it would not boast a motto as proud as '*Liberté, egalité, fraternité*'. The building of Frampton Council (motto: 'Providing *your* services at the best possible value') was a grotesque affair, with brown smoked glass in its windows and a concrete finish. He didn't know how Helen could bear it. He'd once taken a party of boys there when supervising a geography field trip in the place of the department's own teachers, who had all been hit with a brutal strain of gastroenteritis after a departmental outing to a Cantonese restaurant. The restaurant in question had later achieved local notoriety after it was discovered that its top two floors were entirely given over to the farming of cannabis. The council building had been a miserable warren of a place and the boys had wandered around with clipboards, asking the staff questions about business rates in what they had laughably referred to as Frampton's central business district. The only enjoyable aspect of the trip was that Clive had caught a glimpse of something behind the eyes of the council employees that reminded him that other people found their jobs as unsatisfying as he did.

His glass was empty now, so he went inside for a refill and also bought some rolling tobacco and the relevant accoutrements. Back outside he opened up the blue plastic wallet of Gauloises tobacco. It smelt dark and rich and smooth, but the first puff had a sharpness that caught the back of his throat and prompted a cough that took half of his beer to dowse. The second draw was smoother, and by the third Clive felt he had cracked it. No sooner had he smoked one roll-up than he began to roll another. And no sooner had he finished his second glass of beer than he found himself wandering back inside to purchase a third. When he returned to his table a family of four came wandering through the square, pushing bicycles, which they wheeled to the door of the bike shop. They all looked wet but happy. The mother of the group spoke perfect French as they handed back the bikes.

'Enjoy that, boys?' asked the father.

The two boys nodded.

'We can eat here,' the mother said. 'Enjoy some sun.'

'Bonjour,' the father said to Clive as they sat down at the next table and began to peruse menus.

'Bonjour,' drawled Clive, delighted by the idea that he had been taken for a Frenchman.

After a fourth beer Clive stood up, nodded to the family and gave them what he hoped to be a Gallic wave.

'Bonsoir,' they called.

'Bonsoir,' muttered Clive. 'Bonsoir.'

As he started up the hill he heard a cry.

'Ah, monsieur! Ton sac!'

Clive turned back and saw that the father of the group was coming towards him carrying the bag containing the wine and groceries.

'Oh,' said Clive. 'My bag. Thank you.'

*

'I have milk!' said Clive as he strode back in to the gîte. 'I have hot chocolate! I have wine!'

'Oh, very good,' said Helen. They had finished their most recent film and the girls were now out playing in the wet but warm garden. The doors were wide open and the claustrophobia that had enveloped the house for the early part of the day had dissipated entirely.

'And how was your walk?'

'My walk? Yes. My walk. Lovely. Good to get some exercise. Actually, I've found somewhere to hire bikes. We can go out for a ride along the old railway line. If it's warm.'

'And what about supper? What shall we do?'

'I've found a place to have supper too. The little shop is actually a big shop. Actually it's three shops.'

'Have you stopped for a drink, by any chance?'

'I might have had one. After my big walk.'

16

'Oh, not again. Oh, bloody hell.'

It had been a lovely evening in the end. Helen and the girls had followed Clive down to the square and eaten croque-monsieurs in the evening sun. The girls had been particularly taken with Orangina in glass bottles and Helen drank the same beer that Clive had sampled so heavily in the afternoon. The quartet had skipped happily home to the gîte, the rain a distant memory. Now, though, it had returned and was hammering noisily against the windows. Helen was lying on her back with a pillow over her face and Clive was attempting to be soothing.

'It'll pass,' he murmured. 'It did yesterday.'

'It took hours to pass. And it made you so grumpy.'

'Well, I won't be grumpy today. I'll be happy. I promise.'

'Really promise?'

'Look, I'll try.'

'Listen to yourself rowing back already.'

Clive could already feel himself becoming angry, but counted slowly to ten in his head and said, 'Today I shall be bringing all the sunshine that one household could ever need.'

'On second thoughts, I'd rather share a house with a grumpy man than one who wanders around in a state of forced cheerfulness.' With that, Helen burrowed deeper under the duvet.

'I can't think what you mean,' said Clive, pulling back the covers and giving Helen his most wide-eyed grin.

'Stop it. Please. It's saccharine and chilling at the same time. You're like Norman Bates made out of coconut ice.'

'Fine, I'll be grumpy.'

'Silent and grumpy is all right.'

She rolled over onto her side with her back to Clive. He put an arm around her.

'We could make love.'

'We could go back to sleep.'

'We could do both.'

'You find sex with me soporific?'

'No! I find it exhausting.'

'Then you'd better preserve some energy before we next try it.'

'I've just had eight hours' sleep. I'm ready now.'

'Yes, I can feel it.' She reached around behind her and expertly twanged the elastic of Clive's boxer shorts.

'What was that for?'

'To disarm you.'

'Appalling behaviour.'

'You should punish me by giving me the silent treatment.'

'Fine. I will.' Clive peeled back the duvet and climbed out of bed.

'Where are you going?'

'To find some breakfast things.'

'There aren't any.'

'I'll go and buy croissants.'

'Excellent idea. Can you make coffee when you get back?'

He pulled on yesterday's shirt and trousers and then rummaged under the bed for his flip-flops. As he walked out to the car he held his raincoat over his head.

He needed the wipers on full as he drove to the bakery. He had the headlamps on too as he made his way along the valley to Ricarmont. By fiddling with the dial on the radio he was able to pick up an English-speaking station, but not clearly enough to be able to work out exactly which station it was. Further up the dial was a clearer signal for a station playing jaunty French pop. He had no idea what anybody was singing about, but at least he could hear it. He parked as close to the bakery as he could manage, then put his coat on properly and jogged to the shop. He was a familiar enough customer now for eight croissants to bagged up before he had to use any of his halting French. He handed over his coins and said thank you, then put the croissants under his coat and stepped out into the rain again.

'Ah. Hello again.' The voice came from a beaming, confident man of a similar age to his own, whose face he recognised but struggled to place.

'Hi there.'

'Last night. At that little place in Monvachel. We were on the table next to you.'

'Of course you were. Hello. Not great weather, is it?'

'This? Just a shower.'

The man was in sportswear and had, Clive guessed, already been out for a run.

'Have you been here before?'

'We've been coming for a few years, actually. Love it.'

'And does it rain a lot?'

'Hell of a lot. One of the reasons we love it. We used to go further south but it really was just too hot. No, if it's rain you want, this is the place to be. Know where the hottest place in the whole of Europe was yesterday? Aviemore. Unbelievable.'

'I wouldn't mind a bit more sun.'

'Well, good luck. See you around. You like to cycle?'

'Love it,' said Clive, who had probably last been on a bike in about 1976.

'Well, we'll probably see you out on the trails.'

*

Clive lowered himself gingerly into the hot bath and took a deep breath before waiting to see if the temperature was going to defeat him once again. He had run it twenty-five minutes ago but it had been far too hot to even consider getting into. He had also, while doing some stretches, allowed it to overfill, which meant that there was no space for cold water. The chain was broken, so the only way to let any hot out was to plunge his hand in, and he couldn't even bear the heat long enough to do that.

Instead he had sat naked on the edge of the bath, periodically dipping his hand into the water until the temperature had lowered enough for him to hold his fingers under the surface. But what had seemed a bearable temperature for his fingers was still completely intolerable to his feet, and after standing there for just a few seconds he found himself leaping from the bath again, emitting a series of panicked yelps. Why weren't all parts of the body equally sensitive to heat anyway? What purpose did that serve? He could remember Helen showing him, when Sarah was a baby, that the best way to check the bath wasn't too hot was by lowering an elbow into it. He chanced an elbow now and found it to be completely excruciating.

'Christ,' he howled, as he grabbed his arm away. 'Oh Christ.'

'You all right up there?' came a shout from below.

'Just banged my head,' he called back. Banging your head in a house whose proportions you had not yet become fully accustomed to felt to Clive like a far more dignified reason for being in pain than anything that suggested he had not yet – at the age of thirty-eight – managed to master the art of running a bath without incident.

'In the bath?'

'Yes,' called Clive.

'Be careful up there!'

'I'm trying!' he called.

Why it was necessary for a domestic boiler to heat water to this temperature was beyond Clive. You could make tea with it. But then there would be no satisfaction to be taken from never having to wait for a kettle to boil if you always had to wait this long to actually use the bath without the risk of permanently scarring your bottom. Finally, when he was able to hold his elbow under the water and find it if not comfortable, at least tolerable, he climbed in. His skin instantly turned red, but at least he was in. His reading book was, he now discovered, just out of reach and so he just lay there, staring at the peeling ceiling. Probably the wrong sort of paint. Or maybe the steam generated by the water from these taps was so scalding that even waterproof paint stood no chance. It could probably dissolve granite.

He let out a series of slow sighs, and then dipped his lips under the water and blew some bubbles. Almost as soon as he'd arrived home, he had found himself arguing with the girls about just watching films.

'What would *you* like us all to do today?' Helen had asked.

'Something fun. I met a lovely man by the bakery today who says that he and his family absolutely love the rain. He says it's why they come here.'

'Does that mean it rains all the time here?' said Helen, looking genuinely panicked by this possibility.

'It means it rains *some* of the time here.'

'Did he say that this area had anything else to recommend it?'

'Yes.'

'And what was that?'

'He said that it wasn't too hot. And he said that there's loads of great places to cycle.'

Helen looked at the girls, who were still sitting on the sofa waiting to see if they were to be allowed to watch another film.

'Would you two like to go cycling in the rain?'

'No.'

'Never.'

'Oh dear, Clive. Sounds like cycling in the rain isn't all that popular for some reason.'

'I'm trying to be positive. Are you sure you don't want croissants, girls?'

'We had them yesterday.'

'Yes, and I thought you liked them.'

'And the day before.'

'I see. So you're just not hungry? Is that it?'

'Clive,' said Helen quietly, 'why don't you read a book?'

'I'm trying to make everybody happy!'

'Then let them watch a film. Girls,' she called to them, 'Daddy and I have decided that you can watch a film.'

'But . . .'

'Clive. Have a bath. Read a book. Relax. And let us relax too.'

'Are you going to watch . . .' He looked over to see the girls taking something called *Monkey Trouble* out of its case. 'Are you going to watch that with them?'

'It sounds amazing. But no. I'm going to sit with them and read while they're watching it. OK?'

And so here he was. He couldn't reach his book, and he was too hot to relax, but at least he'd managed to do one of the things that Helen had asked of him. The sight of the peeling paint bothered him. It was messy. Mess made him feel wriggly and irritable. Before they'd had children their home had always been neat. And cleaning and tidying it together – doing the washing and drying or folding linen – after a working day gave them an opportunity to talk. It was while folding a bedsheet that Helen first told Clive that she thought she might be pregnant.

Clive was just closing his eyes, with his chin under the water, when there was a knock at the door.

'Naked man in here,' Clive said.

'Lady in clothes out here,' said Helen's voice.

'Come in, come in.' His first instinct, despite years of marriage, was to cover his genitals with a flannel. But there wasn't one to hand. Instead he covered them with his hands, much to Helen's surprise.

'What are you doing?'

'I'm cupping myself.'

'Why? Some sort of experiment?'

So that you don't have to see it.'

'*It?*'

'Well, you know. You might not want to see it.'

'I'm sure it's more fun to look at than *Monkey Trouble*.'

'Do you want to see it?'

'No! I just don't *mind* if I do. It's just there, isn't it? Causing no one any harm, hopefully.'

'Dah-dah,' said Clive, underwhelmingly.

'And there it is,' said Helen. 'It neither delights nor revolts.'

'Oh.'

'Well, it does sometimes, obviously. Delights, I mean. Not when it's looking quite so poached. Is it very hot, that water?'

'Very. The boiler is unbelievable.'

'How are you getting on? You reading?'

'Didn't bother in the end. Just having a think.'

'About school? About a sure-fire route to promotion? Can I bring you a tea?'

'Yes please. Thank you.'

Helen quietly shut the door behind her. He had almost started to enjoy his bath before she had come in. Now he felt suddenly miserable. It wasn't that she had come in and offered him tea that bothered him but the fact that she had mentioned school. He had managed to banish it from his mind. And now, abruptly, it was right back at the forefront again. The school and what it was doing to him and his family was the reason that they had come away in the first place. If he loved working and living in Frampton, it probably wouldn't have occurred to him to go away anywhere else. Helen had said that not only did she want a holiday, she also wanted to 'tell people that they had been on holiday'. Clive felt that they found it easier to be together away from home. Well, that was the idea anyway. That was the problem with holidays, Clive thought. If you think about them too much, then you inevitably start thinking about why you'd needed a holiday. And – worse – what you would be going back to when it was over. An image of all those parents sitting in military rows in that stifling tent swam across his eyes. He thought about Icke and the smug little smile that would flash across his face before he said something deliberately unhelpful in that voice of faux concern. He thought about Crouch and that pinstriped suit of his. Would he be wearing it even now? He probably would, Clive thought. He would probably be wearing it at some all-expenses-paid conference somewhere in the Far East, while he explained to a group of educationalists in Singapore all about the Frampton Character and his wife wandered alone around air-conditioned shopping malls. He thought of Iain Dixon too, probably parking his ridiculous Mercedes on the edge of some cricket field in the Home Counties with a new lady in tow. Mark would be in Italy right now, looking at religious art and being effortlessly happy. And what about poor Wally? Out in the woods, struggling to keep up with his own dogs, a man perpetually alone, even when in company. The thought of all of these people made Clive shudder, even in a bath as hot as this one. He thought about the gloomy, pompous architecture, the grey skies, the polite notices requesting that people stay off the grass, the noise of distant teenage laughter down corridors, of sneering in the refectory, those whispered, needling remarks that he could hear being muttered from the back of the classroom as he bent to write on the overhead projector. And he thought about Findlay and wondered if those folders had hit him or not, and whether it would be punishable if they had. Should he mention it to Helen? All of it made him feel quite, quite sick.

*

'How was that then?' said Clive, coming down the stairs.

'Good,' said Katie.

'Bit silly,' remarked Sarah.

'Well, you've probably watched enough for the moment, haven't you? Why don't we go out somewhere?'

'Have you forgotten to dry your hair, Daddy?'

'No, Katie. I'm very hot is all.'

'Eurgh,' said Sarah. 'You're sweaty.'

'Yes, all right. That's what happens if you have a very hot bath. You sweat.'

'So you get dirty again?'

'Not exactly.'

'What then?'

'Well, it is sweat. But it's clean sweat. All the really foul stuff came out about three-quarters of an hour ago.'

'Do we have to discuss sweat?' said Helen. 'It's bad

enough having to see it. Seriously, drink some water. You must be terribly dehydrated.'

'I'm fine,' said Clive, who was actually now nursing a headache. He had taken three painkillers – technically an overdose, in fact – but was yet to feel their effects.

He crossed over to the sink and filled a pint glass with water from the cold tap, but it was warm to the taste and so he poured it away again and let the water run for longer.

'What's wrong with it?' asked Helen.

'It's hot.'

'That's because I've just washed up.'

'There was still enough hot water to wash up even though I'd run a bath?'

'That's right.'

'Just how much water can that boiler heat? It's terrifying.'

'Sometimes stuff just works, Clive.'

'True, true.'

Their boiler at home was an appallingly temperamental machine. In fact, their entire plumbing system was permanently on the brink of collapse, but still it was only ever patched up and never replaced. It needed, as with so many things in their lives, a complete overhaul. If anyone ever so much as turned on a tap when somebody else was in the shower, there were panicked cries from the bathroom and a frenzied hammering on the walls. All the taps dripped, and neither of the cisterns were watertight. If you lay awake at night – and Clive often did – there were continual drip, drip, drips. This was someone's second home and still everything worked properly, even though it was seemingly unoccupied most of the time. But then why would it be occupied, given that it rained constantly, even in the height of summer?

'What do you think then?' he called hopefully to the girls, when the water had finally run cold enough to drink.

'About what?'

'Going out.'

'It's still raining.'

'Yes, but that's no reason not to go out.'

'We haven't got raincoats.'

'That's what we'll do then. We'll go out and buy you some raincoats.'

'Can't you go and buy them?'

'No, Katie.'

'Please, Daddy?'

'Girls,' asked Helen, 'do you really want to wear coats that have been chosen for you by Daddy?'

The two girls leapt up from the sofa with alacrity.

'Oh, charming.'

'Only trying to help,' said Helen.

'Now then. Who knows what a *hypermarché* is?'

'I do,' said Helen. 'It's a capitalist palace.'

'Exactly. And that's where we're going.'

'We're going to a palace?'

'No, Katie. Not really a palace, no.'

'It's a shop,' said Sarah.

'It's a *massive* shop,' said Helen. 'They sell everything.'

'Great!' said Sarah.

'Is this definitely a good idea, darling?' Helen now looked worried.

'Anyone else have any good ideas?' asked Clive.

But the question did not need to be answered because Sarah and Katie were already running towards the door and out to the car, the rain apparently not bothering them one bit.

17

'Are you sure you're all right to drive in this?' Helen asked as she peered through the windscreen at the wipers which, even on their highest setting, were making little impact.

'I can cope. Might need a bit of help reading the signs. What did that one say?'

'I couldn't see. We won't miss a *hypermarché*, will we? It'll be the size of a village.'

'Do the wipers sound a bit squeaky to you?'

'Yes. Have the rubber bits worn down? When were they last changed?'

'Really no idea. I doubt if it was in the last year. If life becomes so dull that we can remember when we last had new windscreen wipers, then it really will be time to go out and rob a bank or something.'

'That would be fun. We could put tights over our heads.'

'We'd probably need guns too. They don't have to be loaded. It's really about the look.'

'If we wore particularly amazing tights – you know, with a saucy pattern on – then they might be so distracting that no one would notice that we didn't have guns.'

'Have you got any tights like that?'

'Most of my tights are probably even older than the windscreen wipers.'

'Christ. What a life.'

'What are you talking about?' It was Sarah, pitching her voice above the noise of the rain.

'We were fantasising about robbing a bank,' called Helen.

'In France?'

'Probably back home,' called Clive. 'I'm not sure my French is up to robbing a bank.'

'Are we going to rob a bank?'

'No, Katie. We're just fantasising.'

'What's fantasising?'

'It's just wishing things could be the case that aren't. For instance, I'm fantasising about the rain stopping.' said Helen.

'What did that sign say?' asked Clive.

'Couldn't see.'

'Oh for goodness . . . Can we just concentrate on the road a little more, then? Do you know what side of the road the *hypermarché* will be on? Was that on the pinboard?'

'We didn't check. You look that side, I'll look this. Girls, can you keep your eyes peeled for a big shop?'

'Yes.'

'Can we have some music on?' called Sarah.

'Is it all right if we don't?' said Clive. 'Just makes it easier to concentrate.'

'Please?'

Helen switched on the radio, and out came some jaunty European pop.

'Do we have to?' said Clive.

'It's not going to affect our eyesight, is it?'

'It's just a bit . . . There!' exclaimed Clive.

'There!' shouted Helen at the same time.

'What do you mean, 'there'?' said Clive.

'I can see the *hypermarché* up ahead. It's on my side.'

'Yes, but the sign for the exit's on my side. Big blue and red sign.'

'All the signs are on your side. That's how it works.'

'The actual exit must be on this side too. Unless we're meant to plough through the central reservation.'

'Then take the exit.'

'I'm not sure exactly where it . . . Oh bloody hell.'

The brake lights of the car in front had suddenly come on. Clive looked over his left shoulder and overtook it.

'Nifty little move,' he said.

'Where are you going?'

'Well, he braked suddenly, so I thought I'd—'

'That was the exit for the *hypermarché*.'

'Was it?

'Look, there's the *hypermarché*, and all the cars going over that little bridge there . . .' she pointed, 'came off at that exit.'

'Oh for God's sake, why didn't anybody . . . ?'

'It was on your side. It was your responsibility.'

'Oh bloody hell.'

On their left they were now passing the enormous *hypermarché*.

'How were we supposed to . . . ?'

'We were supposed to look for the signs.'

'We *were* looking. I saw the sign.'

'Then why didn't you follow it?'

'Because you put the music on!'

'You didn't take the exit because when you got to it you decided to overtake the person in front of you. Rather than following him.'

Clive said nothing.

'Didn't you? Hmm? Didn't you?'

'Yes. All right. YES. Yes, I did.'

'Where are we going?' called Sarah.

'We're going to the bloody *hypermarché*!' shouted Clive.

'Don't swear at her,' chided Helen. 'Or shout.'

Then she herself shouted, 'Daddy is taking us on a diversion.'

'Oh for God's sake,' muttered Clive. 'Now where do we go?'

'Just keep going. There'll be a roundabout. There has to be.'

'Please can we have the music up?'

'NO! Just everybody look out for signs for a roundabout.'

'You should be able to spot a roundabout without the need for signs. Just don't overtake every time you see a brake light go on and we should be all right.'

'It was a *mistake*. Why are you doing this?'

'I'm trying to help. If you'd rather I said nothing, then I'll say nothing.'

'Yes please,' said Clive.

And on he drove.

'There must be a roundabout soon,' he eventually said.

Helen said nothing in a manner that was almost deafening.

'I said, "There must be a roundabout soon."'

Again Helen said nothing.

'I'm sorry that I missed the exit. And I'm sorry that I blamed everyone else. OK?'

Helen glanced at him, her lips sealed.

'Please speak. I'm sorry.'

'Thank you,' she whispered.

'We'll get to a roundabout, then come back the way we came and hopefully we'll be able to find the *hypermarché*. What's this?'

It was a crossroads, and the lights were on red. Ahead of them was a succession of cars with their brake lights on.

'I'm not going to try overtaking,' said Clive, in what he hoped was a conciliatory tone.

'Glad to hear it.'

The lights stayed resolutely on red.

'This would have been a good place for a roundabout,' said Clive.

The lights eventually turned to green and all four cars in front of them set off again. However, by the time their car reached the the give-way line, the lights turned red again.

'Right,' said Clive, clenching his teeth but remaining, otherwise, outwardly calm. He even attempted to hum along to the tune on the radio.

'Know this one, do you?' asked Helen.

'Know it, love it,' said Clive.

As the French DJ purred at them, the lights turned green again and they finally set off. More road yawned ahead of them, but still no sign of a roundabout. Instead, they came to a town, the name of which they couldn't read through their rain-covered windscreen, but whose one-way system they were quickly and irretrievably drawn into.

'This is crazy,' said Clive after ten minutes of trying not to explode.

'It is.'

'Shall I pull off? Just turn down any street and see what happens?'

'Where are we going?' called Sarah.

'We don't know, darling. We're lost. All we know is that we're in France.'

'And that it's raining.'

'And that the wipers are squeaking.'

'And that we hate French pop.'

'Don't pull off. Just keep following it.'

And so Clive did, until they came to the edge of the town. It was the same edge as they had come in at because they came once more to the crossroads that let only four cars through at a time. There were eight cars ahead of them.

'Is there much of the morning left?'

'Ten minutes,' said Helen.

'Well, it's passed the time,' said Clive.

*

'Do you think everyone in the region has decided that this is the only possible thing to do in the rain?' said Clive as, after finally making it to the *hypermarché* and pulling off the main road, they found themselves in another queue to get into the car park.

'Maybe it is,' said Helen.

'Do you think there's a system?'

'That's made everybody come here?'

'For the car park. How do people at the front of the queue know when there's a space?'

'Well, they'll see a car come out of the exit.'

'Yes, but how do they know that that's someone's who's now left a space free and not just someone who hasn't been able to find a space? Do you follow?'

'I don't know. Maybe you have to memorise the number plate of the person in front of you. You've certainly got long enough.'

'A girl in my class is going to Euro Disney,' said Sarah.

Clive sighed.

'It'll be raining there too,' said Helen. 'And it's probably more crowded.'

'I'm hungry,' said Katie.

No one said anything until Katie spoke again.

'I said, "I'm hungry."'

'I'm hungry too,' said Sarah.

'You should have eaten your croissants!' spat Clive.

'I ate mine and I'm hungry,' said Helen. 'Aren't you hungry?'

Clive nodded sadly. He looked behind him but there was not even the vague possibility of him turning the car around. They had moved forward two spaces since they arrived.

'Maybe there's a café in the *hypermarché*?' said Sarah.

'That's a point.' He turned to Helen. 'Why don't you and the girls just go on foot and I'll try and join you.'

'Yay!' said the girls.

'How far away does it look to the actual building?'

Helen reckoned on about 400 metres. 'We'll get soaked. The girls are in T-shirts.'

'Oh for God's sake. Why did we even come here?'

'To get coats. Or do you mean to France?'

'Both. Oh, this is just . . .' Clive did not have the vocabulary to hand to explain how he truly felt, so instead he used the palm of his hand to sound the car's horn.

'What did you do that for?'

'I'm just . . . cross. And hungry.'

'I'm *starving*,' said Katie.

'That's no need to hit the horn. The people in front will think they've done something wrong.'

The people in front did indeed wonder if they had done something wrong. More horns were now sounding behind them. The driver's door of the car in front had opened and a smart-looking lady in her fifties, quite impervious to the rain, was marching towards them. She bent down at Helen's window, saw that she was a passenger and not the driver, and then checked the front of Clive and Helen's car to realise that she was dealing with British people. She made a questioning gesture – a sort of shrug with added malice – at Clive and then indicated the queue ahead and behind. Then she returned to her own vehicle, the door still open, muttering to herself and shaking her head. She made one final gesture suggesting that Clive was mentally deficient in some way and then climbed back in, slamming her door as she did so.

'Stupid cow,' said Clive.

'Is that fair? You honked at her.'

'I didn't. I was just honking in general. That's allowed, isn't it?'

'No.'

Clive, seeing no alternative outlet for his rising fury, began to pound his own right leg with a clenched fist.

'Look, you've got a raincoat on. Why don't you just get out of the car for a bit.'

'Fine,' said Clive. He faffed about with his seat belt, then got out and slammed the door.

'What's wrong with Daddy?'

'He needs some air. He's just getting a little cross. About things that he has absolutely no control over.'

'Can we have the radio back on?'

'Of course.'

Helen switched the radio back on and turned up the volume. Clive was pacing up and down, until something appeared to catch his eye and he went off to investigate. At this point a vehicle left the exit, and the car at the front of the queue proceeded into the parking area. The other five cars ahead of them all moved forward a length, and then the cars behind them began to honk. Clive, meanwhile, was nowhere to be seen.

'How the hell has he managed this?' muttered Helen.

The honking continued behind them, and just as Helen was clambering over into the driver's seat, the door opened and Clive attempted to occupy the seat too.

'What are you doing?'

'What are *you* doing?'

Helen clambered back into her own seat. Clive shut the door and inched the car forward.

'Where did you just go?'

'You told me to get out of the car.'

'I meant for some air. I didn't mean go for a walk.'

'What happened was I thought that I saw a place, and so I went to investigate it and then a car came and took it.'

'Well, it was probably the car at the front of the queue, wasn't it?'

'Well . . . yes. As it turns out.'

'What do you mean "as it turns out"? Of course that's what happened. I don't think all the bits in your head join up sometimes.'

'I was trying to speed things up.'

'Well, don't. All we can do is wait. Unless you want me to drive and you can go and find us all something to eat. Or you can give me your raincoat and I'll go.'

'Please stay, Mum,' said Sarah.

'Oh, I see,' said Clive. 'You don't want to be left in the car with me. Is that it?'

'Well, who would?' said Helen.

'Fine. I'll go and get some food, and I'll come back and find you here. Unless you've moved. In which case . . .'

'Just go inside the *hypermarché*, find the café and wait there.'

'What if there isn't a café?'

'If there isn't a café, go and find the girls' clothing section and meet us there. You can start looking at raincoats.'

'You want me to wait on my own in the girls' clothing section?'

'Somewhere else then.'

'Fish counter?'

'Do we need fish?'

'It's just the first thing that came into my head.'

'Meet us there then. If there isn't a café.'

'What if there isn't a fish counter?'

'How many contingency plans do we need?'

'An infinite number, given how the day's panning out.'

'Fine. If there's no fish counter, wait by the entrance. And if there's no entrance, that explains why the car park's so full.'

'This fucking place,' Clive muttered as he got out of the car.

There was, it turned out, a café, right by the entrance.

It took up almost as much floor space as the whole of the supermarket in Frampton, and Clive bought himself a *café au lait* at the counter, which he then carried slowly on his wet tray to the nearest empty table. By the time the coffee was cool enough to sip, Helen and the girls had arrived.

'That was quick.'

'We were just lucky, I guess. Have you not got yourself something to eat?'

'I thought I'd wait for you.'

'Well, you shouldn't have. Come and choose some food, girls. Can we bring you something?'

'Anything,' said Clive. 'Anything with cheese.'

Something about the swiftness with which Helen turned away from him told Clive that he had not been forgiven. Did she need time or an apology? It was hard to judge, sometimes. 'It's not normal to apologise this often,' Helen had once told him. He never knew if it was the apologies she minded or the fact that he kept doing things that he needed to apologise for.

'Sorry,' he said, as soon as Helen had returned with a croque-monsieur for him. It had obviously been heated through a number of times. Any solid structure it had once had had been broken down by successive microwaving. The polystyrene plate on which it had been served was struggling to cope with its demands.

'For what?'

'For my behaviour just now. In the car. And out of the car. For honking. And shouting. And not thinking. For allowing the weather to get the better of me.'

'Do you think you behave differently in the sunshine?'

Clive reckoned on this for a while. 'Well, a little better, I'd have thought.'

'A little better is about right. Not wildly different.'

'Are you cross with me?'

'Yes, I'm cross, Clive.'

Across the table, the girls were glumly eating hot dogs containing the pinkest meat that Clive had ever seen.

'I'm sorry.'

Helen looked at him. 'Apology accepted.'

'Thank you.'

'But I don't want to be having this same conversation any time soon. We're on holiday. And some of us are doing our best to have a nice time.'

The girls were looking at each other and sniggering.

'What?' said Helen.

'We thought you'd have a row,' said Sarah.

'We're not rowing,' said Clive.

'We are having a grown-up conversation.'

'Exactly. How are your hot dogs?'

The girls looked at one another.

'Disgusting,' said Sarah.

'Well, I'm sorry about that,' said Helen. 'This is the best we can do in the circumstances. Just put more ketchup on them.'

Katie grabbed the squeezy bottle from the middle of the table and ejected a tremendous squirt of tomato sauce, some of which landed on her plate.

'That's it,' said Clive. 'Everything will be fine if we just put more ketchup on it. Life's like that sometimes.'

He then attempted to slice his own croque-monsieur, and the knife, though plastic and brittle, went clean through both it and the plate.

'Shall we abandon this lunch?' asked Helen.

'Let's,' said Clive, pushing his chair back and standing up. 'Why don't we go and enjoy ourselves instead. And buy some raincoats.'

*

'Do you want to drive, or shall I?'

It was still raining when they finally emerged from the depths of the *hypermarché*. After all the bright strip lighting inside, it took a few moments for their eyes to adjust to the gloom. The girls had each chosen a new raincoat, light pink for Katie and a shade of red for Sarah with just enough orange in it that the two garments clashed slightly. Helen had chosen something dark blue that could be folded and crammed into a fist-sized bag with a drawstring. Amidst the miles of aisles crammed high with plastic the girls' attention had been grabbed by a paddling pool. It would have been large enough to accommodate the whole family, a point illustrated on the box by an almost offensively photogenic family of four all laid out in it on a hot sunny day, against a backdrop of green, green grass and the bluest of skies.

'What do you think, Daddy?'

'I think they look just like us.'

'Can we buy it? Please?'

'I think we'd be tempting fate.'

'Please,' asked Katie.

'If the weather gets better, I will come back and buy it. All right?'

They had, without really intending to, also bought a lot of wine, bread and cheese and they needed a trolley to convey it all over to the far side of the car park where Helen had carefully backed in.

'I'll drive,' Clive said.

'If you're sure.'

'It's no trouble. I don't mind.'

Clive was in fact anxious to get behind the wheel again to prove to his wife that he was capable of keeping his cool in the driver's seat and already a changed man. He would not allow himself to be flustered by any difficulties. They loaded up the boot and all climbed in.

'Back to the gîte?' said Clive, who started the car, checked that the gearstick was in position for first, looked both ways and pressed down on the accelerator. The engine made a rough noise and the car shot backwards and crunched into whatever metal object was behind it. No one spoke at first, the tension caused not so much by the crash as by their uncertainty about how Clive would react.

Clive, sensing that this was a test he had to pass, made a circular shape with his lips and slowly blew out a very long breath.

'Right,' he said. 'Well, there we are.'

He turned off the engine and felt the gearstick, which he released with the clutch and heard two clicks.

'Right,' he said again. 'OK.'

He gathered himself and then said, as evenly as he could, 'Did you, by any chance, leave the car in reverse?'

'I think I did,' said Helen quietly. 'Sorry.'

'It's fine,' said Clive, a little too quickly, glancing in the rear-view mirror to see that behind them was a sleek green sports car. Helen leant over and saw it too.

'Ooh,' she said.

'I'll go and inspect the damage.'

Clive got out of the car and soon came back wearing a relieved expression.

'It's fine,' he said. 'The bumper's fallen off. But it's fine.'

'Their bumper?'

'No, ours. There's a little crash barrier between the cars. That's all we hit. The other car's fine. Luckily. It looks very expensive.'

'But our bumper's come off?'

'Yes. But that's still good news really. Well, it's not great, obviously. But at least we haven't hurt the other car. I might be able to just click the bumper back on. I'll see.'

'I'm sorry for leaving it in reverse.'

'Honestly, it could have been a lot worse. You all right, girls?'

'Yes,' they choroused.

'Will this take long?' asked Katie. 'We want to watch a video.'

'And you will,' said Clive, 'just as soon as I can sort this out.'

'Great.'

Helen said nothing but looked Clive directly in the eye, and he knew at that moment that, even though it was taking every fibre of his being, he was passing this test. He climbed into the driver's seat, fired the ignition and eased the car forward a foot or so to give him some space to work with the bumper. Then he got out and went to the car's rear to take a closer look. It really was lucky that the crash barrier was there. It wasn't a high one, but it must have been just high enough to reach the bumper as they reversed, which had caught on it and been wrenched off. The bumper had a couple of dents in it but it was still roughly the shape that it was meant to be and the little pins for fixing the bumper to the car were still in place. He bent down and examined the underside of the car to see where the pins slotted in and lined up the bumper underneath them, bending the metal back where he could to make it straighter.

'If I can do this,' he thought, 'and do it calmly, I will be a hero.'

Then he picked up the bumper, took a step back to get an overview and collided with the crash barrier. His first reaction was one of pain as the metal lip of the barrier dug into his heel. His next was of precariousness as he began toppling backwards and, his hands being full, was unable to steady himself. Then he fell full length backwards onto the bonnet of the sports car. He hit it with his shoulders first, and then his head, and then finally heard the metal bumper he had held aloft come crashing down against the windscreen. There was the sound of metal hitting treated glass followed by that of plastic cracking. He lay where he landed, looking straight up into the clouds above him, and felt the rain hitting his face. Then he closed his eyes and felt the drops on his eyelids.

'Clive?'

Helen was standing next to their car now, her face a perfect combination of concern and confusion.

'Did you see that? Or just hear it?'

'Both. I was turning around to talk to the girls and then I saw this sudden flurry of movement. Are you all right?'

'I don't know. I've not tried moving.'

She took a step closer and examined the situation. 'Did you trip?'

He bit into his lower lip and nodded. Helen stepped over the crash barrier and lifted the rear bumper off the sports car's bonnet and windscreen. The low, slanted windscreen had a crack across it and a windscreen wiper had snapped.

'Do you want a hand up?'

'I just want to lie here for a moment.'

'You're getting very wet.'

'I don't really mind. I think I might have another bath when we get back.'

'OK. You lie there for a bit. I'll just see if I can get this back on.'

She stepped back over the barrier with the bumper, knelt down and pushed each of the pins back into the retainer holes until the final one clicked into place. Then she climbed back into the car, found a scrap of paper and a biro and wrote a note explaining, in modest French, that it was their fault and giving the driver of the sports car their contact details back home in Frampton. They could deal with all this later. She certainly couldn't be doing with a furious French person turning up at the gîte and having to explain just what had happened to them. This sort of communication, she felt, could be more safely dealt with from opposing sides of the English Channel. She popped the note under the sports car's one remaining windscreen wiper and offered Clive a hand up.

'Do you want to drive or shall I?' she said.

*

'No luck?'

Clive stood shivering in his towel at the bottom of the stairs in the gîte.

'No. It's just not getting hot. Perhaps we've used all the week's hot water in one day.'

'You're shivering, you know.'

'I know.'

'Go and get dressed in some dry clothes and we'll light the fire.'

The girls were already lounging on the sofa, the soundtrack of *The Lion King* ringing out around the sitting room. Clive nodded and turned on his heel.

'Are you cold, you two?' asked Helen.

'Mmm,' said Sarah.

'"Mmm" as in "Yes," or "Mmm" as in "What?"?'

'What?'

'Are you cold?'

'Bit.'

'I'm cold,' said Katie, a state of affairs that seemed a little hard to believe given the sheer number of cushions that she had piled up around her.

'Daddy and I are going to light the stove. Does that sound fun?'

'Mmm.'

'How's *The Lion King*?'

'We've seen it before.'
'I know. But are you enjoying it?'
'Mmm,' said Sarah.
'We've seen it before,' yelled Katie, crossly.

18

'Oh my God, it's actually sunny.'

Helen undid the catch and then pushed the window open to allow the fresh air into the bedroom. Clive was still in bed, awake but with his eyes closed. He managed to say, 'Oh thank God.'

'It doesn't sound like the girls are awake yet. Let's go and drink coffee outside.'

'Perfect,' said Clive. He got out of bed and made his way to the bathroom.

If, twenty years ago, he had been shown a photograph of the pale, greying and slightly bloated figure that he now saw in the mirror, he wouldn't have recognised himself. Nor would he have placed the man in the photo in his thirties. He felt an ache in his bladder and moved over to the loo to perform a long and slow piss. Helen then came in wearing the same very short shorts that she had worn on their first walk to the next village and a bikini top. 'I'll use the downstairs,' she said.

'You look excited about the sun.'

'I can't wait.'

She disappeared again, and Clive splashed cold water on his face and behind his ears.

*

Downstairs the smell of fresh coffee already filled the air. Clive opened up the double doors and Helen carried the things outside on a tray.

'What a difference a day makes,' she said as she put down the tray on the metal table outside. They selected the least wonky of the chairs and sat opposite each other, Clive squinting into the low sun.

'Do you want to swap places?' asked Helen.

'I'm fine.'

He was going to be a model of relaxed cooperation today, and to acquiesce to all demands. Perhaps a holiday version of himself really existed, if he made enough of an effort.

'Go on. Swap with me. Your face is all scrunched up.'

They got up and swapped places and Clive was now perfectly positioned to catch sight of the barbecue about which he had fantasised.

'Barbecue later? If the weather holds?'

'We'll see.' Helen plunged the coffee and poured it, then took a sip and closed her eyes, letting the sun hit her eyelids. 'This is actually civilised, isn't it? When the sun's out.'

'It's perfect,' said Clive. 'Perfect. You look very beautiful in the sun, you know.'

'I hope I look beautiful all the time.'

'Well, you do. But the sun enhances your beauty further.'

'You look nice.'

'I'm feeling a bit fat, actually. I was just examining myself up in the bathroom. My tummy's growing.'

'Well, no one comes on holiday to lose weight, do they?'

'That's a point. Shall I go and get croissants?'

'Just relax. The girls will be down soon. Just enjoy this.'

When the girls did come down they were just as excited as their parents by the sight of a sun-bathed garden, and immediately scampered off around it, re-exploring the nooks and crannies they had found on the first day and going off to explore the outhouses. Clive went inside to make himself toast, and came back out to find that the girls too had settled around the little table.

'What do you want to do today?' he asked. 'We could go out on bikes if you like? Perfect day for it.'

'I'd just like to stay here,' said Sarah.

'We could get the paddling pool!' said Katie with sudden excitement.

'Yes, the paddling pool!' said Sarah. 'Can we? Can we? Can we?'

Helen looked at Clive. 'Can we?' she said.

'Of course we can,' said Clive. 'I'll go. Anyone want to come with me?'

*

Clive drove alone with the windows down and the radio on. The English-speaking station he'd found was not so crackly now it wasn't raining, and he was able to listen to the news for sometimes minutes at a time uninterrupted. He drove slowly to make sure that he didn't miss the turn-off, spotted it just in time and followed the winding road around to the bridge that took him over the main road and down towards the entrance to the car park where yesterday had gone from bad to considerably worse. The car park was, mercifully, deserted in comparison to the previous day, and Clive parked carefully and slowly in as empty a spot as he could find.

He went in and bought the paddling pool and also got himself a pair of imitation aviator sunglasses so that he could stop wincing into the sun in the way that irked Helen. He relished the pleasurable sensation of the sun on his arms and on the back of his neck, although he could feel a little point on the top of his head where he couldn't remember ever feeling the sun hit him before. He felt his crown with the tip of a finger and realised that he was touching skin where there definitely used to be hair. It wasn't a big spot, but to the touch it was undeniably a little bare circle. He sat in the driver's seat and tried to lean forward in such a way that he could look at the top of his own head in the rear-view mirror, which he couldn't.

*

'Paddling pool!' Clive announced as he sauntered into the garden.

Helen was still sitting at the table in the bright light, the empty cafetière in front of her and a book on her lap. The girls ran over and took the box from him, ripping it open.

'Careful, girls. We'll need the box again. We'll be taking it home with us, won't we?'

'You found yourself some sunglasses as well.'

'What do you think?'

'Very handsome. Slightly pinkish hue to the lenses. Is that what you were after? Pretty.'

Clive took them off and examined them. 'Oh, so they do. They looked sort of silvery in the shop. Do they look all right though?'

'Who are you trying to impress?'

'You.'

'I'm impressed.'

He put the glasses back on and sat down. 'Do I have a bald spot?' he asked.

Helen laughed. 'Not a big one.'

'So I do?'

'Yes.'

'Why didn't you tell me?'

'I thought you knew.'

'How long's it been there?'

'Oh goodness, Clive. About six months, I think. I've stopped noticing it.'

'Six months?'

'About that.'

Clive leant forward and cast his mind back over the last six months: all those lessons he had taught, all those evenings at the boarding house, all those hours in the staffroom being bored out of his mind, all those nights in the pub with Mark, all those afternoons he had spent wandering from pub to pub to make sure that the pupils weren't drinking in them. Sitting on the steps outside the theatre on that that ruddy trip to Stratford. Lying dazed beside the stumps during that cricket match; that first conversation with Flora. His memory of each and every one of these occasions now had to be updated slightly and altered to reflect the fact that he had been through all of those things with a bald spot. And he was, presumably, the last to know. Every time he had sat down in a chair it would have been visible to anyone who was standing nearby. As he drove a minibus it would have been visible to those sitting behind. As he knelt down to retie a shoelace in his classroom or bent forward to open one of the drawers in his desk. Perhaps it could have been seen by all of his pupils as he wrote on the whiteboard. That class he had taught, the one Findlay was in, for instance. It was a teacher with a bald spot they had been cheeky to, a teacher with a bald spot who had thrown those things out into a corridor, where they may or may not have hit someone. It was as if he'd discovered he'd been walking about with his flies undone for half a year.

'What's wrong?'

'I was just thinking about my bald spot.'

'It's really not that big.'

'But it is there.'

'It's absolutely there. It's not important though, is it? It's what happens to men.'

'Not to all men. Mark doesn't have one. Crouch doesn't have one. Icke doesn't have one. And even bloody Wally doesn't have one.'

'Well, all right. Not everyone. But lots of people. It's completely normal. It looks fine. Like it's meant to be there.'

'You think I'm meant to be bald?'

'Well, if it happens, it happens. It's not a reason to despair, is it? There's just more of you to tan.'

'I bet the owner of the green sports car doesn't have a bald spot.'

'It might be a woman.'

'True. But if it is a man, I bet he doesn't have a bald spot.'

'Oh, he probably does. He's probably completely bald. That's probably why he bought a sports car.'

'So you think it's something that you need to compensate for?'

'I think it's something that a *certain type of person* thinks they need to compensate for. Not you.'

'I hope not. It's just a bit of a surprise, that's all. A reminder that the wheel is turning.'

'Don't worry about it. I don't. Forget about it. But at the same time, do remember to put sun cream on it.'

'Sun cream. That's a point. Have the girls got it on?'

'We all do.'

'Well, don't let me forget.'

The girls had now completely destroyed the box that the paddling pool came in and had rolled the pool out on the grass. It really was very big indeed.

'What happens now?' called Katie.

'We blow it up,' said Clive and went over to give them a hand. It worked in sections. They took a nozzle each and tried to inflate it.

'It doesn't work,' said Sarah. 'There's no air going in.'

'It just takes time. It's going to need a lot of air.'

'It'll take ages,' said Katie.

'You've got to squeeze each side of the nozzle. Pinch it with your teeth as you blow.'

The girls tried, but it was no use.

'I tell you what, why don't you two go and play? Daddy can do this, and then I'll come and get you when it's ready to fill. You can help me get the water in.'

The two girls immediately ran off to play tag, leaving Clive kneeling down and puffing away furiously.

'Do you want a hand?' called Helen.

'It's fine. Really. It's just a bit tedious, that's all. You carry on. Have you had any breakfast?'

'That's a point. I'll go and do that. Do you want anything?'

'Some water?'

It took Clive nearly half an hour before the base was filled, and then he lay down on the grass next to it to get his breath back for the next assault. How many lungfuls would it take to fill the bloody thing? He was nearly hyperventilating now. Still, whatever the pain, if he did it uncomplainingly, he could win some affection. He found the first of the nozzles for the sides and began to blow into it. He really hadn't thought it would be this difficult when he'd begun. He stopped again and struggled for breath. Amidst all the torn cardboard there was a piece of white paper flapping about. He picked it up and saw that it was the instructions. There were a couple of rudimentary diagrams and then words in small type: instructions in Chinese, French, Dutch and German. Finally, at the bottom, were the instructions in English.

'It is highly advisable to use a foot pump with special nozzle (both available separately).'

As Clive sighed Helen came out with a tall glass of water for him, which he drank in one go.

'How's it going?'

'Slightly trickier than I thought it would be,' he said stoically. 'It turns out you're meant to use a foot pump.'

'Maybe they sell them in the bike shop?'

'Unlikely, I'd have thought. Even if they did, do you know the French for "special paddling pool attachment"?'

'Could you mime it?'

'Not without a queue building up behind me. I'll just have to do it the hard way.'

'Think of how grateful your daughters will be,' she said, giving him a peck on the cheek. 'More water?'

'Please.'

Clive wiped the sweat from his forehead and recommenced blowing. It made his head ache. Was that caused by too much oxygen going into his brain or too little? Best just to push on through.

An hour and a half later it was done. Clive closed up the final nozzle and stood up, arms aloft.

'Success! Success and exhaustion!'

Helen looked up from her book. 'Well done. I'll miss the sound of you huffing and puffing. I'd rather got used to it.'

'I feel incredibly light-headed. Where are the girls?'

Helen called for them and they ran around the side of the house. They were both carrying sticks and had rubbed dust all over their faces.

'What have you two been up to? Swallows and Amazons?'

'What and what?' asked Katie.

'We're fairies,' said Sarah. 'These are our wands. This is our make-up. We turn stones into hamburgers and trees into palaces.'

'Excellent. Well, this . . .' he indicated with a flourish, 'is your paddling pool.'

'Where's the water?' asked Katie.

'Well, it's still in the taps. But this bit has taken all my time so far.'

'Daddy's been working very hard for you two.'

'Thanks,' called Sarah over her shoulder as they ran off to restart their necromancy.

'Right,' said Clive. 'They seemed impressed.'

'They're having fun,' said Helen.

'I know. I know. Even so. Oof.'

'How are you going to fill it?'

'I hadn't thought. Do you suppose there's a hose?'

The two of them wandered around the outside of house. There was a tap underneath the kitchen window on the other side but no hose in sight. Even if there had been, it would have had to be very long. The outbuildings threw up no treasures either, other than a plastic bucket with no handle. The two looked at each other.

'Oh God,' said Clive.

'Don't catastrophise,' said Helen. 'Why don't we drag it round and fill it straight from the tap?'

'Brilliant,' said Clive.

'We can't leave it there, obviously. It'll be in the shade. Do you think we could drag it round again once it's full?'

'Honestly? No.'

'We don't have to fill it today. We can get a hose next time we're out. Unless you fancy going back to the *hypermarché*? Or I could go.'

'We should have gone earlier. Then we could have got the foot pump too.'

'Yes, but we didn't know then, did we?'

'Look, we can't go back to the *hypermarché* again. But we've got to fill it today. It might not even be sunny tomorrow. We'll just have to do it the hard way. I'll use the bucket.'

'We can use the washing-up tub as well. We'll do it together. It won't take too long.'

Even as she said this they knew that it was not an honest assessment. But silent complicity in a shared lie enabled them to make a start on their task. Clive had never really had cause to consider before just how crucial a component of a bucket the handle is. A full bucket with a handle can be dragged, or even swung. A full bucket without a handle, though, has to be picked up and held close. And if the substance that the bucket is full of is water, then the bucket becomes slippy and, as one moves, the bucket jiggles with you, its contents bob up and down, and they are poured down your front. You finally reach the paddling pool and the bucket that began its journey nearly full is now half empty, and a task that began as merely daunting has become Sisyphean.

The path around the back of the house was narrow, too, and Clive and Helen kept getting in each other's way as they turned the corners.

'Why don't you fill the tub from the tap in the kitchen?' Clive asked.

'I don't want to splash water in the house. It's tiles. They'll get slippy.'

'They'll dry. We're all outside anyway. It's a much quicker route too.'

'Then we should both fill it from the tap in the kitchen.'

'But then we'll get in each other's way again. Trust me. One inside, one outside. That'll be the most efficient way.'

'Without a hose?'

Helen adopted the kitchen as her source of water and they stopped getting in each other's way quite so often, but the task became a lonelier one. It was so hot, and hard work, and speech became difficult.

'Shall we just stop for a bit?' said Helen eventually, having poured another tubload in.

'We can't. It'll never get filled.'

'Well, can I stop for a bit then?'

Clive emptied his bucket and stood bent over for a little while, stretching the aching base of his spine. 'I'm going to carry on.'

'You'll wear yourself out.'

'I just want to get it done,' he said.

I just want, he thought, to achieve something, to be responsible for some sort of success, however minor.

Helen lay down on a sunbed with her hat on and Clive threw himself into the task once more. Using the kitchen tap and the washing-up tub made things a lot easier for him, and in another forty-five minutes the job was done. When he saw that the water was up to within just a few inches of the pool's uppermost rim, he threw the tub down on the grass. His clothes were drenched with tap water, his head and arms with sweat, and he dropped down onto his knees like a pilgrim at the end of the Santiago de Compostela trail. He could have wept, if dehydration hadn't made this a practical impossibility.

'Well done, darling,' said Helen. 'Another glass of water?'

'Oh God, yes. Girls!' he shouted. 'The paddling pool's full. Come and see! Come and play!'

The girls rounded the corner at full speed, crying, 'Brilliant!' and 'Hooray!', kicked off their jelly sandals and jumped straight in.

'Freezing!' said Sarah.

'Too cold,' said Katie, and the pair hopped straight out again.

'It'll just take a little while to warm up,' said Clive. He kicked off his shoes and socks, and then rolled up the bottoms of his trousers.

'You'll soon get used to it. Look.'

Then he stepped into the pool to demonstrate this. Goodness. The girls were right. It really was shockingly cold, especially on a day like today.

'See!' said Sarah.

'Well, it's only cold at first. I'll count to ten and it'll be fine. Well, a minute. Why don't I give it a minute? Then it'll be fine.'

'We'll come back when it's warmer,' said Sarah, and led Katie off to the far corner of the garden.

When Helen came out Clive was standing alone in the paddling pool. He stepped out of it.

'The girls not had a go yet? Are you hogging it?'

'They've had a go, and they said it was too cold.'

'Lunch in half an hour?'

'Great.'

'I'll just go and pull a few things out of the fridge.'

But when Helen departed, the sight of no one playing in the paddling pool that he had gone to the *hypermarché* to buy at such expense and that had then taken an age to inflate, and a further age to fill, infuriated him, irrespective of how cold it was. So he stripped off down to his underpants and got in by himself and lay flat on his back, with his head resting on the side of the pool, and grew more used to it. The cold water slowly became just cool and then lukewarm, and finally it was completely bearable. Relaxing, even. And when, twenty minutes or so later than planned, Helen came out to tell everybody that lunch was on the table if anyone wanted it, Clive had already gone a pinkish hue – pinker, even, than his new sunglasses – all over.

'Are you all right in there? Clive?'

Clive was, in fact, asleep.

'Hmm?' he said, opening his eyes and lowering his sunglasses.

'Lunch. If you want it.'

'Oh right. Yes. I'm quite comfortable here actually.'

'Well, you can have it whenever. You'll just have to battle the flies for it.'

'Fine. Thank you.'

'Know where the girls are?'

'I heard them shouting about climbing trees a while ago.'

'I'll go and look for them. You do look comfortable, actually. Bit pink perhaps.'

'Really?'

'Little bit. I'd come in for a bit of shade if I were you.'

Inside, what had looked merely pink underwater looked altogether redder out of it.

'Gosh, is that sore?' asked Helen as Clive, wet pants removed and replaced with a towel, bent over the table to fork some smoked sausage onto his plate.

'A little.'

'You need some aftersun. Seriously.'

'Fine, I'll go and put some aftersun on.'

He tried to be calm but this was tempered by the fact that his towel came loose as he reached the bottom of the stairs and he had to grab it with both hands. He cursed as he realised that the length of the towel was not quite sufficient to reach comfortably about his own diameter.

He went up to the bathroom and inspected the damage. A whole morning in the sun, three-quarters of an hour of it all but naked, had wreaked havoc on his fair skin. His shoulders were redder than anything else, but even his thighs and stomach were a deep pink, with clear lines and white flesh demarcating where his boxer shorts had protected him. His groin was now the only white part of his body, and what a depressing site that was: white and spongy, his damp genitals suffering from the compacting effect of having been submerged in cold water for forty-five minutes. He picked up the squeezy bottle of aftersun from the window ledge and slathered it generously all over himself, its instant cooling effect making him tingle. He rubbed at it and rubbed at it, but he had put too much on for the skin to absorb fully, leaving a white, oily residue all over his body. He gave it a further fifteen minutes to sink in, then got dressed again, his skin slippery under the soft linen. He felt lardy.

Flies were buzzing around his plate when he went downstairs again, and he shooed them away before sitting alone to eat. He added some mayonnaise to his plate and regretted it immediately after the first taste – now feeling as oily on the inside as he did on the outside. He could hear splashing outside, and looking out through the double doors he could see, on the paving slabs, the shadows of Helen and the girls now all playing in the paddling pool. He put his empty plate in the sink and then went and stood in the doorway to the garden. The sun was higher now, and the temperature greater.

'Feeling any better?' asked Helen, while simultaneously trying to prevent the two girls from wrestling her under the water.

'A little.'

Helen gave in to the girls' efforts as they pushed her onto her side, squealing with delight as she became submerged.

'What a happy scene,' Clive thought. And then, realising that he was not part of the scene, he stepped away from the door, picked up his book and went and sat in the armchair by the unlit stove, there to stare into the distance. The book remained unopened on his lap for over an hour.

19

The next morning the rain was descending again. Clive, who had slept poorly anyway, had woken early to go the bathroom and was now standing in there, looking out of the window at the torrential dawn. Wind was whipping through the conifers and making the windows rattle. One side of the paddling pool looked to have collapsed, and water was spilling from it onto the already saturated lawn. Clive pressed his forehead against the pane. Was rain this depressing in England? At least you expected it there. And at least you didn't have to watch it come down while also suffering the after-effects of sunburn.

He went downstairs and put the kettle on, then tidied some of yesterday's plates into the dishwasher. There were three empty wine bottles by the sink. Clive's last memory of the night before was of standing alone by the kitchen sink and eating, quite needlessly, an entire garlic sausage. That was probably why he he'd slept badly, that and an afternoon and evening of complete inactivity. But there was no point fighting the rain or his family. When everyone was up they would all drive to the *hypermarché*, purchase as many videos and bottles of wine as they fancied, and the girls could watch films all day while he and Helen read until it was time to start drinking. Perhaps a glass of wine at lunch? Maybe two, followed by a nap. Then they could open another bottle at six. Or half five even. Why not five itself? Or four? He could start now. No, he had to get out. It didn't matter that it was raining. It didn't matter that it wasn't yet six in the morning. What time would that bakery open? Early, he reckoned. He could drive there now. Better than that, he could walk there. It might take a couple of hours, but he would feel better for it. He could walk himself sane again.

He went upstairs to the bedroom and got dressed, then nudged Helen awake.

'What time is it?'

'Early. I'm going out for a walk.'

'Is it raining?'

'I'm afraid so. Hammering down.'

'Oh for fuck's sake.'

'I know. When you get up can you and the girls come and collect me from that bakery? Doesn't have to be for a couple of hours.'

'You're going to walk there? In this weather?'

'Yes.'

'You're mad,' she said, and rolled over.

Five minutes later he was padding along the side of the road, and his sturdiest shoes were already wet through. He was thirsty too. And his sunburn made all movement so uncomfortable that at times it felt as if he was only progressing inch by inch. But he was going to walk to that bakery no matter how long it took. They were horrible conditions, but that was all the more reason to keep going. He wanted Helen to be impressed with his fortitude. How nice it would be for her to have something to be impressed by. He could be a hero of sorts, rather than a balding man who might be facing the loss of his job and who knew what else when they got back. He walked on, his scorched skin still screaming under his clothes, the taste of the garlic sausage rising in his throat. At first he sidestepped the puddles that had gathered by the side of the road, but after a while there didn't seem any point and he just walked through them. He was a pilgrim now, on an arduous journey to his own self-worth.

Forty minutes later he stopped for shelter under a tree at a kink in the road. His feet were so sore that he took his shoes and socks off and bathed his feet in a puddle. A car went past, then stopped and reversed. As it drew level, the driver's window came down and sitting there in the dry and the warm was the self-assured family man he had first encountered outside the *tabac*.

'How's it going?'

'Terrific,' said Clive, standing barefoot in a puddle at seven o'clock in the morning in the pouring rain.

'Need a lift anywhere?'

'I'm fine. Really. Enjoying it. Just like you do.'

The man wrinkled his nose. 'Well, we normally do. But it's been just that bit *too* wet this year. We were thinking of going home early. Or heading south. Get a bit of—'

It was only at this moment that the man realised that Clive was not wearing socks or shoes.

'Are you sure you don't need a lift anywhere?'

'Really. I'm fine. Just giving these a quick soak, and then I'll be heading on. I love a morning walk.'

'Right. Well, that's commendable. We'll see you about.'

The man looked for a moment as if he was about to say something else, but then thought better of it. The window went slowly up again and he drove on, leaving Clive to stand and watch as the car disappeared from view.

*

By the time he could finally see the bakery in the distance, Clive was in what Helen would have called an 'absolute state'. His bottom half was soaked through and freezing. His upper half, with the exception of his head, was dry and incredibly hot. He was dehydrated and hungry, and had a headache so brutal that it felt as if a set of barbecue tongs had been forced through his left eye socket. His soaking hair fell across his forehead in wet strands. He examined his reflection in somebody's rain-specked window and recoiled, partly at the sight of himself and partly at the fact that the occupant of the house was staring back out at him. Clive's looks matched those of a man who had recently befallen a rapid succession of catastrophic events. His face, though it felt incredibly cold, was hot to the touch. His teeth, not yet even brushed, were chattering.

He felt guilty about even entering the bakery in this state but he had to get out of the rain, and he needed food and water. The little bell above the entrance rang merrily and he wiped his feet ineffectively on the door mat. It was so warm in there that he found it unsettling. The smell of freshly baked bread and pastry hit his nostrils with a power that nauseated. The lady behind the counter gave him a smile that started warmly and then quickly petered out as she took in his appearance fully.

'Bonjour, monsieur.'

'Bonjour. Bonjour. Un croissant, s'il vous plait. Et un café au lait. Et un verre d'eau. S'il vous plait. Merci.'

'Un croissant. Un café au lait. Un verre d'eau.'

Clive pointed at little row of smart, circular tables along one side of the bakery. 'D'accord?'

'Oui, oui. Bien sur.'

She gave him a solemn nod and then went into the back room, from which the sounds and smells of bakers at work were emanating. Clive pulled out the wooden chair nearest to him and collapsed so hard onto it that he thought for a moment it might give way. It certainly made enough of a crunching noise for the lady who had just disappeared to put her head back around the corner to check that everything was as it should be. She closely inspected Clive and her furniture at some length and then retreated once more.

There was a spring-loaded metal box on the table, stuffed with small and slightly waxy serviettes decorated with the name of the bakery. Clive, with difficulty, managed to extract a handful of these and began trying to wipe the rain and sweat from his face and hair, but their size and texture meant that all he succeeded in doing was moving the liquid around. When the lady brought him his glass of water there was a little pile of wet, scrunched-up serviettes on the table in front of him and he looked, if anything, even more dishevelled.

'Mon mari,' she said, 'il parle anglais.'

'Ah,' said Clive. 'Bon.'

Sure enough, her husband – a friendly, flour-covered man – came out of the back room, slapping the fine, white dust from his hands.

'Ah, it is you,' he said. 'My wife, she says there is wet man out there.'

'Ha. Yes. I am very wet. I've been for a walk. Probably not very clever.'

The man shrugged. 'We are men. We are stupid, yes?'

'Sometimes,' said Clive.

'Sometimes!' repeated the man, and then laughed loudly and for a very long time.

Clive tried to join in but couldn't.

'How is your holiday?' the man asked when he had stopped laughing.

'Oh,' said Clive, 'magnifique.'

'Your family, they like it here?'

'Oh, very much. And they like your croissants too. Delicious.'

'This is good. This is very good.'

His wife came back into the front of the shop, and the baker took this as his cue to leave. He gave Clive a powerful pat on the shoulder, contacting squarely with the worst patch of Clive's sunburn, and walked off whistling. Clive drained the glass of water, sweat now stinging his eyes, and waited patiently for his coffee and croissant. When they arrived he immediately ordered another of each, and it was only when the second round arrived that he realised he had forgotten to bring his wallet.

*

It was another half an hour before Helen strode into the bakery with Sarah and Katie in tow.

'What's happened to you, Daddy?' said Sarah.

'I went for a walk.'

'Was it fun?' asked Helen.

'I'm drier than I was when I first arrived. Luckily there's a hand drier in the loo, so I've stood with my trousers and socks under that for twenty minutes.'

'And are they dry?'

'Drier.'

'Can we have a croissant?' asked Sarah.

'I'd like a cake,' said Katie.

'You can have what you like as long as your mother's brought her purse.'

'Did you come out without money?' Helen asked in astonishment.

Clive pursed his lips and nodded. 'Whole thing was a bit spur of the moment. Still. Done now.'

'I've got money. Go and choose something, girls.'

Sarah and Katie went off to the counter while Helen took a moment to really let the full magnitude of Clive's state set in.

'Are you actually all right?' she asked.

'I think so. How's your morning been?'

'We've had a lovely time. Do you want another coffee?'

'Please.'

Once Helen had settled the bill, they progressed from the bakery to the *hypermarché*, where the girls chose a selection of videos and Helen and Clive – whose shoes made a horrible squelching noise everywhere he walked – bought more cheese and wine. When they got home the girls parked themselves in front of the television, where they would stay for the remainder of the day, and Clive, once he'd bathed and redressed, dropped into the armchair opposite Helen's. The stove burnt – much as the rain outside descended – incessantly, and the first bottle of wine was opened at half past three in the afternoon. The girls helped themselves to food and finally put themselves to bed at half past eight, just as Clive was uncorking what Helen reckoned to be their fourth bottle of wine.

'This is the last of the white,' said Clive.

'I think I'll stop after this,' said Helen. 'I can hardly read any more. I'm going to drink an awful lot of water and have a very long bath.'

But for Clive, there simply was no stopping. When Helen had gone upstairs, Clive promising to be up in a moment, went into the kitchen to start on the red. They were out of firewood now, and Clive, who couldn't face the prospect of a journey to the outbuildings, was reduced to putting the old magazines and supplements from under the coffee table into the stove, as well as bits of cardboard packaging that he fished out of the bin. When he got up to open the second bottle of red, he took a Camembert out of the fridge and ate the whole lot in one go, prising it from its flimsy wooden container using a fork while leaning against the open fridge.

He still got to bed before midnight, but woke two hours later to be sick into the toilet, causing a downward hunch so violent that his forehead collided with the metal hinge of the toilet seat and blood also trickled into the bowl. He sat on the edge of the bath holding, for want of anything else, a clump of wet loo roll to his head. Then he climbed back into bed, empty and sore, and his wife woke briefly to quietly inform him that he was an arsehole.

Outside, the rain continued to fall.

20

'Do you actually love me?'

Helen's eyes had been open for less than ten seconds when Clive uttered these words. The sun was streaming through the curtains and they could hear the girls playing downstairs. It was the sort of morning that croissants and orange juice existed for. Instead Clive lay there, practically stuck to the sheets, dry-mouthed and with his mind racing enough to ask a question such as this.

'Well?'

'Well what, Clive?'

'I said, "Do you actually love me?"'

'Clive, why don't you open a window?'

Clive got slowly out of bed and braced himself for the first hammer blows of a hangover. But they did not arrive. His vomiting, though foul, had at least saved him from some further agonies. He was dehydrated and foggy but not to the extent that he would have to hide under the covers for the rest of the day. He wanted to get on and make amends.

'So?'

Helen rolled over so that she had her back to him and pulled more of the duvet over herself.

'Is that your answer?'

'That's me telling you I've only just woken up. You haven't even said good morning. Let alone sorry.'

'Well, I am sorry. I don't know why I drank so much. Frustration maybe. I know this is unhelpful, but I just need to know that you love me.'

'What you need is to shower.'

'Are you cross with me?'

Helen sat up now. 'Oh, take a fucking guess, Clive! You behave like a monster all day, then you drink and vomit all night, and then you wake up and start demanding answers to big questions.'

'I'm sorry.'

'I tell you what. I'll have a shower, Clive. You stand there and think. And you'd better be a more bearable person to be around today or . . . you had just better be.'

And with that she got up and left the room. Clive couldn't decide whether she was giving him another chance or telling him that there would be no more chances for him to get it right. All he did know was that she hadn't answered his question.

*

It stayed sunny and the family had decided to hire bikes and ride along the old railway line. Katie was not confident about cycling on her own and so the relentlessly helpful man from the village *tabac* had suggested that he borrow something called a *rosalie* that Clive and she could ride together. Clive was led behind the shop and showed a machine that looked like two bicycles attached side by side. There were two sets of pedals at the front, one steering wheel and two bench seats. Next to the steering wheel was a handbrake. They could take four people, the man said, but were great for two.

Helen and Sarah were on bikes and were waiting for Clive and Katie as they pedalled around to the front of the shop. The two sets of pedals were attached to each other, so that it was only necessary for one of them to pedal in order to make the whole set go round. Their progress was stately enough, even though Clive found that the effort required to pedal was far greater than that needed for a normal pushbike.

Sarah and Helen set off down the hill towards the track. Behind them Clive and Katie made good, if nervous, progress and pulled out onto the wide road that swept further down to the valley floor.

'Are you happy?' he asked Katie.

'Yes,' she said. 'Can we go faster?'

Two cars had already overtaken them and Clive was feeling the pressure of being a slow road user.

'I think we need to be a bit careful while we're on the road, darling. Once we turn off we'll speed up a bit.'

But their speed was not something over which Clive had much control. The *rosalie* was heavy, and as they cycled downhill it began to accelerate. I hardly need to pedal, thought Clive, I can just freewheel. He tried to lock his feet where they were, but found that as long as the front wheels of the *rosalie* were turning, so too were the pedals. As they turned faster, Clive's feet continued to spin with them. Up ahead he saw a car pull out and start climbing the hill in their direction, so he gripped the wheel harder and tried to hold his line. By the time the car had passed them, they had reached a speed that left Clive giddy with fear. Katie, oblivious, was screaming happily. Clive, meanwhile, was sickened by the sight of his own legs pedalling away so furiously. A creeping, burning pain began to run up his calves. He had to get his feet off the pedals. And soon, very soon, he would have to stop. Helen and Sarah had turned left to travel south, and there was no way he could make that turn safely at this speed. He needed to get his feet off the pedals and apply the brake. Gingerly – and it was this caution that cost him, he later bitterly reflected – he tried to lift his feet. But as he started to lift his right foot from the pedal, that same pedal completed a full cycle and struck his heel hard, forcing it into the mechanism and the chain that linked the two pedals. The pain was almighty and instantaneous, running from his toes to just above his knee. Helen, by now some distance ahead, was unsure if the scream that she heard was one of fear or despair, and turned her bike around to look. She saw Clive and Katie's *rosalie* stopped at an angle, and her concerned daughter holding the hand of a father with his eyes tightly clamped shut. She and Sarah pedalled back up the hill.

'Are you all right?' she asked. 'This is a steep place to stop. The brakes must be good.'

She looked down to where her husband was jabbing his finger and saw that that the brakes had played no part in the vehicle's stopping. Clive's right foot, in a bulging white trainer, was jammed deep in the chain mechanism and absorbing all of the pressure and weight of the *rosalie*.

'Bloody hell,' said Helen, and put the handbrake on. This relaxed the pressure from the chains and, by pedalling backwards with his left foot, Clive was able to slowly create space to waggle his right foot free from the mechanism. Still he couldn't speak. Instead he took a series of big, sharp breaths and shut his eyes, tilting back his head. His shoe felt as it was full of blood, his foot as if it had burst.

'We were going really fast!' said Katie, excitedly.

Helen looked on, waiting for her husband to say something. His teeth were clenched and his face was empty of all colour. He wore the effortful expression of someone clinging to a mast. Finally he opened his eyes and looked up at the blue sky.

'Thank you,' he whispered.

'My pleasure. You all right?'

Clive took this question as a challenge. 'Yes,' he said. 'Just a bit of pain. Let's carry on.'

'You're sure?'

'Absolutely.'

Maybe it would be fine, he told himself. He could will his foot to be all right.

'What happened?'

'I don't know. I just stopped pedalling and my foot got hammered into the mechanism.'

'It's fixed-gear.'

'It's what?'

'Fixed-gear. If the wheels are turning, then the pedals are turning. That's why there's a handbrake.'

'Did the man tell us that?'

'I don't know. But that's what it is.'

'I see. Of course.'

And why hadn't the man who'd just hired it out explained all this? Maybe that was what he had been saying when Clive had kept nodding and saying, 'Oui, oui. Oui, oui.' It did seem likely. The man had, after all, been pointing at the pedals and at the wheels. Still, he'd keep the foot moving and he'd somehow try to be upbeat. Life would go on. Time would somehow pass.

*

They had cycled for two hours before they stopped for lunch. There was enough of a breeze to take the edge off the sun and the girls kept hooting with delight. Clive was pushing through the pain, desperate not to mention it. While the others were setting out their picnic, Clive took himself behind a bush on the pretext of having a pee and removed his right shoe and sock. The whole foot was a light pink colour, with bruising on the heel and just above his toes. It was incredibly swollen. Getting the shoe and sock back on took him an age but he worked hard to disguise his pain as he walked back to the picnic blanket.

Two and a half hours later though, after they had returned to the hire shop, Clive could conceal his agony no longer. He walked up the hill to the gîte so slowly that Helen said, 'What are we going to do then? Doctor? Chemist?'

'Maybe I just need to sit it in some cold water? Take a couple of painkillers?'

'Come on,' she said, and picked up the car keys from the kitchen table.

They all drove to town and waited outside as Clive went into the shop and fetched arnica. Then, back at the gîte, he took off his shoes and socks and sat on the sofa, rubbing the oily cream all over his puffed-up foot, from which all colour had now drained other than that of the bruises. The girls flopped in front of the television and picked at some cold things, then went out to play in the garden. Helen opened a bottle of wine and sat outside reading. Clive lay back and stared at the ceiling, a pose in which he remained for some hours, until it was quite dark outside and the rest of the family had come back in.

'Are you just going to stay there for the rest of the day?' asked Sarah.

'I might,' said Clive. 'Daddy's in a lot of pain.'

'Why?' said Katie.

'My foot!' exclaimed Clive. 'I nearly chopped the bloody thing off.'

'Don't take it out on her,' Helen chided him.

'Sorry,' said Clive. 'Sorry, Katie. I'm just in a lot of pain, and it's not going away.'

'I see,' said Helen. 'So shall we just leave you there? Are we allowed to ask if you're OK, or will that cause further outbursts?'

'I have raised my voice once today,' said Clive. 'At a person, anyway. I have tried, all day, to be bearable, to not moan, to cover up how much my foot hurts for fear of irritating anyone. I'm trying. That's all I'm doing. Trying.'

'Thank you,' said Helen. 'Thank you for trying.'

'But . . .' He tailed off.

'But what?'

'Doesn't anybody feel even a tiny bit sorry for me?'

'We all feel sorry for you, Clive,' said Helen. 'Just not as sorry as you feel for yourself.'

She walked off to the kitchen to find more wine, leaving Clive looking back at his two daughters, their faces cloaked in puzzlement.

'I'm sorry, girls,' he said. 'I'm sorry that I'm like this. And that I make your mother like that.'

They didn't reply to him, but then they had no idea what he was talking about. It was Katie who came over to the sofa and sat down next to him.

'You look very sad, Daddy,' she said.

Clive pulled a face.

'Do grown-ups ever cry?' she asked.

'Yes,' said Clive. 'Yes, they do.'

As he said this, silent tears began to stream from his eyes. Helen, still in the kitchen, was unaware of them.

*

The next morning, Helen said that it was time to leave. They would get new ferry tickets, whatever the cost, and they would go home. Helen drove to Dieppe to buy new tickets for that evening.

It was Helen who'd woken first. She got out of bed and opened the shutters, and it was the light that then spilled into the room that woke Clive. He lifted his head and watched as she opened the drawers of the chest and got dressed, then got down the suitcase from the top of the wardrobe and began to fill it.

'What are you doing?' he asked.

'Packing,' she said.

She had her back to him.

'Are you leaving?'

'We're all leaving.'

Clive was about to ask why but then realised that he already knew. She would tell him that he was the reason they were leaving, he was sure of it. A hundred reasons why this wasn't the case came to him in an instant, but he lacked the courage or fight to give voice to any of them. If he started an argument now, it wouldn't matter if he won or lost; the end result would be the same. So instead of asking why, he simply asked, 'When?'

'As soon as possible,' she told him. 'I'm going to drive to Dieppe now and buy tickets for whichever ferry we can catch first. Whatever the cost.'

'OK. Yes. Good plan,' he said. As if it was a decision that they had reached together. He had no idea if it was just the holiday that was over or everything.

When the girls came down for breakfast and asked where their mother was Clive told them about her trip to Dieppe. He imagined that he was being the bearer of bad news and was taken aback by the ambivalence with which the girls greeted his telling them that they were going home.

'OK,' said Sarah, and went upstairs to pack.

'Can we keep the videos we've bought?' asked Katie.

'Yes,' said Clive. 'I've no idea if they'll work at home, but we can keep them.'

And so they all packed their suitcases, tidied the house, loaded the car and drove off to Dieppe, leaving just enough time to make their crossing.

*

Clive could still remember so clearly the ferry journey back to Patras when they returned to the Greek mainland from Corfu. They could have taken a shorter route to Igoumenitsa, but they fancied travelling through the night and getting as much time in the Corfu sun as they could. Although it was late, the sky was still quite light, and they had enjoyed a supper and drinks near the port, sleepily dragging their luggage onboard and then, having deposited it in their cabin, going out onto the deck to hold hands, look up at the stars and kiss in a quiet corner. They kissed until it was too cold to stay outside, and then went hurriedly but carefully down to their cabin, Clive undoing his shirt as Helen fumbled at the lock. They didn't need to speak about what they were going to do in those days; they would give each other a look and then it just happened. Against the locked door, on the floor and on each of the bunks. No wonder they had been able to sleep so easily on the hard benches in Kiato the next day.

*

The car deck on the Dieppe—Newhaven ferry was a less romantic proposition altogether. Clive, the last driver up the ramp, turned off the engine and looked behind him to see that both girls were fast asleep, as they had been throughout the check-in process. Because they had booked at such short notice, there were no cabins left, and so they would just have to find somewhere in a communal area to lay the girls down, before scooping them up again at four in the morning when they got back to the UK.

'Well,' said Clive, 'it's a shame it's worked out like this.'

'Worked out?' said Helen.

'Yes.'

'Do you honestly think that it has just "worked out" like this, Clive? Honestly?'

'We have been very unlucky with the weather,' he said.

'I tell you what we have been unlucky with, Clive. We've been unlucky with you.'

'Me?'

'Yes. I know the weather's been bad. But we still could

have managed. The biggest problem with this holiday has been you.'

'I'm not sure that that's completely f—'

'It is completely fair. It's been you. The girls and I, we could have coped. We could have managed. We'd have eaten nice food, and watched films, and relaxed. And if and when the sun came out, we would have gone out and we would have enjoyed ourselves. Maybe not a lot, but a little. Enough. You, however, have made enjoying ourselves completely impossible. You've been utterly miserable. It is not possible to have fun when your bloody depression or whatever it is just looms over us all the entire time.'

'I'm not depressed, I've just been—'

'I tell you what you've been. You've been a miserable fucking nightmare. You've made stupid choices and stupid decisions. You've brought us all down. Don't talk about the bloody weather. The biggest, darkest, gloomiest cloud in Normandy has been you. You have ruined this. Completely ruined it.'

'Look, I just—'

'Don't speak, Clive.'

'Can I just—'

'No. You can't. You can think. You can think about the extent to which you've ruined this. You can think about who you are. You can think about what you're doing to us. You can think about how you can change. You can think about how you can stop fucking things up. You can think about everything. But don't fucking speak. Because it's your fault we're leaving.'

'It was you that said we should leave,' said Clive.

'Yes. Because of you. Because of the way you behave. Because you always fail to notice the impact your behaviour has on others until it's too late.'

'Look, it's not been easy. It's rained a lot, and . . .'

'Don't be pathetic, Clive.'

'Oh fuck off, Helen,' said Clive.

Then the shouting really started, a good ten minutes of it, and the car shook and bounced as if its occupants were expressing lust rather than anger. The girls pleaded with them to stop, but they were ignored. Helen had a lot more to say to Clive, but the task of breaking up the quarrel finally fell to one of the men in orange overalls who had been directing the traffic on the deck and who knocked on the driver's window and then pointed at his watch, signalling that it was time that they went upstairs and joined the rest of the passengers.

'I love you,' said Clive, not to the man in overalls but to Helen.

'I said, "Don't speak,"' she said.

PART THREE

July 1998

21

It was the night before the end of the half-term holiday and, once the girls were in bed and the kitchen was tidy, Clive had taken his whisky glass to the sitting room and was sitting in his armchair in the corner. He was thinking, as he so often did, about the past.

From the recent past, he was mulling over that evening's attempt at a family dinner. Both he and Helen, without giving voice to it, had hoped that this might be an opportunity to draw a line under what had happened on their holiday and to look towards the remainder of the term. But when Clive had gone upstairs to tell the girls that it was time for supper, he discovered that his youngest daughter had just spent the preceding three-quarters of an hour having her face and torso decorated with stars by her older sister with a pen. Then, when Helen had come upstairs to see what the delay was, it was discovered that the pen in question was the permanent marker intended for writing names on school uniform. 'I could put Katie through the washing machine and those stars wouldn't come off,' Helen had said. Dinner was then further delayed as Helen phoned a practical friend to learn that before Katie could be taken to school the next day, they would have to find an open chemist and purchase some alcohol rub or else she was condemned to arrive for lessons with her face still mapped with this grotesque constellation.

Over dinner both Clive and Helen attempted to talk about the future, but the girls kept dragging the subject back to their dismal French holiday. Clive had offered up the notion that he had really hoped that a holiday away together would have made them feel like they used to feel when they went away. 'Remember what it was like when we were in Greece? In Corfu? Paxos?' he had asked.

'I don't really,' Helen had replied.

Instead the pair had pored over every excruciating detail of their abortive trip to Normandy. It was exhaustive – as far as Helen was concerned, at any rate; Clive had still not raised with his wife the incident with Findlay that had given cause to so much worry and turmoil within him and had thus coloured his mood while they were away.

It was this aspect of the slightly more distant past that Clive now considered as he allowed himself to pour another finger of whisky into his glass. As much as the implications of the single lesson he had taken on that Friday concerned him, there was also the issue of the actual facts. If this business went any further, he would have to give his side of the story in full, and each time he thought about the incident, he found that he remembered it slightly differently. Clive had once heard a policeman on the radio describing how rarely different eyewitness accounts of a crime actually match up. Now he found that even his own recollections of the event were inconsistent with each other. Once Crouch had described the folders that Clive had thrown hitting Findlay, that had become an image in Clive's head. That image then sometimes became indistinguishable from a memory. Had he actually turned back towards the rest of the class before he saw where the folders went? Or had he actually seen them not hit the boy? He had been sure two weeks ago but he wasn't sure now. That squeal he could sometimes hear when he recalled coming back into the classroom, was it the boy or the door? Had it happened at all? He had to get a version of events straight in his own mind, but would it be the correct version? All he definitely knew was that if he had hurt the boy, he hadn't meant to. But that, he knew, would not be enough. Perhaps if he described it to Helen, he would be sure of things. Just saying it out loud would help him solidify his recollections. But then the prospect of explaining it to Helen at all was a terrifying one. With luck, he would never have to.

He tried to put all of these thoughts to one side, and then began to mull over something that had happened nearly a year ago now. He had been sitting in that chair drinking whisky at the end of August until one in the morning and turned off the radio before the news headlines. He had missed the news, therefore, that the Princess of Wales had been in a car crash. Instead he had heard it first thing the next morning. It was an odd moment of history for him to feel nostalgic about, but he could still remember that hug that Helen had given him when he went up to the bedroom to tell her. She knew something big had happened because of the look on his face, she had later told him. He had gone in, closed the door behind him and relayed the facts.

'She was in a car crash. Paris.'

Helen had said nothing, but climbed straight out of bed, wrapped her arms around him and held him. It felt natural. They had gone downstairs and drunk coffee together side by side on the sofa, watching the television news. When the first sounds started coming from the girls' bedroom, they had looked at each other and instinctively knew that they needed to tell them. They had climbed the stairs together and walked into the girls' bedroom holding hands. It was Helen who told them, kneeling on the floor between their beds. It was Clive who put an arm around Katie when she sobbed that she 'didn't know that princesses could die'. Clive had cried too, not for Diana but for his daughter. Perhaps it was that feeling he felt nostalgic for: the four of them standing in a knot together, holding each other tightly.

He had had to go into work later that day for the start of the school year. The staff all had to convene early in the afternoon and Mark Taylor, put completely on the spot by the headmaster, had spoken brilliantly about collective grief and how little we speak about death. 'We don't talk about it, not because we're not interested in it, but because we're afraid of it,' he had said.

Clive had been envious of him at the time for being the sort of person who could not only improvise a speech like that but also be reassuring. He envied him now simply for not possessing all the feelings that Clive did.

I wouldn't mind an event of that magnitude striking now, thought Clive. That would bring them all together again. And it would distract from the Findlay business. It also occurred to Clive that Mark would never be guilty of a thought like that.

22

'Thanks for making the time to come in, Clive.'

'My pleasure, Headmaster.'

He had been waiting for a summons to see Crouch all week. Now it had finally arrived. Clive decided to tackle the issue head on.

'I assume, Headmaster, that this is about Findlay?'

'No, no. It isn't, actually.'

'Well, I must say I'm rather relieved to hear it, Headmaster,' said Clive. Relief was in fact rushing through him like wind. He closed his eyes for a moment, and then said, 'I think it was just a small incident that was totally blown out of all proportion.'

'Well, let's just see what happens on that score, shall we? We may well be going to be talking about it, Clive. Just not here. Not now. Due process must be followed. It's all in the hands of the boy's parents, as things stand.'

'But you've heard nothing from them?'

'I've heard no word as yet, but that doesn't mean that they don't intend to take things further. They've had the half-term holiday to think about it. I think if they were going to say something they'd have said it by now. But we must wait and see.'

'I see. Well, I've bumped into him a couple of times this week and he's not said anything.'

'Are you worried, Clive? I don't think that you should worry.'

'Because you don't think anything will come of it?'

'Because worrying is not the Frampton way.'

Never had such a meaningless statement been delivered with such gravity.

'I'm uncertain how I should feel, to be honest. But I did assume that was why you'd asked me here.'

'Oh no.'

So if not Findlay, what?

The headmaster let out a long, satisfied sigh and then uncrossed and recrossed his arms, as if to mark a shift in tone. 'Been a good start to the second half of term, Clive?'

'Yes, I think so.'

'Helen good? The girls? Someone told me you went to France over the break.'

'They're well, thanks. France. Yes. We did. Quite a difficult time for various—'

'I love France.'

The headmaster beamed as he said this, as if he was proud of the fact. But Clive had no idea whatsoever how to respond to a statement of such mundanity and so he took a sip of his coffee and then sucked air through his teeth. Really he just wanted to know why he had been called up, apparently out of the blue on a Friday afternoon, by the headmaster's assistant and summoned to a meeting. It had sounded urgent, so naturally Clive had assumed it was about the incident with Findlay. Not so urgent that the headmaster didn't keep him waiting for fifteen minutes after he had arrived. And now clearly not so urgent that there wasn't time for small talk.

'Do you know what this is about, Linda?' Clive had asked her when he arrived at the school office. 'Is it disciplinary?'

'No idea at all. He'll be ready in a moment. Can I make you a coffee?'

'Thank you, Linda. Yes please. Milk and none. He didn't sound angry or anything, did he?'

'He never sounds angry. He just asked me to call you and have you come over.'

'Hmm.'

He had already finished the first cup of coffee long before Crouch's door had opened, and so it was his second cup of the afternoon that he was now nervously swallowing while he waited for the headmaster to get to the nub of the matter. When he'd first entered, Clive had been directed to sit in an armchair, but then rather than sitting down himself the headmaster had embarked on a slow lap of the room, peering at the photos on the wall of his own study as if he hadn't looked them over a hundred times before. Was this a status game, Clive wondered, struggling to find a way of sitting comfortably on the high-backed chair.

'And how's Flora getting along? Well? Settling in? Robert seems pleased.'

'I think she's doing very well,' Clive said.

How am *I* doing? he thought.

'Robert said she'd made a very good start. Has an easy way with the pupils.'

'Well, I've not seen her teach, of course, but she certainly seems to be happy. Clearly knows what she's doing.'

'Yes. Very good CV, we thought. Interviewed extremely well. And it was her idea to come across for a few weeks. Get to know the place.'

'Yes, she mentioned that. She's very . . . impressive, I suppose.'

'Yes,' said Crouch, as if the thought had never occurred to him. 'Impressive. Very good way to describe her. And the boarding house? All good? Been on duty much?'

'Sunday night and last night. Absolutely fine. It's been redecorated over the break, I see. Looks very smart.'

'Yes. Very much so. Arabella chose the colour scheme, you know.'

'Did she?'

'Yes. And *personally*, I think she's done a very good job. But then I suppose I would say that, wouldn't I?'

'Well, I think you're right, Headmaster, for what it's worth. Some excellent choices by Arabella.'

'Helen OK? The girls?'

Clive only had one free period on a Friday afternoon and he was already halfway through it.

'Headmaster, would you mind telling me why I'm here? If it's not about Findlay, that is.'

The headmaster immediately moved from the position he had taken up behind Clive's chair and sat down behind his impossibly large oak desk.

'I'm sorry, Clive,' he said. 'Is there somewhere you need to be?'

'I've a lesson that starts in twenty minutes.'

'My apologies. My apologies. Let me begin. It's not a big thing.'

'Right.' Clive placed his coffee cup down carefully on the arm of his chair and folded his hands in his lap.

'I wouldn't do that if I were you. Bit thin, those arms. I've witnessed a fair few spillages from this vantage point.'

'Right. Sorry.' Clive picked up the cup again and took another sip.

'Thank you. It's not a problem. The fabric's actually stainproof. But even so. We don't want coffee all over you, do we?'

'We don't,' said Clive, struggling to conceal how testy this meeting was now making him.

'Tennis,' the headmaster suddenly said.

'I'm sorry?'

'Tennis. Ever played tennis?'

'No.'

'I want you to start coaching it.'

Clive couldn't quite believe what he was hearing. He had had dreams less surprising and illogical than this, and so he sat there waiting for the headmaster to explain himself.

'You look surprised, Clive.'

'I am.'

'Then allow me to explain. What do we produce at Frampton?'

'Produce?'

'What is our end product?'

'Well. Lots of eighteen-year-old boys, by and large. Hopefully with good A level results.'

'It's more than that though. Isn't it, Clive?'

'Yes,' said Clive, after a pause.

'Would you care to expand on that?'

There must be a right answer to this, Clive thought. 'Well,' he said, 'hopefully they're also good people. Nice. Polite. Helpful. Interested in things. Healthy.'

'I'll tell you what we produce, Clive. It's all-rounders.'

'Of course,' said Clive. 'All-rounders.'

'And in what sense am I talking "all-rounders", Clive?'

'In . . . in all senses?'

'In all senses, Clive. Boys – young men, really – who are good at lots and lots of different things. Who excel across a range of fields.'

Across a range of fields. *Christ.*

'A range of fields. Yes.'

'And we do it well, don't you think?'

'Sometimes,' said Clive, although the headmaster's furrowed brow told him that this was not the correct response.

'I think we do it *very* well, Clive. But do you know what else I think, Clive?'

Clive shook his head.

'I think we could do it better, Clive. Even better. And do you know how I think we can do it even better?'

'More tennis?' suggested Clive, his confusion now writ large across his face.

'Yes,' said the headmaster, much to Clive's surprise. 'At least in your case. If we're going to turn out all-rounders, if becoming all-rounders is what we demand of our boys, then I think that we should demand it of ourselves, don't you?'

'Alternatively,' Clive said, 'we could help them become all-rounders by being specialists ourselves.'

'Frankly, I disagree. We should all take on extra responsibilities.'

'Is this a cost-cutting measure?'

'It most certainly is not a cost-cutting measure, Clive. Anything but. It is an opportunity for us all to enrich the lives of ourselves and each other and, by extension, the life of the school.'

'But I don't play tennis. I don't know anything about it.'

'The fact that you don't know anything about is precisely why you should coach it. A new skill.'

'I don't need a new skill. And the boys don't need me coaching them. If they want to learn tennis, they should have a proper tennis coach. Shouldn't they?'

'You will become a proper tennis coach, Clive. You'll be adept in no time.'

Clive could feel an anger rising from deep within him. If he went home and told Helen that he had to start coaching tennis, she'd probably go spare. Telling her he wanted to join a tennis club would be a different matter, of course. If Findlay's parents had made a further complaint, he would probably have acquiesced, but as they hadn't he could simply see no reason to.

'Are you doing this to anyone else?'

'I'm going to roll it out across the whole school.'

'And will you take be taking on additional responsibilities yourself?'

'Yes, I shall.'

'What?'

'Well, I'm not totally sure yet. Leading trips, possibly.'

'Perhaps you should teach French? If you like France so much.'

That would free up a member of the French department, Clive thought, to come over here and start telling other teachers that they have to start coaching tennis.

The headmaster emitted a mirthless laugh. 'Clive, I can sense a certain reluctance on your part. And I can quite understand your desire to scrutinise such a plan. But it's a plan that's going ahead.'

'Why are you telling me this now? Why not right at the beginning of term?'

'I was planning on introducing the plan *incrementally*.'

If anyone had ever been so pleased with themselves for using the word 'incrementally' before, then Clive certainly hadn't been there to witness it.

'It's a plan that is still being developed, Clive. And we can do things like that here at Frampton, because our flexibility is so built in. Linda's been a huge help, of course. She's working out a grid of what everybody should be doing. She's terribly good at grids. I'm taking a little advice. Sounding people out. Doing it case by case.'

'Look, Headmaster. If you are sounding me out, then I think that the idea of me teaching tennis is ridiculous.'

'But Clive, all teaching is good.'

'Not bad teaching.'

'Clive. You're a good teacher.'

'I'm a good history teacher. I know the subject. I stand at the front of the class and I know what I'm going to talk about. It makes sense for me to do it. But for me to teach tennis, at any level, is plainly ridiculous. I've never even owned a racket.'

'I think you'll surprise yourself, Clive.'

'Who else has agreed to take on teaching something for which they have no aptitude and in which they have always declared absolutely zero interest? Anyone?'

'Have you always declared absolutely zero interest in tennis, Clive? Is that true?'

'Look, I don't hate it. I just don't ever think about it.'

'Well, we have to start somewhere, don't we?'

'Headmaster, I honestly believe that I am not a good place to start.' Clive was trying to state this as moderately as possible but did himself no favours by instinctively standing up and putting the coffee cup down on the arm of the chair as he did so.

The headmaster stayed seated. 'Have you always been a rebel, Clive?'

'I'm not a rebel.'

'Oh, I think you are. And do you know what? I admire you for it. Honestly. And I know that we can harness that rebel spirit of yours. And put it to use on the tennis courts. You're someone who doesn't like to play by the rules. Trust me. I understand.'

'Well, I can't play by the rules of tennis. I don't really know them.'

'Yes, Clive. But you can learn them!' The headmaster was up on his feet now, exhorting Clive with outstretched palms. 'And once you've learnt them, you can teach them to others. You see? We can all do a little bit more, can't we?'

Or we can do less and do it better, thought Clive.

Clive and the headmaster stood looking at each other. The headmaster's eyebrows were raised. He was asking a question. All Clive had to do was answer it in the affirmative and all things would be well. That was how it was supposed to work.

'I can't do it,' said Clive. 'I teach a lot of lessons every week. I have other pastoral responsibilities. And those are just the official ones, not the ones that get sprung on me. And I have a family. Who need me. I can't suddenly take up tennis, or anything else for that matter. But good luck with your plan. Now, if you'll excuse me, I really do have a lesson to teach.'

The headmaster took several seconds to digest this unusually defiant outburst from Clive. He was used to Clive being sulkily acquiescent. That was a little tedious, but at least bearable. And, most importantly, what needed to be done got done. This new trait was not at all welcome and the headmaster communicated as such with his eyes, which he narrowed like a cat's. He extended the index finger of his left hand to smooth his moustache before speaking.

'Have you anything else to say, Clive?'

'Yes. If you'd asked me to coach tennis because we're short of tennis coaches, then I would have considered it. If it would mean that more boys who wanted to play tennis could play it, then, you know . . . great.'

'I see. But . . . ?'

'But this approach of asking me to do it in order to . . . *improve* myself? I'm afraid not.'

'We are short of a tennis coach, as it happens.'

'Then I suggest that's the first thing you tell the next person you try to convince.'

Clive was certain that he detected an admiring look from the headmaster. It was probably because Clive had shown some decisiveness. A degree of fortitude. He was standing up for himself. All part of the unique Frampton Character.

The headmaster said nothing at all as Clive walked out of his office. In the room outside, Wally and Iain Dixon were sitting awkwardly side by side on a sofa.

'Oh hello, Clive,' said Iain. 'Any idea what these meetings are about?'

'It's just a chance for you to express yourself, really,' said Clive. 'Thanks for the coffee, Linda.'

'Did you leave the cup in there?'

'Yes, sorry. It's on the arm of the chair.'

'Oh, he won't like that.'

'I dare say. See you all later.'

As he jogged down the stairs, Clive felt suddenly glad that he'd been invited for that meeting. It had felt absolutely fantastic.

*

There were no sports matches planned in the second half of term, a nod towards focussing on academia in the run-up to the summer exams. Saturday afternoons were now free to the boys for the purpose of studying. It soon became clear that this strategy had somewhat backfired, as hundreds of boys were left with nothing to do from lunchtime onwards and so disappeared off into town to acquire cigarettes, alcohol and any mind-altering substances that Frampton could muster, which was most of them. By three in the afternoon those staff charged with knowing the whereabouts of the boys realised that they had absolutely no idea where they were.

At five in the afternoon Clive walked to the supermarket at the other end of town with Sarah and Katie in order to buy milk and the ingredients for a Sunday roast. To get to the supermarket on foot was a far harder task than it was by car, and to approach it from the centre of the town involved crossing two roads leading off a roundabout and then going through an underpass that emerged at the foot of a car park, at the far end of which stood the red-brick superstructure bedecked with black-and-white branding. It had had a different owner two years before, and a different one again two years before that, one supermarket giant after another taking it in turns to lose interest in the Frampton market. Normally it was necessary to follow a somewhat haphazard pedestrian route that had been marked out in yellow painted lines zig-zagging between the cars, but today the car park was largely empty and contained rather more abandoned trolleys than it did cars. It was a windowless building, bathed in a curious yellow light that always made it feel as if it was quarter to nine in the evening, regardless of what time one actually entered the store.

'What would you like to do, girls? Shall we split up into groups to get what we need?'

'Can Sarah and I go round together?' asked Katie.

'Of course. Why don't you two get milk, flour and eggs? I'll get meat and vegetables. If I can find any.'

'They have everything here, don't they?' asked Sarah.

'They claim to. If we haven't bumped into each other, then I'll see you at the meat counter in ten minutes.'

He placed a hand basket into Sarah's grasp.

'And don't put anything in here I haven't asked you to get. No sweets.'

'What about ice cream?'

'Fine. Get ice cream.'

The girls walked off in completely the wrong direction and Clive began to stroll along the vegetable aisle, listening to – or at least hearing – a series of almost totally unintelligible announcements being made over the tannoy. Clive reckoned that he could hear fewer than one word in five with anything remotely like clarity. Bargain. Selection. Deals. Today. Store. As he bagged up loose carrots and potatoes, he tutted at the sheer pointlessness of these broadcasts and at the doubtless inanity of the information that they were so spectacularly failing to convey. Would hearing them in their full glory be even worse than their being incomplete, he wondered. He placed the basket at his feet and stared into it at the carrots and potatoes in their flimsy polythene bags, like disappointing newborn kittens. They didn't look very exciting. Get some vegetables, Helen had said. There should be something green, probably. Peas? Peas would be safe. Everyone likes peas. He would have to go to the frozen aisle. He picked up the basket and rounded the corner, and saw at the far end of the supermarket two figures he thought he vaguely recognised. Teenage boys in hooded tops. Moving too fast. Conspiratorial. They disappeared down an aisle and so he made his way to the end of the store as swiftly as he could. As he turned the corner into the furthest aisle, he saw them again at the far end, where the spirits were stored. They each held a bottle in their hands. He was about to shout, but they would be too far away. They were absorbed in a frantic conversation, so he might still have time. He put down his basket, doubled back on himself and jogged along the parallel aisle. When he reached the end of it, he tiptoed around the corner and stopped to see if he could identify the boys by their voices. They were whispering, though, and it was hard to hear them above the sound of the tinny, incoherent proclamations still booming out of the tannoy. Something about meat, cat litter and bathroom products. Perhaps some appetising confection that combined all three?

'Let's get these. It's the cheapest.'

'Shall we try and get one each or should one of us try and buy both? Less risky?'

'I'll get these. You get fags.'

'What's your new ID like? How old does it say you are?'

'Nineteen.'

'That's more realistic than mine. Says I'm twenty-six.'

Clive was fairly sure of their identities now and so he stepped out and around the corner, coming face to face with Matthew Dunster and Michael Hicks, who immediately began to radiate panic. For a moment Clive wondered if they were going to try and run. They had been so obviously caught in the act that it was hardly worth them even attempting to conceal their guilt and yet they both instinctively put the bottles they were holding behind their backs. They looked at each other and then stayed where they were.

'Good afternoon, gentlemen.'

'Hello, Sir.' Dunster.

'What brings you here?'

'Just a bit of shopping, Sir.' Hicks.

'Really? Good idea. Nice quiet afternoon for it.'

'Yes, Sir.'

'Thought you might take advantage of a free afternoon and have a drink, did you?'

'Yes, Sir,' said Dunster, quietly.

'But unfortunately you've bumped into me and that's somewhat put a hole in your plans, hasn't it?'

'It has, Sir, yes,' said Hicks.

'So I think that what you had perhaps better do instead is let me return whatever that is to the shelves and then you should go back to your house and do something else for the afternoon and evening, and hope that I don't decide to tell anyone less nice than me where I bumped into you and what it was that I found you trying to do. What is it you've got?'

The boys withdrew their hands from behind their backs to reveal that they were each grasping a bottle of the supermarket's own-brand vodka. Clive put out his hands and they each passed him their bottles. He spoke calmly and quietly.

'Very silly idea this, boys. Very silly. Nearly every teacher who lives in this town shops here. If you're going to buy something you shouldn't, don't do it somewhere where you're going to get caught. And if you're going to get pissed, don't do it on this stuff. Go somewhere out of the way and have a few beers. You might be sick that night or have a headache the next day. Drink a bottle of this stuff and you'll end up in the back of an ambulance having your stomach pumped and then suffer the indignity of being collected from the school sanitorium by your very disappointed parents on account of having been sent home for a couple of weeks by the headmaster. Do you understand me?'

'Yes, Sir.'

'Hicks?'

'Yes, Sir.'

'Good. Then you'd better leave these with me and keep your noses very clean indeed for the rest of the weekend. The reason there's no sport this afternoon is so that you can study. Not so that you can go out on the town like a couple of lunatics. Go on. Disappear.'

Clive watched the two boys scurry off towards the exit. They paused briefly at the tobacco counter and looked back to see Clive still watching them. He raised a pair of incredulous eyebrows at them and they looked sheepishly at him before continuing on their way. After they had disappeared through the exit Clive looked for the place on the aisle where they had found the vodka, and was about to replace the two bottles on the shelf when his eye was caught by the price label. It really was astonishingly cheap stuff. Might make a nice change, he thought, and went off to put the bottles in his own basket. Then he went to find the girls, who were waiting at the meat counter with no milk, not enough flour, far too many eggs and an enormous amount of ice cream.

23

For the past few weeks, Clive and Helen had been living in the shadow of the holiday to Normandy. He had still heard no more about Findlay's accusations, although the boy had been, whenever Clive had any contact with him, unusually diffident. Clive's tensions on that front were easing a little, although the sinews between he and Helen had undoubtedly tensed and twisted, and in the weeks that followed it would remain to be seen whether they would slowly loosen and unclench or if lasting nerve damage had occurred. Sometimes in the mornings when Clive opened his front gate and turned left to walk in the direction of the school, he realised, if it was cold, that he had a slight limp. The stiffness in his ankle took his mind straight back to Normandy. For men of another generation there would be an inherent heroism in that.

Yet life had returned to something a little bit like normality once they had returned to Frampton. They had both gone back to work, and on his free evenings Clive focussed his attentions on looking after the girls. Helen began to socialise more, to meet up with colleagues from work and other people from the school who lived in the town. She was often out in the evenings, and Clive marvelled at how someone could find so many things to do and people to see in a town as small as Frampton. By the time she got back, Clive was usually sitting out in the garden, drinking wine and smoking roll-ups in the dark, and they would sit out there and talk about their days as if they were flatmates. They would take turns using the bathroom and read until one of them switched off their bedside light, a cue always taken by the other to mean that another day was now over.

At the school, Clive kept his head down as much as possible following his little showdown with the headmaster, and tried to keep out of trouble with Icke too. This was made easier, in part, by Flora's presence around the department. She possessed an innate optimism and lightness of touch that the department had been somewhat lacking previously, and now that she was starting to take some lessons and not just observe, they all had less crowded teaching timetables. How strange, Clive thought, that he had initially resented her appointment. Now it was a source of relief every day that she was there. There would be gales of laughter in the departmental staffroom, and something about her had softened Icke's manner. Flora acted as a buffer between Icke and Clive, and she also loved the actual craft of teaching, which rubbed off on the rest of them. Still, if Flora wasn't about, Clive made a point of keeping out of Icke's way. This was not a tactic that had escaped Icke's attention.

'Oh hello, Clive, you're still here, are you?'

It was morning break, and Clive was just making his way into the main staffroom.

'Very much so, Robert,' said Clive, as cheerfully as he could manage.

'I feel like I haven't seen you for weeks.'

'Well, I've certainly been about. Teaching, mainly.'

'Glad to hear it. Although not as much as you used to. Thanks to Flora.'

'Well, I'd not really noticed that there was a problem before, but there seems to be the right number of us now, doesn't there?'

'I suppose,' said Icke, after a moment's thought, 'it's about having the right number of people with the right attitude.'

It was hard for Clive to perceive this as anything other than direct criticism, but he held his nerve and just about managed a smile.

'Well, nice chatting with you, Robert. I'll let you get your coffee.'

As Icke turned his back the smile fell rapidly from Clive's face. Anger could well within him so quickly now. At home it was numbed, but he saved up his emotions for when he was at work. He fantasised about marching after Icke, grabbing him by the hair and then slamming his head into the coffee machine repeatedly, hopefully as boiling liquid was pouring out of the front of it. He wanted there to be blood. Instead, he placed his coffee cup back with the others and helped himself to a glass of water from the sink. He went over to the corner of the room where Wally was sitting, looking unusually desperate. This impression wasn't helped by the fact that he, once again, had one of his hands heavily and clumsily bandaged, following an incident caused by the headmaster's insistence that Wally teach one lesson of woodwork a week in order to 'broaden his skill set'. In Wally's case, this experiment had only lasted fifteen minutes before the school nurse had to be summoned and pupils had to help Wally into a chair.

'How's the hand, Wally?' said Clive, taking a seat.

'Stitches out next week, hopefully. Can't wait. As long as it's healed properly. It's been a nightmare walking the dogs with only one working hand. And they just get stronger and stronger.'

'Is he going to make you go back to woodwork?'

'I sincerely hope not.'

'You should have told him no in the first place.'

'I didn't realise that was an option. Nobody did, except you. Even Dixon agreed to take on another skill.'

'You mean him volunteering to help with the gardening club?'

'Exactly.'

'Well, what neither you nor the headmaster have realised is that there isn't a gardening club.'

'Isn't there?'

'No.'

'Well, maybe I could do that too.'

'I wouldn't. I'd just keep your head down.'

'That's your new mantra, isn't it? Going well?'

'It was. Just bumped into Icke by the coffee machine. I've avoided any contact with him for a week, and the one time I speak to him, he makes a snide remark about my attitude.'

'You have to ignore him. Bet your department's a nicer place to be since the lovely Flora arrived.'

'Yes. Much nicer. Although calling her "the lovely Flora" wouldn't endear you to her.'

'Why not?'

'It sounds creepy, Wally.'

'Does it?' Wally looked very concerned by this.

Clive nodded.

'I'm very sorry, Clive. I didn't mean to be—'

'It's all right, Wally. I was just warning you. Don't take it as an insult.'

'I mean, she is lovely. Isn't she? Divorce isn't much fun, but she always seems to be pretty upbeat.'

'Probably relieved to be away from him. Whoever he was.'

'Yes. Another teacher, wasn't it?'

'Exactly,' said Clive. 'So presumably unbearable. Like we are.'

'Well, quite.' Wally managed a little chuckle, but the remark had clearly given him pause for thought. 'Do you really think that?'

'No, Wally. I hardly think anything any more.'

'Your foot any better?'

'Getting there. I've had quite a bit of physio on it. The limp comes and goes. If I'd been limping the day that Crouch wanted me to coach tennis, though, it might have been less tricky turning him down. Then he wouldn't have so much cause to hate me.'

'Does he hate you?'

'Well, I don't know about hate. But my "card is marked", apparently.'

'Is it the Findlay thing? I can't believe anything really happened, did it?'

'That's gone quiet for now.'

'Who told you your card was marked? Him?'

'Can't say.'

'Linda?'

'Yes.'

'On school property?'

'Pub.'

'Oh dear. You don't want him on your back.'

'Well, quite. Oh God, here he comes.'

The headmaster had indeed come into the staffroom but had not yet assumed his speaking position, and so Clive took this as a good opportunity to quietly slip away.

'Perhaps see you at lunch, Wally. Enjoy what Crouch has to say. I've got an appointment with a window I need to stare out of.'

*

As Clive crossed the quad, he thought of Icke's infuriating comment. He couldn't even keep that man onside by staying out of his way. What did he mean 'the right attitude'? Clive's attitude was that he should be allowed to teach without this sort of petty threat hanging over him. He couldn't resist aiming a kick at the neatly manicured lawn that he was walking along the edge of. 'Keep Off The Grass.'

What was the point of having grass if you weren't allowed to walk on it? It was entirely cosmetic. The only person who ever walked on the grass was the man who cut it. It was all about looking the part, about creating something that looked nice in photos for the prospectus or when prospective parents were looking around the wretched place. It was purely symbolic, like so much of Frampton; creating the appearance of perfection was so much more of a focus for the school and the headmaster than attempting to pursue the real thing ever was. Wouldn't it be fun to get hold of a mole and bury it under there somewhere and then see what sort of damage it could do? A spate of molehills appearing the morning of Speech Day would be an absolute delight to behold. Clive took a careful, guilty look around and then crossed an edge of the lawn. Keep Off The Grass, indeed. Not if you don't say please.

He still had twenty minutes to spare before his next class started, with a group of seventeen-year-olds who still had a year to go before their exams. He had been teaching them for nearly a year now but still didn't quite feel he'd got a handle on them. Maybe he was losing his touch. He had taught a few of them for their GCSEs, but there were a number he hadn't taught before and some new boys who had only started school that term. Normally what people thought was easier about teaching A levels was that your class only contained people who were there by choice. That was the theory at least. But in an environment like Frampton that couldn't really be guaranteed. The boys had all sorts of pressures exerted on them by their parents and the school itself. History was a subject that it was felt looked good on university application forms, and so bright people might be steered in that direction at the expense of something that they were genuinely passionate about. Some of the boys in this class appeared to have no interest in the actual subject whatsoever, only in how to do well at it. Icke asked the teachers in his department to show the pupils 'model templates for high-scoring essays'. Identify and repeat 'key words'. Refer back to the title at the beginning and end of every paragraph. Start with the conclusion. They weren't teaching history, they were teaching the boys how to be good at exams. And the boys, understandably, were happy to take on board anything that might make the exams easier. They just wanted to learn the facts and the magic essay algorithm; it was hard to get the boys interested in discussion and interpretation of any issue wider than these facts. And these boys were horrifyingly confident, thinking little of telling Clive just how they would like to be taught. Clive's suspicion was that the attitude they had towards teachers was inherited from their parents. There was a man who had rung Clive up a couple of years ago to complain that Clive kept giving his son low marks. 'I have to wonder if you're teaching him well enough,' said the man, who owned his own chain of petrol stations.

'I see,' said Clive. 'But I'm afraid he doesn't apply himself all that well.'

'Then it's your job to make him apply himself. That's what we pay for.'

'Yes, I appreciate that.'

'I hope you do, Mr Hapgood, I hope you do. Because there's a little saying that I proscribe to: "Those who can, do; those who can't, teach."'

'Very good,' said Clive. 'If that's your view, then I'm not sure there's much point in our talking, is there? And I wouldn't worry too much about your son. He's very bright.'

'I know he is.'

'He's so bright, in fact, that he knows the difference between "proscribe" and "subscribe". Lovely chatting.'

He had ended up having to explain himself in Crouch's office but had received only the gentlest ticking off. The headmaster, it later turned out, had previously had issues with this particular parent. During a phone conversation about the boy's poor behaviour, the man had suddenly asked Crouch how much he earned as a headmaster. Crouch, taken aback by the man's directness, had actually told him, and had then suffered the indignity of the man snorting derisively that he didn't generally take advice from people from that far down the pay scale and wasn't about to start now. Clive's source for this was Linda, who had an unfortunate habit of listening in to the calls that she put through to her boss, and the even more unfortunate habit of repeating some of the things she had heard when she had consumed three glasses of the house Sauvignon in the Crown.

Clive retrieved his rolling tobacco from his desk drawer; he reckoned he had just enough time to go for a smoke and be back before class started. There was an alleyway that ran behind the history department to the area behind the science block where the school's minibuses were parked and the boys often smoked. Teachers weren't meant to smoke on school property either, so Clive often went there. As he walked down the alleyway, three boys coming the other way looked rather startled to see Clive.

'Hello, Sir,' they shouted incredibly loudly, and Clive heard scurrying and sprinting from the other end of the alley. The boys looked rather pleased with themselves for warning the other smokers off and Clive gave them an accusatory glance, but he was secretly relieved by their actions. It was inconvenient to catch the boys smoking, and it was hypocritical of him to tell them off. Now he'd have the place to himself. He sat down on the footplate of one of the buses and rolled up and lit a cigarette, which he smoked so quickly that he felt light-headed when he stood up. His emergence from the alleyway was spotted by Icke, walking back to the department with Flora after break. The boys too were arriving for lessons, their files tucked under their arms.

'Everything all right, Mr Hapgood?'

'Perfectly, thank you.'

'Saw you rushing off during break time. Wondered if you'd been taken ill.'

'No, no. Just had something urgent to do.'

Icke stopped. 'Oh yes? What was that?'

Clive wracked his brain for a response, and infuriated himself with the answer he eventually managed. 'Lesson planning.'

'Lesson planning. Well, better late than never, I suppose.' Icke gave a curt little smile before pushing off, leaving Clive with Flora.

'That was a spectacularly stupid answer, wasn't it?' Clive said.

'Didn't make you look great. Was it true?'

'No. I walked out early so I didn't have to listen to Crouch and so I could go and have a smoke. Was that the right choice?'

'I think the smoking is probably the worse option in the long term, but in the short term, yes. Entirely wise. He said nothing at all for twelve minutes solid.'

'Still pleased you came here?'

'I think so,' said Flora, pushing a lock of light brown hair behind her ear and clearing her throat. Had it been light brown before? Clive wondered. Or was this a new colour? He liked it.

'Good. Who've you got now?'

'Fourth form. And you have lower sixth.'

'Very good, Ms Wilson. Very good indeed.'

*

It was half past eight before Clive made it home. He could hear talking further down the hall as he let himself in the front door. A man's voice.

'Hello?' called Clive.

'We're in the kitchen,' shouted Helen.

The man in the kitchen was a little older than Clive, but in considerably better shape. No grey hairs either. A jawline straight out of an advertisement for shaving products.

'Clive,' he said, 'how do you do?' He held out a hand to Clive and flashed him a smile. Strangely square teeth.

Clive took the hand and shook it.

'This is Martin. He's on the council. We were just talking about the planning committee.'

'Rather a dry subject,' said the man.

'I'm sure it's not,' said Clive. 'Don't let me disturb you.'

'We're almost done,' said Helen as Clive went to fill up the kettle.

'There's wine open,' she added, and pointed to the table where two full glasses stood next to a bottle. 'There's probably a glass left in it.'

'I'd better not,' said Clive. 'You two can finish it.'

'How's your boss?' said Martin.

'My boss?'

'Julian Crouch.'

'Oh, I see. Have you had any dealings with him?'

'We play golf together sometimes. When we have time.'

'Do you?' said Clive.

'Martin does a lot of sports,' said Helen. 'Marathons and things.'

'Half-marathons,' said Martin, as if he was talking about hopscotch.

'I think I will have that glass actually,' said Clive, turning off the kettle. 'What party are you?'

'Party?' said Martin.

'Town Council. What party are you?'

'Oh,' said Martin. 'I'm Independent.'

'I see.'

'Martin was only elected in May,' said Helen.

'This ward?'

'Mountway.'

'Oh, very nice.'

'Yes, it's interesting.'

Clive got down a glass and emptied what was left of the bottle into it. 'Well, I'll leave you two to it.'

He went and sat down in the living room and turned on the television to see a bit of the news. A report from Hebron. He could hear that there was still talking in the kitchen but it was not loud enough for him to make out any of the words. He dialled Mark's number, but it went, after many rings, to the answerphone. It had done that a lot lately. When he went to take his glass back to the kitchen, Helen and Martin were both standing next to the sink and had to move apart for him to put his glass down on the worktop.

'Excuse me,' said Clive, and Martin smiled at him.

Then he returned to the television and carried on watching the news with the volume a little lower.

'Nice to meet you, Clive,' Martin called through a few minutes later as he let himself out of the front door.

Clive heard Helen loading glasses into the dishwasher and turning it on. He listened to her quietly carry out a succession of indiscernible tasks and fill a glass with water before she finally came into the sitting room and sat on the arm of the sofa. Clive turned off the television with the remote control.

'Who is Martin?'

'A town councillor.'

'I know that. But who is he? What's his other job?'

'Has his own company. Something to do with computers.'

'Just passing, was he?'

'No,' said Helen, crossly. 'He rang up and asked if he could come round for a few minutes for a chat. And so I said yes.'

'Great.'

'I'm going to have a bath.'

'Right then.'

Helen closed the door behind her and Clive turned the television back on. Last night's whisky glass was still on the shelf and there was a good inch or two left in the bottle.

Golf and half-marathons, thought Clive.

*

Clive laid out breakfast for the girls the next morning, and then kissed them each on top of their heads before shouting up the stairs.

'That's me off.'

'What?' called Helen

'I'm going.'

'OK.'

'Bye.'

'Yes, bye.'

'Have a good day, darling,' said Clive quietly to himself as he opened the front door. They'd lived in that house for years but he still managed to trap his knuckle behind the knob of the Yale lock three times out of five. This time it caught the fold of skin just on the underside of where his index finger bent. He sucked at it as he opened the front gate and turned left towards the school. He really did have some last-minute lesson planning to do today, and he wanted to be the first to the staffroom in the history department. Two boys walking in the other direction were whispering as he approached and then went silent as he passed them.

He unpacked his briefcase, found the folder he was looking for and then made for the kettle. As it boiled, he stared at Icke's special cup and imagined the sense of giddy satisfaction he would feel if he picked it up and tossed it back over his shoulder. The sound of smashing. The look of hurt on Icke's face.

The door opened and in came the cup's owner.

'Clive, good morning.'

'Robert. Kettle's just about to boil. Coffee?'

'Not for me, thanks.' Icke removed his coat as if he meant business and then hung it on the only hook on the back of the door. 'I had a call from Mr Crouch last night. Quite late.'

'Oh yes?'

'About Jonathan Findlay. All very worrying.'

Clive felt a sudden coldness deep inside him. 'I see,' he said. 'I thought the fuss had died down. It's not been mentioned for weeks.'

'Yes,' said Icke. 'It hadn't. But I believe that the parents have been having a bit of a think.'

'Look. I sent a boy out of my class for misbehaving. It's really not an uncommon event in a school like this.'

'That's certainly true.'

'Yes,' said Clive, spooning some instant coffee into a mug. 'It sounds as if he's just taken being sent out very badly. It was weeks ago.'

'Even so,' said Icke. 'The headmaster called me about it. Wanted to get a few of the facts straight.'

'If he wants to get the facts straight, then he should talk to me.'

'I suppose he just wanted to check how things looked from my perspective. What was it that he actually did?'

'He was rude about my teaching.'

'Was he?' said Icke, and momentarily the beginnings of a smile appeared on his face. Not for long. A couple of frames and then it was gone again.

'And so I told him to get out.'

'So what's this about you hitting him?'

'I didn't hit him. I threw some of his things into the corridor and he says he got hit by one of them.'

'Injured, apparently.'

'That's what he claims.'

'And you deny it?'

'I don't deny that I threw his things, certainly. As for his being hit . . .' Clive threw up his hands. 'I suppose it's his word against mine. I fail to see how you could shed any light on it.'

'Do you know what the headmaster asked me? He asked who did I trust more in an instance like this, you, or the boy.'

'And?'

'Well, it's quite a question, isn't it?'

'And what did you answer?'

'I didn't. I said I'd speak to people.'

Clive started to pour the hot water into his mug. 'Well, I would hope that you would support me.'

'Oh, I will,' said Icke. 'Of course I will. But it's a worrying state of affairs if questions like that have to be asked. Don't you think? I'm just a little worried that the thing could reignite.'

The door opened and Flora was standing there, looking full of the joys of life. It was definitely a different colour, her hair. He could see that now.

'Hello, everyone. Well, you two. All right?'

'Good morning, Flora,' said Icke. 'I'm well, thank you. Clive, do you know that you're bleeding?'

He nodded at them both and then departed. Clive said nothing until after the door had shut, then looked down and saw that blood was dripping from his finger where he'd caught it on the lock at home. He sucked it again.

'Wretched man,' he said.

'You all right?'

'Do you recall an incident that occurred before the half-term holiday? Jonathan Findlay was involved.'

'No. Is he OK?'

'I sent him out of my class.'

'Oh, that. A few boys have mentioned it. It's all fine though, isn't it?'

'I thought it was. But Icke just said that Crouch suddenly called him about it last night.'

'Why now?'

'I've no idea. But the night before half-term, Findlay's mother had obviously spoken to Crouch about it. Said I threw something at him and it hit him.'

'But you wouldn't do that.'

'Exactly. But I got called to see Crouch at his house.'

'Oh yes? I was asked round there for a drink the other night.'

'Just you?'

'Mark was there. Mark Taylor. About six of us.'

'I see.'

'Just an informal thing. Nothing important was discussed.'

'No scandal?'

'Well, hardly any. Apart from the decor,' she added in a whisper.

Clive laughed. 'Those cushions.'

'God, those cushions.'

'They were wearing matching jumpers the night I was there. Lavender.'

'Well, I'm sorry to have missed that. What are you going to do?'

'About their jumpers?'

'About Findlay.'

Clive let out an anguished groan. 'I really don't know. I'll just have to see how it plays out, I suppose.'

'They're taking it further?'

'Icke is giving that impression. It's basically my word against Findlay's, and I really don't know which of us is more likely to be believed.'

'Robert must back you, surely?'

'He says he will. I don't know if he means it though. How are you getting on with him?'

Flora eyed Clive carefully. 'We're getting on well, actually. And I really don't want to get caught up in your battles with each other. I know you two have problems, but from my point of view he's very encouraging.'

'Yes, of course. You have to make up your own mind about people, don't you? I understand completely. What I think about him should have no bearing on what you think.'

'That's right.'

'Obviously,' Clive added, 'I'd respect you more if you decided that you hated him too, but there we are.'

*

Clive arrived in the main staffroom at break time feeling a little queasy. In each of the lessons that he'd taught that morning, some boys had made references to the Findlay incident again, and several made passing comments about his temper. He used to enjoy pupils being cheeky. It gave him a chance to be cheeky back and to mess around a little. Now it just tired him. He kept his mouth shut for fear that he'd go too far, as he clearly had with Findlay. At one point during the lesson with the fifth form he'd dropped his marker on the floor by mistake, and when he had made a slightly cross noise about this, someone called, 'Please don't throw anything at us, Sir,' and everyone else had laughed. 'Very good,' was all he'd impotently said in response.

Clive managed to get a coffee and then took a seat next to Wally, who was staring into space. He had clearly cut his face shaving that morning, and looked sore all over. There were still small bits of tissue with blood on them clinging to his neck.

'All right, Wally?'

'If I threw myself into a gorge,' said Wally, 'do you think anyone would mind? Apart from the dogs.'

'I'd mind,' said Clive. 'What's wrong?'

'I just fail to see the point of life rather too often. I was teaching just now and I suddenly just stopped talking. I could see the boys weren't listening. I test them sometimes. Say things that are definitely not true to see if they're really concentrating, and I just got nothing from them. I looked out at them all; no one was looking up. People were doodling and looking at magazines, and I just tailed off. I don't think they even noticed. I went and looked out of the window. When the bell went they just got up and walked away. It's all so pointless.'

'Sorry about that. But yes. It is pointless. This whole place is just a wanker factory. We should down tools. Don't throw yourself in a gorge though.'

'I won't. I wouldn't have the nerve.'

'You know you've got some tissue on your neck?'

'Have I? Oh God. I thought I'd got it all off. I've been teaching with those stuck to me. No wonder people can't bear to look at me.'

'It doesn't look that bad.'

Wally started feeling blindly around his own neck. 'It's having to shave with the wrong bloody hand. My sodding woodwork injury. That wretched man.'

'Crouch?'

'Yes. Do you know,' sniffed Wally, 'that they have little parties at their house? Little gatherings for teachers. I've never been invited to one.'

'Nor me. Not that I mind.'

'Well, quite. I'd rather not be out at night. It's better for the dogs, really.'

'Sure.'

Over by the coffee machine he could see Iain Dixon talking to Flora. He was making her laugh, and it made Clive feel sick and angry. Mark Taylor was in conversation with Elizabeth Jones across the room and he made a thumbs-up sign with eyebrows raised. Clive shrugged back theatrically, just as Crouch swept into the room with Linda following behind. He had a habit, Clive noticed, of accelerating just as he entered a room so that if someone was following him they always found themselves floundering to keep up, lending him yet more import. Poor Linda was actually carrying a clipboard for him today and, having coughed for everyone's attention, he then just silently put an arm out for her to place it in his grasp. Whether it was by accident or design, the fact that Linda was the only person in the room not by this point looking at Crouch and thus not to notice this gesture was too delicious a sight to behold. Clive giggled slightly as Crouch was reduced to eventually asking quietly, 'Linda, are you there?'

'Headmaster?'

'The clipboard?'

Crouch, attempting to hold his composure, smiled at the room in a wide arc, and in so doing pulled his hand away from Linda just at the moment that she was passing him the clipboard, so that it clattered to the floor. It landed at Crouch's feet, so he had no possible excuse for not picking it up himself. Mark, just out of Crouch's eyeline, was beside himself with glee.

'Right,' said Crouch, after he had picked up the clipboard and smoothed his hair. 'A few things today. Is there anyone who enjoys woodwork? We are *still* a teacher down, owing to an injury. Not that that sounds like a particularly attractive advertisement, but I'm told that what happened to Wally here was jolly unlucky.'

He flashed a smile at Wally, who received the remark as it was intended: to belittle him. He sank down in his chair and reddened.

'As well as *preventable*,' added Crouch, with less of a smile. 'Now. We have a number of outings this week – the last set of outings before we move onto the exam timetable, and a rota for drivers is currently being drawn up by Linda. Please keep an eye out for notices. Thirdly, the Bishop of Swindon is going to be coming to talk to . . .'

At this point Clive felt himself gripped by an acute drowsiness and a mighty yawn rose up so expeditiously within him that he let out a surprised sound as it emerged, like a wave breaking in an otherwise calm sea.

'Mr Hapgood?' said the headmaster.

'Excuse me,' said Clive, and coughed dryly with a closed fist against his chest.

'Are you struggling today, Mr Hapgood?'

Clive, needing to say something, said, 'I'm not really sleeping at the moment,' and then realised that this was true.

'I'm sorry to hear that,' said Crouch. 'I wonder why. Anyway, if I could have your attention for just one more moment and then you could perhaps have a power nap before your next lesson.'

The laughter that followed was more polite than malicious, but Clive felt no better for that.

'I have just one more thing to say to you all, and it is rather important, given the events of last half-term.'

Clive was suddenly very awake indeed.

'Frampton,' went on Crouch, 'is a good school, with a good reputation. It is excellently resourced. I think that we are very lucky to have both the pupils and the staff that we do. *But* – but we must not allow ourselves to become complacent. We have standards. And those standards are to be upheld.'

There was a slight unease developing in the room, a restlessness caused by the audience being uncertain if this was just one of those speeches that Crouch liked to make from time to time, or if he actually had something to say.

'How the boys behave is, of course, of considerable importance. But of equal importance is how *we* behave.'

Standing two along from the headmaster, Icke was nodding solemnly in agreement. He was holding his special cup. Did he carry it between the staffrooms, or did he have a version in each? Either, thought Clive, would be pathetic.

'We cannot expect the pupils in our care to behave as they should if we *ourselves* do not behave as we should. There are boundaries in place, and they must not be overstepped. And if they *are* overstepped – or if people assert that they *have been overstepped* – then we have measures and *protocols* in *place* to investigate, and we will take action if necessary.'

The room was completely silent now, save for Elizabeth Jones sniffing. The laughter had well and truly dissipated.

'Sorry to end on a sober note, but there we are. Enjoy the rest of your break. And Mr Hapgood, a word if I may. At your convenience, of course.'

Conversation in the room recommenced only gradually.

A lot of looks were exchanged, but nothing could be said with the headmaster still in the room. Clive, on the receiving end of a number of enquiring stares, breathed out slowly and then lowered his head into his hands. Wally turned to Clive and said, 'Has something happened that everyone knows about but me? What is it? What's going on?'

'I have no idea,' said Clive. 'No idea at all. Hope your morning improves.'

He got up and walked purposefully over to Crouch, who was now engaged in a quiet conversation with a nodding Icke.

'Headmaster?' said Clive, as loudly and as unselfconsciously as he could manage.

'I had better leave you two to it,' announced Icke, and withdrew like an oleaginous grand vizier.

'Shall we talk outside?' said Crouch.

The room was still full.

'No,' said Clive. 'I think here's fine.'

'As you wish. Linda?'

He passed Linda his clipboard, which she took silently. As she walked away, she caught Clive's eye and then shot Crouch a look of something not far from hatred. Clive nodded back at her with a smile.

'Linda's terrific, isn't she?' said Clive.

'I'm sorry?'

'Linda. Your assistant.'

'Oh, yes, Linda. Terrific. Yes.'

'Yes. I think she's really great.'

Crouch was momentarily off-balanced by this line of conversation. 'Yes, she's . . . she's a very good . . . *person*. A very model of efficacy.'

'I certainly think so. Anyway. You wanted another word.'

'Yes.'

Clive looked around the room, not to see other people but so that they could see him. It was when you were left alone with these bastards that there was trouble. He wanted witnesses. He caught Mark's eye and tried to beckon him over, but Elizabeth Jones was in full flow. He could hear her saying something about closure. Or was it brochures? Whatever it was that she was banging on about, Mark wore a mask of pure patience. Crouch lowered his voice.

'This business with Findlay. I don't know if you're aware, but unfortunately it has raised its head again. Findlay's mother has been in touch with me and – I'm afraid – is keen to take the matter further. So I think that the sensible way to proceed with this matter is for us to sit down with the boy and his parents and try to get to the bottom of just what happened.'

'A formal meeting?'

'No, no. Quite informal, in fact. Just a chance for people to speak openly.'

'And who'll lead this discussion. You?'

'I shall be there, but I don't think that would be appropriate. I shall ask another member of staff to chair it. And Linda will take notes, obviously. We must be seen to be taking this – that is to say, we must actually take this – seriously.'

'It sounds very formal. Chairing. Notes. Why don't I just sit down somewhere with Findlay?'

'No, Clive. I think that could risk further damage.'

'I think we'd probably be able to come to a sensible arrangement.'

'Arrangement?'

'Agreement, I mean.'

'Yes. But no. The boy's mother wants to speak to you. In person.'

'Oh, for God's sake.'

'I thought that perhaps Robert Icke would be a good person to lead the discussion.'

'Icke? Oh come on. I need someone who'll be on my side there as well, at the very least.'

Crouch raised a sceptical eyebrow. 'Robert Icke? He'd be completely professional. Totally trustworthy.'

'Perhaps he's a bit too involved?' said Clive. 'It happened in his department.'

'What about Wally?' said Crouch brightly.

Now Clive lowered his voice. 'No! Not Wally. He'll be absolutely . . . he'll ring up and say he can't be there because one of his dogs is sick. Or he'll bleed everywhere. It should be my choice. Mark Taylor.'

'I shall have a think, Clive. I shall have a think. Anyway, I can't stop long. There's someone rather interesting looking around the school today and I thought it might be good to meet them.'

'I see . . . Any idea when this meeting might—'

But Crouch was now mentally elsewhere, Clive's misdemeanours safely stowed away for now.

'Someone *very* interesting, in fact.'

'I'm sorry? Who?'

'The parent I'm helping show around today.'

'Well, that's great. But I must say it's really not very helpful having this hanging over me.'

'Would you like to know who it is?' Crouch stood there expectantly, waiting for Clive to play the game. 'Obviously, we are always very discreet about this sort of thing.'

It was as if they hadn't been, just seconds earlier, discussing the disciplinary threat hanging over Clive at all. The headmaster touched the side of his upper lip with his tongue, as if about to share some saucy titbit.

'It's someone who . . . well, let me put it like this: do you like Formula One, Clive?'

'No,' said Clive.

'Oh,' said the headmaster. 'Well, perhaps you won't have heard of him. Ah, Mark.'

Mark had finally escaped the clutches of Mrs Wilson and was hurrying towards them. 'Headmaster.'

'Do you like Formula One, Mark?'

'Er, I follow it a bit.'

'Guess who I'm showing around later this morning?'

Clive no longer existed as far as Crouch was concerned. Mark raised an enquiring eyebrow and gave him another thumbs up. Clive gave a thumbs down and moved away towards the door.

'Stirling Moss?'

'No. It's . . .'

But Clive was already away and jogging towards the gates to find a place to smoke. And coming in through the gates as he walked towards them was Jonathan Findlay.

'Ah, Jonathan,' he said, and stopped.

But Findlay carried on walking. 'Sir,' he said quietly.

Clive called after him. 'Look. Jonathan. Please. Could we just have a conversation?'

Findlay had stopped now, but he wasn't speaking. He hadn't even turned around yet.

'Jonathan. Please?'

Clive walked back to Findlay so that he could look him in the eye. Findlay acknowledged him but looked down.

'Look, Jonathan, we really need to talk. I'm sorry about what happened. I really am. I didn't mean for you to be hurt. I didn't know that you had been hurt. If you were hurt, that is.'

Findlay looked up. 'I've been told not to speak to you.'

'Who by, Jonathan?'

'I've been told not to speak to you.'

'Yes, but who by? The headmaster? Your parents?'

'I'm not allowed to speak to you until after we've had the meeting.'

'If you and I spoke now, we might not even have to have the meeting. You. Me. Your parents. The head. It doesn't have to happen. You can make your own mind up about things. Please.'

'I've been told not to speak to you,' said Findlay, and carried on his lonely way.

24

'And you didn't think to tell me?'

'I didn't want you to worry.'

'Because you didn't want me to worry or because you're embarrassed? What a ridiculous thing to keep from me.'

Clive had been loading plates into the dishwasher. The girls had gone to sleep half an hour ago, and Clive and Helen had eaten some leftovers together in something approaching silence. Clive had asked Helen how work was, but had glazed over when Helen had mentioned the planning committee again.

'Am I boring you?'

'No. I'm just worried.'

'About what?'

And so he told her. He told her about what had happened with Findlay. He told her that was why he had needed to go and see the headmaster the night before they'd gone on holiday. He told her that was why he had been stressed during their holiday. Every detail of the story that he shared with her caused more displeasure than the last.

'So what you're telling me is that now you're facing what sounds like a disciplinary hearing?' asked Helen

'Yes. It's tomorrow morning, the meeting. They told me this afternoon.'

'Tomorrow morning? He's moved fast.'

'It could all be over by lunchtime tomorrow.'

'The whole business?'

'My job. Maybe my career.'

'Oh, Clive.' Helen's eyes filled with water.

'I'm really sorry,' Clive said.

'Why did you do it?'

'I didn't do it.'

'Then don't be so melodramatic. Please don't frighten me. It won't be the end of your career. Anyway, it's impossible to leave that school without excellent references.' This wasn't a thought that Clive found particularly cheering. 'No matter what you've done.'

'Or haven't done.'

Helen looked away from him. 'Why don't you call Mark? See if he wants a drink. I've got some things to do here. I think you should go out.'

'Are you sure?' asked Clive.

She didn't reply.

'What have you got to do?'

Helen sounded exasperated now. 'Some work stuff. A couple of phone calls. Have a bath.'

'Fine,' said Clive. 'I'll ring Mark.'

Helen stopped and turned at the door. 'They've just got to find out what happened. Of course they do. I mean, did you throw something at him?'

'No,' said Clive. 'Of course I didn't.'

'Well then. Just tell the truth.'

It was so hard to convince him, sometimes, she thought, just how much she cared.

Mark had answered on the third ring. 'I'll see you in the Crown in five minutes,' he had said, and so there they were, sitting in the non-smoking section.

'I'll get these,' said Mark. 'Tetley's?'

'Yes please.'

He had come back with two bags of peanuts, and shovelled a handful into his mouth before taking his first sip. 'So,' he said, placing down his glass. 'What's happening?'

'Crouch hasn't spoken to you? You've not been asked to attend a meeting? Please tell me that you have.'

'I haven't, I'm afraid.'

'Oh bloody hell. What do you know?'

'I've heard a bit of talk, obviously.'

'Who from?'

'Everyone.'

Clive cursed under his breath.

'Well, people talk, Clive. Of course they do. No one listened to Crouch this morning without being instantly curious. And the boys too. They've been talking about it.'

'How well do you know Findlay?'

'Only a little bit. Not as well as you, I'd have thought. I was asked to keep an eye on him. When the parents divorced. I tried, but he wasn't very forthcoming. I thought it was you he spoke to.'

'It was. Tomorrow, though, I'll be talking with him again. And with his mother. Maybe even his father. Crouch. Is there any way you could come with me? Crouch wants Icke there to "chair" the meeting. That's not going to be balanced.'

'Yes, of course I'll come.'

'Thanks, Mark.'

'If it's allowed.'

'Surely it has to be. Bloody Findlay.'

'He's all right, I think. Enjoys a bit of fuss, perhaps. I'm surprised by all this though. Maybe he felt humiliated.'

'He must have done. This sort of thing must happen all the time.'

'What sort of thing?'

'Just things . . . getting out of hand. Someone getting cross and slightly overstepping the mark.'

'Did you overstep the mark?'

Clive took a long sip of his beer. 'I certainly shouldn't have thrown him out of the class. He was being a bit rude. Nothing more. And they had all been annoying, not just him.'

'Have you said that to Crouch?'

'No.'

'And will you?'

'I don't know if that's wise. I mean, if I ask someone to leave, that's at my discretion, surely? I had warned them.'

'Yes, that's probably fair. Don't tell Crouch you regret throwing him out. You need to show certainty.'

'You're right.'

'And did you throw something at him?'

Clive looked at Mark. Honest, decent Mark.

'I might have.'

'Might have?'

'I threw his stuff.'

'At him?'

'Towards him.'

'Did you see it hit him?'

'I don't know, Mark. I just don't know. I was still con-cussed. Well, a bit. I shouldn't even have been in school.' Clive pushed his stool back and took a look around the pub. 'What a fucking mess,' he said.

'This place?'

'Frampton. This business. I'm most annoyed with myself. For giving Icke and Crouch a reason to go after me. Fucking hopeless.' Clive drained his glass. 'You want another?'

Mark's glass was still two-thirds full but he assented. Clive returned to the table and put the two fresh pints down and Mark asked, 'How's Helen?'

'Not very talkative. It's a bit of a nightmare at home, to be honest. A silent nightmare. You're lucky.'

'Me?'

'It must be pretty uncomplicated.'

'Because I'm a chaplain?'

'Because you're single.'

Mark said nothing.

'I thought I might find you here.'

Clive turned to see Flora standing there, a long navy blue overcoat on and a handbag slung over her shoulder.

'Hello,' said Mark as he stood.

'Flora,' said Clive, starting to rise too.

'Nobody needs to stand up for me. Are they still doing food?'

'They're certainly doing peanuts,' said Mark. 'Let me get you a drink.'

As Mark went to the bar, Flora removed her coat and hung it on a hook on the pillar, then sat down on the empty stool next to where he had been sitting.

'What sort of day have you had, Clive?'

'Not great. This bloody thing's totally blowing up.'

'About Findlay? You'll be fine. You just need to be honest.'

'Exactly,' said Clive. 'Still, I could do without it. Icke's not being very helpful.'

Flora put her hands up. 'I can't get involved, Clive. I can be a character witness, but I can't get involved in your thing with Icke.'

'It's not a "thing". He just hates me.'

'And you him.'

'Yes. Maybe more so. Have you only just finished?'

'Marking. Planning. Photocopying.'

'You can do as much as you like, can you?'

'I haven't been photocopying, Clive. I wouldn't dare touch that machine without the expressed blessing of Robert Icke. It's not my place to tread on sanctity.'

Clive smiled at her. 'You're too good for this place, Flora.'

'What are you talking about? I like it. Trust me, it's better than where I was before. Much better. Be grateful. There's a lot of good people here.'

'Mark, you mean?'

Flora gave him a look. 'Yes. Among others. You're a good person.'

'Whether or not that's true is going to be a finding of a disciplinary hearing.'

'Really? Is that what's happening?'

'In effect.'

'It'll blow over.'

'I hope so.'

'Sauvignon blanc,' said Mark, placing a large, full glass in front of Flora and sliding onto his stool.

'Are you two here for the long haul?' said Flora.

'I might be,' said Clive.

'I can't be, I'm afraid,' said Mark. 'This has got to be my last one.'

'You'll stay for another, Flora?'

*

'Another' had turned out to be somewhat open-ended. Mark, who was going to have no more, in fact stayed for two more before reluctantly taking his leave.

'I've got to write a sermon for morning chapel now,' he said, making his way uncertainly to the door.

'Just tell them about the evils of drink,' Flora said.

'I think I'll switch to wine now,' said Clive. 'Shall we order a bottle?'

'I'll get it. I've not even got my purse out yet.' She put her handbag on the table and rummaged in it. Out came a retractable umbrella, a set of keys and two novels about Spain. Then a diary, some tablets in a numbered blister pack and finally a red leather purse. 'Got him. Back in a sec.'

She dropped her things back in the bag and sauntered to the bar. Clive watched her go. He envied her freedom. Her certainty. She seemed happy too. Even happier than when she'd arrived.

'Talk,' she said, placing the bottle and two glasses down.

'Talk?'

'You're drinking. People normally drink about things. Especially if they're going for it on a weeknight.'

'I don't know,' said Clive. 'Yes, stuff's bothering me. But I don't want to bother you. You're happy.'

'So could you be.'

'Could I?'

''Course. Just let it out.'

Clive poured them each a glass and then held his aloft. 'Cheers.'

'Cheers. So?'

'I fucking hate this place.'

'Really?'

'I hate it. I know there's good people. I know there are. There are people I like. People I love. But there's too much other stuff.'

'Is it the school, or the town?'

'It's both, I think. Well, they're inextricably linked. The school's why I'm here. I mean, I'd like to like it. I'd love to like it. It was Helen who wanted to come here. She didn't really like our old life.'

'Did you?'

'I loved it.'

Flora gave him a sceptical look.

'Honestly. Didn't mind where we lived. And I loved teaching there. I was actually doing some good.'

'You do good now, Clive. Would you go back there? Really?'

'Like a shot,' insisted Clive.

'Really?'

'Yes. But it would most probably be alone.'

'Does Helen like it here?'

'She likes her job. Seems to really like it at the moment. Started hanging out more with people from work.'

'Is that so bad?'

'Well, no. Clearly not. But it's just a new thing. We're kind of having . . . well, it's just difficult. Can I ask, why did you get divorced?'

Flora looked at Clive, then said, 'You don't want to get divorced.'

'No. No. Of course I don't. I'm just interested. What happens when it really goes wrong? What's that like?'

Flora took a sip of her wine, and then another. 'Really?'

'Really.'

'Well, first you stop wanting to talk to each other so much. Then you stop wanting to be around each other. Then you stop liking each other. Then you start disliking each other. Then you start finding each other a little bit more irritating each day. Then you start wanting to hurt each other. Then you finally admit these things to yourself. Then you admit them to each other.'

'When do you stop loving each other?' asked Clive.

'You don't, necessarily.'

'Right.'

'But there's lots of different types of love, aren't there?'

'What about sex?' he asked.

'What about it?'

'When do you . . . I mean, when does that . . . ?'

'I'm not going to talk to you about sex, Clive.'

Not aggressive. Factual.

'Fair enough. Understood.'

Flora changed the subject. 'And the school?'

'It's just. It's just wrong, isn't it? Why are the pupils even there? Why aren't they at normal schools?'

'I doubt there's such a thing as a normal school.'

'I mean a comprehensive.'

'Like the one you taught in?'

'Yes.'

'And did you go to one too?'

'I went somewhere like this. Maybe that's why I hate it so much.'

'Hate?'

'Have a problem with it then. I look at the boys here and I think of what I was like at their age and I project it onto them.'

'Is that fair on them, Clive?'

'Probably not. Why have these people been sent here? What's happening at home?'

'Well, it could be anything. Some of them live overseas. Some of them have divorced parents.' Flora's compassion was genuine.

'Yes, but loads of them don't.'

'People want their children to have a good education.'

'And do you think they get it?'

Flora thought. 'Academically, they do.'

'Exactly. What about the other stuff? The fucking entitlement of these children. And that's them as teenagers. What'll they be like when they're grown-ups? You've seen the way some of the parents behave. No wonder their children are arrogant little fuckers.'

'Not all of them.'

'No, not all of them. But enough of them for it to be a worry. There's a whole world out there that's nothing like this. Some of them won't be prepared for it. Some of them don't even need to be prepared for it. They'll never see it. Schools like this are fundamentally dishonest. Look at someone like Crouch. Do you think he's an honest man? Really?'

'I don't know.'

'He's not. He's an arsehole. The self-importance of the man! Or someone like Icke. They wander round the place thinking that they really matter. And it's infectious. The boys get fed the idea that this is a really special place. And that they're special people. And that they really matter.'

'Everyone matters,' said Flora.

'Yes, of course everybody matters. But people here think that they matter *more*. They're taught that they do. "The unique Frampton Character." They're fed this bullshit, and they believe it. This place isn't unique. There's loads of mediocre private schools like this one.'

'Would you prefer to teach at a really fancy one?'

'No. I'd prefer it if they didn't exist. All buttresses and beautiful lawns you can't walk on. High walls. People get to the age of fifty and they're a top barrister at some amazing chambers and they think that it's because they went somewhere like this.'

'It is, though, isn't it? I'm not defending it ideologically. But the two are related. They've been given a head start. Confidence.'

'Confidence is a trick. They think they *owe* the school. They come back for Old Boys' days. And Speech Day. And give money for dining halls or theatre seats. The school owes *them*. It always has. But they've been complicit in all this. Letting it go on and on. There shouldn't be schools like this. *We're* complicit. It's . . . unjust.'

'Do you ever think you should just try and enjoy life, Clive?'

'I'd love to. Just not here. Not working at a school like this. I can't square myself with it ideologically.'

'What about when you're sober? Is it easier then?'

'A little bit.'

'You like teaching?' she said.

'Yes, I think so. You?'

'I love it. Why don't you go back to the state sector?'

'I might. I might.'

'Well then. There's a way out. There's always a way out.'

'Is there?'

'Yes.'

Flora was refilling their glasses now, the bottle already empty.

'I know I'm banging on,' said Clive.

'It's fine,' said Flora. 'It's good to talk.'

'It is, isn't it? Do you really understand me though? I know I'm ranting, but it's not just drink. Do you understand me?'

'I do. I really do. Just remember to look for the good in things, Clive. There's always good.'

'In everyone?'

'In everything.'

'Even me?'

'Don't fish. Yes. Even in you.'

'Thanks, Flora.'

'You're welcome.'

They chinked glasses.

'You're great, Flora.'

'Thank you.'

'You're really great. Shall we have another bottle?'

'If we can talk about something else.'

'Can we talk about how everybody knows your business in a place like this?'

'Let's not.'

'Fine. Fine. Let's talk about Spain.'

'I'm reading about Spain at the moment.'

'I know. I saw.'

'We want to go in the summer.'

'We do?'

'A friend and I.'

'Great. Do it. Go anywhere that isn't Normandy. That's what I think.'

'What about the rest of France? Is that safe?'

'No. It's all too close to Normandy.'

As Clive returned with their next bottle, Flora said, 'What does Mark think about the disciplinary thing?'

'I thought you didn't want to talk about it?'

'I just wondered what Mark said.'

'He said he'd try to help.'

'Good. He will too. You know that, I hope. He likes you. He says you've been his best friend here.'

'He said that tonight?'

'He said it the other day. He worries about you.'

'Well, he shouldn't.'

'*You* worry about you,' she said.

'Exactly. So no one else should have to. Oh God.'

'What?'

Clive was suddenly panicked. 'Dixon. Iain Dixon. He's just come in.'

'So?'

Clive watched Iain walk to the bar. He was wearing a slightly rakish hat, which he put down next to the pumps while he chatted to the girl serving there. Iain glanced at his watch while the girl was talking to him.

'He's probably waiting for Frank Harper. He's a gossip too.'

'What are they going to gossip about?'

'You and me, sitting here pissed.'

'We're not that pissed.'

'We will be after this bottle.'

'True.'

'It's OK. He's not seen us. I'm going to drink this glass and then go and have a word.'

'Why?'

'Draw attention to us being here together like this. If I go and draw attention to us, he'll think it's innocent.'

'It is innocent.'

'Exactly. And I want him to think that. So trust me. That's what I'll do after this.' Clive pretty much drained his first glass from the new bottle, and then poured himself another. 'You ready for another?'

Flora drained hers too. 'Go on then. It's fun drinking on a weeknight.'

'Do you not normally?'

'Maybe a glass. But not like this.'

'You should try it more.'

'Who have you got first thing tomorrow?'

'Before my hearing? Sixth form. You?'

'Sixth form. Same as you.'

'Oh yes.'

'See, you are pissed.'

'I'm going after this one.'

'Same.'

They finished their next glasses and then got up to leave.

'I'll walk you home, Flora.'

'No need. Although I am definitely drunk now. Not as drunk as you though.'

'It's fine. Let me have a piss.' Clive lurched off to the far side of the bar where the toilets were. Iain was still deep in conversation with the barmaid.

'Honestly, Karen, you'd like the West Country. I'd take you there myself if you'd let me.'

In the loo Clive struggled with his fly for nearly half a minute and then steadied himself with his free hand above the urinal. There was a faded advert on the wall for

Murphy's Irish Bitter. The tiles were cool, so after he had zipped up he stood there with his forehead pressed against them for a while, trying to get some clarity. He found none.

He patted Iain on the shoulder as he walked back past the bar, and Iain spun round.

'Hello, Clive. You just come in? Let me get you a drink. This Findlay business sounds like a ball-ache.'

'I'm fine. Just going. I've been here for ages. With Flora.'

'Flora's here too?'

'We're just going. She came in for food, but there wasn't any.'

'You have been here a while, haven't you?' laughed Iain.

'It's not even closing time,' said Clive. 'Goodnight, Iain. Goodbye, Karen.'

Flora was still putting her coat on. It's what she'd been doing when Clive had left the table.

'You all right?'

'Sleeves,' she said.

'Can I help?'

'It's done now. No, sod it. I'll just carry it.'

They walked to the door. Clive pulled it open and they stepped out onto the street where the air hit them hard.

'Well, that was fun,' said Flora. 'Bit of spontaneity. I like spontaneity.'

Which was when Clive kissed her. Or tried to. His lips were probably an inch from hers when she put her hands on his chest and gently pushed him back.

'Clive. What are you doing?'

'Oh my God, Flora. I'm sorry. I'm really sorry.'

'You're out of your fucking mind.'

'I know. I'm sorry.' He turned his back to her and ran his fingers through his hair. There was already cold sweat creeping across his brow.

'You should go home, Clive.'

'I should.'

'To your wife.'

'Oh, Jesus Christ.'

Flora started to walk away from the pub in the direction of town. Clive called after her. 'Flora. I'm sorry.'

She waved him away. 'Go home and sleep, Clive. Big day tomorrow.'

As he watched her walk away, he took his tobacco from his pocket and tried to roll himself a cigarette, but it was beyond him. He dropped two lots of tobacco before he gave up and threw the whole lot down into the gutter. Then he dropped his lighter too and ground it under his foot before starting out for home, his heart pounding.

When he got there, he undressed in the sitting room and cleaned his teeth in the downstairs loo using the brush and toothpaste that he kept in there for late nights and early mornings. The house was in total darkness and he climbed the stairs as slowly as he could. Their bedroom door was ajar, and he pushed it gently open. It made no sound. Then he tiptoed around to his side of the bed and climbed painstakingly in beside Helen, trying to disturb the mattress as little as possible.

'How was Mark?' said Helen.

'He's good. Sends his love.'

'What was his advice?'

'To be honest.'

'Sounds sensible.'

She fell straight back to sleep, and Clive lay on his back next to her, his eyes wide open and his heart dancing to the beat of pure panic.

*

He woke up at quarter to six, his pillow wet with sweat. Helen was still fast asleep, and so Clive showered and dressed, then went into the kitchen and made a coffee. He felt awful, but he knew that the hangover was nothing to do with it. He went into the downstairs loo and retched into the basin, then looked up at himself in the mirror and said the word 'idiot'. He had to get out of the house, so he went back into the kitchen and poured the coffee down the sink, returned to the downstairs bathroom and brushed his teeth with his back to the mirror, unable to even look at himself. He couldn't keep still. He grabbed his coat and bag, went out of the house, turned left at the gate and walked towards the school and the history department. He could get there early, maybe have a chance to see Flora before anyone else did. He would apologise to her. He would beg for her discretion. And what would she do? He had no idea. These were the thoughts still going through his head as he realised the door to the history department wasn't opening, no matter how many times he rattled the door handle. Then the bell behind him in the quad rang out and he realised that it was still only half past six in the morning. The service department wouldn't be opening up for another hour. The place was completely abandoned. He could walk across the grass if he wanted. He had to go somewhere. He swung his bag over his shoulder and set out for the river, like a cat who knew it was about to die. There was a path behind the bus park that led to the little footbridge, and from there he could walk along the bank or cross the river and start climbing into the woods. He chose the bank and walked away from the town until he could just see its two spires in the distance. There were just a few dog walkers about, and they said hello to him genially. He was surprised, at first, by their friendliness, until it occurred to him that of course they had no idea of what was going on in his head and his life and had no reason to despise him. It was a thought that cheered him, and he felt the first pricks of optimism in days. He tried to carry it with him as the time came for him to walk back into town but it steadily receded the closer to town he got, replaced by gloom twinned with doubt. The door to the department was now unlocked, and someone had already boiled the kettle in the staffroom. There was a cup next to it with dry coffee granules waiting. Flora?

'Morning, Clive.'

Icke.

'Hello, Robert.'

'You're in early.'

'Always. Well, sometimes.'

'Shall we say occasionally, and leave it at that?'

Clive couldn't remember the last time he'd heard Icke make a joke. He found it unnerving but nevertheless reached for a little smile. 'This your coffee?'

'Yes.'

'Not using your usual mug?'

'I've moved it to the main staffroom. They're at a bit more of a premium there.'

How is it, thought Clive, that you can be such a tiny, boring man and yet right now I would still rather be you than me?

'Mmm,' said Clive, spooning coffee granules into a cup of his own, then pouring the boiling water in.

'Term's flying by, isn't it?'

'I'm finding it a bit more of a slog than you, perhaps.'

'Yes. Well. I know there have been one or two difficulties, but I think this department's generally running along pretty well. Don't you?'

'Yes,' said Clive. 'All very satisfactory on that front.'

'Flora's such a good addition, isn't she?'

'She's fitting in wonderfully, Robert. Wonderfully.'

'You think she's happy? I know you two talk.'

Clive felt himself redden, though he couldn't be sure if it was due to anger or embarrassment. Icke was incapable of addressing him in a way that he didn't find needling.

'I'm—'

'You do talk, don't you?' Icke was blowing on his coffee now, infuriatingly.

'We do talk, yes.'

'Yes, Iain Dixon said he bumped into you in the pub last night.'

'Oh, did he?'

'Yes. Told me on the phone. Said he felt a little in the way, actually.'

'What?'

'He was only joking, I'm sure. He does joke, Iain. Can't help it. Like you. Well, like you used to be. Bit more serious now, aren't you?'

'He wasn't remotely in the way,' spat Clive. 'We were just leaving when he arrived. I went over and spoke to him . . .' Clive suddenly stopped. 'Hang on a minute. This was only last night. He rang you to tell you about it?'

'No need to be so defensive, Clive. He just happened to mention it. We were talking about something completely different. That's all.'

'At half past eleven at night? What?'

'A private matter,' said Icke sternly.

'Fine,' said Clive.

'Have you heard about the headmaster's plan?'

'About what?'

'About this Findlay business. For today's little chat? Well, meeting. Get it all out in the open.'

'You're involved, are you?'

'The headmaster has asked me to chair the meeting.'

'Has he?'

'Yes. I think that's sensible. Don't you? I'm sure things can be dealt with speedily if we're all honest with each other.'

'Let's hope so.'

There was a whoosh of sound and colour as the door swung open and Flora was suddenly standing there, brightly dressed and with a big smile on her face.

Clive, meanwhile, could feel all the colour draining from his own.

'Hello, you two!'

'Ah, Flora. Good morning. You seem very jolly today.'

'I am very jolly today, Robert. Very jolly indeed.'

'Excellent. Well, I shan't take up any more of your valuable time.'

When Icke had left, still blowing on his coffee, Flora's smile relaxed somewhat.

'Hello, Flora,' said Clive quietly.

'Clive,' she said. He guessed that they were standing eight feet apart, and would have preferred the distance to have been at least double that.

'Can I make you a coffee?'

'Please,' she said.

'Are you really feeling jolly?'

'No. Not at all. I feel absolutely disgusting. But this is how I cope with hangovers at work. It's a trick my ex taught me; if you've got a hangover, you should bounce into work being very jolly and then people say, "Oh, you're looking very jolly today," and they don't notice that you're anything but.'

'Do you have to keep it up all day?'

'No. Just each time you walk into a room. It's brilliant.'

Clive felt the side of the kettle and turned it on again. 'Flora. About last night . . .'

'Let's not talk about last night.'

'I'd love it if we didn't. Icke just said that Iain Dixon saw us.'

'Saw us what?' There was a note of terror in her voice.

'Just that he saw us. Felt that it was worth mentioning to Icke in a late-night phone call.'

'Well, that's all right, isn't it?'

'I hope so.'

The kettle clicked again.

'I'm really very sorry,' said Clive, staring hard at a spot on the floor about three feet in front of her.

'Let's not talk about it,' said Flora. 'Nothing happened.'

'Exactly. Nothing happened.'

25

'Right then,' said Julian Crouch. 'I think we're quorate now. Shall we begin?'

Wally had been the last to arrive, and it was a tense silence that he had finally broken by doing so, with Clive, the headmaster, Robert Icke, Linda, Jonathan Findlay and his mother and father all in awkward attendance. Findlay looked even less like he wanted to be there than Clive did. His mother crossed her legs in a way that made Clive's throat feel dry. She and her ex-husband sat next to each other and appeared to have as much of a connection as two strangers forced to sit next to one another in a busy train carriage.

Eventually Wally had come panting into the headmaster's study with sweat dripping from his forehead and temples.

'I'm so sorry, everyone,' he'd said. 'I went to your house, Headmaster. I thought we were meeting in the study at your house, not this one. Arabella put me right. All right if I sit here?'

He sat down in the only empty chair in the circle, next to Linda, who – always well prepared for such occasions – passed him a box of tissues.

'Thank you,' said Wally, and proceeded to mop his brow with the first of the three tissues necessary to complete the job. He then gave Clive a little smile. Clive's request for Mark to be present at the meeting had been rebuffed.

'The purpose of today's little chat is really to clear the air,' said Crouch. 'I thought perhaps that you might like to speak first, Mr Hapgood?'

Clive, vestiges of his hangover still remaining, wasn't sure if he was supposed to stand when he was speaking or remain sitting, and he was halfway through attempting the former when Crouch's eyebrows suggested that the move was not necessary.

'Sorry,' said Clive, and sat back down. 'Well, let's see. Some weeks ago, I was teaching Jonathan's class – I wasn't meant to be; I was suffering from concussion, and they're not my class anyway – and things got a little out of hand. They were playing pranks and misbehaving, and I became cross. Jonathan was one of the boys involved in the bad behaviour and it was him, I'm afraid, who, in retrospect, bore the brunt of it. I had told the class that . . .'

Clive broke off because Mr Findlay had snorted at his use of the word 'brunt'.

Findlay's mother was already imploring him to speak. 'Jonathan?'

'Shall we let Mr Hapgood finish what he has to say?' said Icke.

'Let him speak,' said Mrs Findlay.

'Very well,' said Icke.

'Which of us do you mean?' said Clive.

'Jonathan,' said Mrs Findlay. 'It's him that this happened to. Not you. He's the victim.'

'Would you like to say anything further to your original statement, Jonathan?' said Icke.

'No,' said Jonathan.

'Say something, Jonathan,' whispered Mrs Findlay.

'No,' Jonathan whispered back.

'Right,' said Icke. 'Clive? Sorry, Mr Hapgood?'

'Well,' said Clive, 'I asked Jonathan to leave the room. He put up some resistance, with the support of others, it must be said, and I'm afraid that this angered me further. When he did eventually leave the room, he chose not to take his possessions with him, despite having been told to, and so I made sure that they – somehow – got to the corridor.'

'And how did they get there, Mr Hapgood?'

'I threw them,' said Clive quietly.

'I beg your pardon, Mr Hapgood?'

'He threw them,' said Mr Findlay.

'Threw them?' said Icke.

'Threw them,' said Clive.

'At him?'

'No, I wasn't really aiming them anywhere.'

'But did you throw them towards him?'

'That's certainly the direction they went, yes.'

'But you don't assert that that was your intention?'

'I don't really understand,' said Clive.

'Did you mean to throw them towards him?'

'Well, I was facing towards him when I threw them. I certainly didn't intend for them to end up behind me.'

Icke raised a quizzical eyebrow.

'I think we're possibly getting a little bogged down in the semantics here,' said Crouch.

Clive couldn't bear the way that the headmaster so regularly misused words, but felt that now was not really the time to put him right.

'It's possible,' said Icke.

'Did you or did you not thrown my son's things at him?' said Mrs Findlay.

'Yes,' said Mr Findlay.

'No,' said Clive.

'Jonathan?' said Mrs Findlay.

Jonathan Findlay said nothing.

'Sorry, when *was* this?' asked Wally.

Linda, struggling to write this all down, let out a sigh.

Icke began again. 'Tell us what you think happened please, Jonathan.'

Jonathan Findlay sank even lower into his chair.

'Speak, Jonathan,' instructed Mrs Findlay.

Findlay pursed his lips for a while, breathed out slowly and then began. 'We were all being badly behaved. All of us. Not just me.'

'What sort of thing, Jonathan?' Icke said.

'Hiding his stuff. Swapping his markers.'

Mrs Findlay tutted.

'Norman got told off a bit. No one else, really. Rogers was a bit rude to him. Nothing really happened. Then I said something and that was when Mr Hapgood got really angry. That's when he told me to leave.'

'And what was that, Jonathan?' asked Icke. 'What did you say to him?'

'I can't remember.'

'Mr Hapgood?'

'It was about my teaching ability,' said Clive.

'In praise of or critical?' asked Icke.

'Well, obviously it was critical,' said Clive. 'I wouldn't have asked him to leave if he'd put his hand up and said that he thought I was a good teacher. Would I?'

'I'm just trying to get to the bottom of what happened,' said Icke.

'He said I can't teach.'

'That's not quite what I said,' said Jonathan.

'I thought you said you couldn't remember what you said,' countered Clive.

'Well, I can.'

'And what was it, Jonathan?' asked Icke.

'He said the words "I can't teach" and I said, "I always thought that actually." That's all.'

Mr Findlay opened his palms to the room with a 'so what?' look on his face.

'Is that right, Mr Hapgood?'

'Yes. Yes, that was it. That's what he said.'

The room considered the seriousness of what it was that Jonathan Findlay had said and came silently to the unanimous conclusion that it wasn't very serious at all. Icke eventually gave voice to this opinion. Mr Findlay added that it was almost certainly a fair summation of Mr Hapgood's talents.

'It might be, Mr Findlay. It might be,' agreed Icke.

Clive looked at his head of department with impotent loathing and said, 'Thank you, Robert.'

'Merely speculating,' he replied. 'Trying to consider this from all the possible angles.'

'I think Clive's a very good teacher, actually,' said Wally, helpfully. 'Not that I've actually seen him teach,' he added, somewhat less helpfully. 'But he's a pretty decent bloke. That much I do know.'

'Yes,' said Icke. 'But what we're trying establish are the *facts*. Was it unfair of Mr Hapgood to remove Jonathan from the class in the first place, and did he then throw objects at the boy which *struck* him? If so, did he do so *intentionally*?'

'Yes, yes and yes,' said Jonathan's mother.

'Yes, yes and yes,' said Mr Findlay, as if she hadn't spoken.

'Yes, I don't know and no,' said Clive.

'Could everybody please speak more slowly?' asked Linda, taking notes furiously.

'What were the three questions again?' said Wally.

'The three questions were . . .' began Icke.

'*Wait!*' demanded Linda.

Everybody waited until Linda had finally stopped writing, after which she took one of the tissues from her box and blew her nose angrily. She attempted to stuff the scrunched-up tissue into the pocket of her dress and realised that it didn't have one, and then looked around for a bin to put it in. Others joined this search for a bin, and when at last all possibilities within the room were exhausted, the headmaster remembered that there wasn't a bin in this room. 'Linda usually takes my rubbish,' he said, struggling to conceal his irritation that this meeting wasn't running as efficiently as he'd hoped it would.

'Why don't I take it?' said Wally eventually, and shoved it into the pocket into which he had earlier thrust the tissues that he had used to mop his brow. As he did so, a baffled look ran across his face and then he pulled from the pocket two bone-shaped dog chews and a small see-through vial with a red lid.

'Ah,' he said. 'It's for fleas,' he added, in response to the headmaster's enquiring stare.

The offending items were thrust back into the pocket and Icke cleared his throat. 'Now, where were we?'

'Two yes, yes, yeses and one yes, I don't know and a no,' said Linda.

'And what were the three questions again?' said Wally.

'Never mind what the questions were,' said the headmaster. 'If I may speak for a moment, the gist of where we have got to is that Mr Hapgood and others are in disagreement about the events of . . . actually, when was this, Linda?'

'That's what I asked,' said Wally.

'I don't know,' she said. 'No one has said.'

'It doesn't matter when it was,' said Mrs Findlay. 'What matters is that it happened.'

'Or didn't happen,' said Clive.

'It did happen,' said Mr Findlay.

'There we have it,' said Icke.

'You haven't actually asked Jonathan what happened yet,' said Mrs Findlay.

'Yes, I have,' said Icke defensively.

'Only what happened in the classroom. Not out in the corridor.'

'That's true,' said Linda, checking her notes. 'Unless that happened while I was still catching up with something else that had been said.'

'Very well,' said Icke. 'What happened out in the corridor, Jonathan?'

All eyes looked to Findlay. Clive could either hear someone drumming in the next room or his own heartbeat.

Findlay said softly, 'He threw a folder at me, and it hit me.'

'You're saying that he deliberately aimed a folder at you and he was successful?' said Icke.

'I'm not sure it sounds like behaviour that I'd equate with success,' said Findlay's mother.

'What I meant—' began Icke.

'I know what you meant,' she said.

'Sorry, Mrs . . .' He wasn't sure whether she would want to be called 'Mrs Findlay' or not. He cleared his throat and continued. 'Right then. Clive?'

'Yes?'

'What do you have to say in response?'

'In response to what, sorry?'

'To Jonathan's description of your actions.'

'I see. Well, I disagree.'

'With all of it?'

'No, as I said, I did throw his things towards him.'

'So what is it you're denying? That something hit him?'

'What I'm denying is intent to hit him, and knowledge that it hit him.'

'So it might have hit him?'

'Well, it could have,' admitted Clive. 'But I didn't see it. I wasn't there.'

'You weren't *there*?' said Mr Findlay.

'In the corridor. I didn't see it. I threw the things at him and then turned back to the classroom.'

'Sorry,' said Wally, 'were you in the classroom or the corridor? I'm finding it very hard to piece all this together.'

'I was in the corridor,' said Jonathan.

'Clive? I mean, Mr Hapgood?' Wally said.

'Both, probably,' said Clive. 'I was in the doorway. But I'd turned around very quickly. So I didn't see where the things I threw went.'

'You must turn around *very* quickly,' said Mr Findlay.

'Look. I didn't see it,' said Clive. 'That's all I can tell you. I was concussed.'

'Any witnesses?' said Icke. 'Could the other boys see what was happening? Through the doorway perhaps?'

'You'd have to ask them.'

'*Has* anybody asked them?' said Jonathan's mother.

Icke and the headmaster exchanged looks.

'On this specific point?' asked the headmaster.

'Yes.'

'On this specific point . . . er, Mr Icke?'

'No,' said Icke eventually. 'Lots of other things yes, but on this specific point no.'

Mr Findlay emitted a sigh that was halfway to being a roar. 'Is everyone who works in this place completely imbecilic? For the fees we pay, I thought we might be assured of at least basic competence, but clearly this isn't the case. I've driven a hundred and forty miles for this. Still, I'm grateful to Mr Icke here for phoning us and encouraging us to take the matter further, as it's given me a chance to see for myself just what goes on here.'

Icke blushed and avoided Clive's stare.

'Should I be writing this down?' said Linda.

'I don't think so, Linda, no,' said Crouch.

'You can write what you like,' said Findlay's mother. 'My son says that this man threw something at him, and this man is trying to deny it despite the fact that he claims he didn't see what happened, unlikely as that may sound. It's his word against my son's, and essentially this man is calling my son a liar. Is that a fair summation of events?'

'I think . . . yes,' said Icke.

'I haven't called him a liar,' said Clive.

'You've implied it. You didn't see what my son said happened. You have no evidence to suggest that nothing hit him. We only have your word that it wasn't intentional if it did. My son, on the other hand, says that it happened and had a cut on his chest to prove it.'

'Will anybody speak up for me?' said Clive to the room.

Icke was looking at his own feet, as were Crouch and Jonathan. Mr Findlay was staring at him icily. His ex-wife had her arms crossed and was looking at a fixed point on the ceiling. Linda was writing down the words 'Will anyone speak up for me?'. And Wally had just discovered some worming tablets that had come loose from a tube in his other pocket and was struggling to get them back in. Having managed to deal with about half of them, he looked up to see that the rest of the room's occupants were looking at him. Clive was silently pleading with him to say something. Anything. Wally stopped what he was doing with the worming tablets and opened his mouth. Then, realising that he couldn't think of anything to say, he closed it again and resumed the job of feeding the tablets back into the tube.

*

Clive walked around the quad, barely able to contain his rage. The apology that he had just been forced to make to both the boy and his parents in front of everyone else in the room had been beyond excruciating. As Findlay had been almost as embarrassed about it as Clive was, he had made no response, leaving silences that Clive felt compelled to fill with further apologies. 'I am sorry for your injuries,' Clive had said. 'I am sorry for effectively calling you a liar. I am sorry that you think that my teaching is inadequate.'

Goodness knew what the rest of them were all doing now. Clive had finished his humiliating climbdown and then asked for permission to leave the room. Perhaps they were discussing whether the apology was adequate and, if not, whether further action should be taken. His anger, he knew, required a focus. He had to be in a calm state by the time he got home later. He couldn't bring any more anger into that home. He needed to get it all out now. There was only one thing he could do. He carried on his way around the quad and went through the archway that led into the steps up to the staffroom. The place was reassuringly empty, and so he went over to the shelf by the sink and located what he was looking for: Icke's special mug. There it was. He took one last look towards the door, then raised the mug above his head and threw it down hard onto the floor. It smashed satisfyingly, and in just the way he'd hoped it would. Not into pieces so big that it could be glued back together. Not into such tiny fragments that it wasn't recognisable. He was standing there, revelling in his action, when the door opened and Iain Dixon walked in.

'Oh dear, Clive. Did I hear something break? Nothing valuable, I hope.'

'Not to me,' said Clive.

'Are you all right, Clive? You look a little discombobulated.'

'I'm fine, actually,' said Clive, turning to face him. 'But do you know what, Iain? You can be a real arsehole sometimes.'

Iain shifted his weight onto the other foot and took a sideways look at Clive. 'Are you sure you're all right, Clive?'

'And do you know what else, Iain? When you call your pal Icke tonight, you can tell him that he's one too.'

*

'I'm home,' shouted Clive cheerily as he came through his front door some hours later. He could see the girls at the kitchen table, doing their homework.

'Hello, Daddy.'

Clive put his things down by the front door and went through and kissed each of them on the head. Katie clung to him.

'Where's your mother?'

'Upstairs,' said Sarah. 'Wondering where you are.'

He went upstairs and pushed the door open. Helen had her back to him and was looking at herself in the full-length mirror that they had meant to put up long ago but still rested against the wall.

'Could you do this up for me?' she asked.

She was in a black dress that clung to her, and was just putting on her earrings. Pearl. Small ones. He could smell perfume. Quite mild. Rosewater?

'You look amazing.'

'Thanks.'

'Where are you going?'

'Oh for fuck's sake, Clive.' She turned to face him. That lipstick. Red and dangerous.

'What?'

'It's tonight.'

'What is?'

'Our meal.'

'Our meal?'

'My work meal. Out at Fencham. The people carrier's here in ten minutes.'

'Who'll be there?'

'Clive, have you been listening to anything I've said this week? The town councillors. The county councillors. The outgoing mayor. That lovely lady from the Chamber of Commerce. And we're not allowed to discuss business. There'll be speeches.'

'Will Martin be there?'

Helen bristled. 'Everyone will be there. Including Martin. Now do me up.'

She turned her back to him and he came over and slid the zip slowly up, watching as the light freckles on her back disappeared from view. When he got to the top, he held his hand there for a moment and then put his forehead on her shoulder. She rested her head on his.

'Have a lovely evening, Helen.'

'Thank you.'

'Have the girls eaten?'

'Fish fingers. There's more in the freezer.'

*

The girls had wanted so many stories that he didn't get downstairs until after half past nine. He filled his glass with whisky and then got out his school diary, searched for a number and dialled it. No answer. He tried Mark, and there was no answer from him either. He turned on the television and allowed fifteen minutes to pass before trying the first number again. Nothing. He waited another fifteen minutes. And then another, before dialling again.

'Hello?'

'Flora,' said Clive, jumping up from the armchair. 'It's Clive.'

'Oh, hello, Clive. Sorry, I've just got in. Are any of these messages on the machine you?'

'No. Been anywhere nice?'

'Yes, as it happens. How was the meeting this afternoon?'

'Bad. Dreadful. Really just awful. Icke was foul. Turns out he put Findlay's parents up to it. Crouch was there but he might as well not have been. Wally was beyond useless.'

'Did they say why Mark couldn't do it?'

'No. But probably because he's my friend.'

'Wally's your friend.'

'Yes. But Wally's Wally.'

'I know.'

'Still, it's over. I think. I had to apologise to the boy and his parents and I've heard nothing more.'

'So everything will be back to normal?'

Clive sat back down in the chair.

'Well, will it?'

'I hope so. Listen, Flora, are things OK between us?'

There was a silence from the other end of the line.

'Flora?'

'I thought that might be what this phone call's about.'

'Yes. Well. Are they? I just feel really dreadful.'

'Well, don't. Forget it happened.'

'I can't pretend nothing happened.'

'Nothing *did* happen.'

'Is that how you honestly see it?'

'Look, Clive. You were drunk. I was drunk. You tried to kiss me. I stopped you. You accepted it. That's all it was.'

'You seemed cross.'

'Well, I was. You did something stupid. Or tried to. As I said, nothing really happened. I'm not cross now. It's over.'

'What's over?'

'Last night. We don't need to talk about it again because nothing happened. We're colleagues. We're friends. And we'll be perfectly happy if we just don't mention it again.'

'I'm just a bit unclear as to why it happened, I suppose.'

'It didn't happen, Clive. But if you tried to make it happen it's because you were drunk and you weren't thinking. It's passed. We can move on if we don't talk about it.'

'I'm just worried.'

'I'm not going to mention it to anyone, if that's what's worrying you. You've nothing else to worry about. You made a stupid mistake. It's not like you're moping about town in love with me, is it?'

This time the silence came from Clive's end of the phone.

'Clive?'

'You're right, Flora. You're absolutely right. I'll stop worrying.'

'Good.'

'As of tomorrow, everything will be back to normal. It never happened.'

'It never did. I'll see you tomorrow.'

'Yes. Goodbye, Flora.'

'Bye.'

Clive replaced the receiver in the cradle and then stood up and went over to the shelf to refill his glass. A wave of tiredness came over him, and he leant against the shelf for a moment with his eyes pressed closed. When he opened them again, he looked around the room as if it were a stranger's house. He crossed back to the armchair and slowly lowered himself into it, then shut his eyes again.

He awoke when he heard a large vehicle pulling up outside. The whisky glass was on the table next to him, untouched. There were some lengthy goodbyes and then a fumbling with the lock before he heard the front door open.

'Hello?'

'Sitting room,' he called.

Helen teetered in and sat down on the edge of the sofa. She looked so beautiful and happy.

'How was it?'

'Great, thank you. Really great. Really relaxed evening.'

'Would you like to go to bed?'

'Are you drunk?'

'No. Are you?'

'A bit. I need a glass of water.'

'And then do you want to go to bed?'

'Yes, Clive. To sleep.'

'How was the company? Who were you next to?'

'Brian Griffiths on one side. Know him?'

'I think so.'

'Martin on the other.'

'Oh really? And how was he?'

'He was really fun, Clive. Actually.'

'Do you think he fancies you?'

Helen stood up. 'Would you care if he did? Would you? Really?'

'I'm just asking.'

'Well then. He might.'

'What are you going to do about that?'

She looked at him as if he was deranged. 'I'm not going to do anything, Clive. Why would I?'

'I have absolutely no idea.'

'Good.' She sat down again. 'Pass me your whisky.'

He did so. Helen took a small sip, followed by a larger one. 'I tell you what was interesting though.'

'What?'

'I saw Mark there.'

'Mark? What, on his own?'

'No. He was with your new colleague. Looked very sweet together.'

'Flora?'

'That's it. Flora.'

'Did they see you?'

'No. They left long before we did. Nice though, isn't it? It would be good for him to be with someone. Don't you think?'

'Yes, I suppose so. He has been a bit hard to get hold of lately. I wonder if that's why?'

'Maybe it is. How exciting.'

'Yes,' said Clive. 'Well, that is good news. Probably keeping it a secret.'

'Maybe that's why they went out of town, away from prying eyes.'

'Except yours.'

'I wasn't prying.'

'Of course not.'

'No need to talk to me like that. I wasn't. You can be so sharp sometimes.'

'I know. And yet you still haven't asked me how the meeting went today. About Findlay.'

'The meeting. God. How was it?'

'The meeting I had today that would decide my future? That one? It was fine. As it happened.'

'Is everything sorted?'

'Do you care?'

'Why are you being like this, Clive?'

Clive thought. 'I'm being like this, in all honesty, because I sometimes feel like I'm misunderstood.'

Helen stood up and drained the glass she was holding, then put it down on the arm of the sofa. 'You are misunderstood, Clive.'

'I'm glad you realise this.'

'It's you that doesn't realise, Clive. It's you that misunderstands you, Clive. We all understand you perfectly well.

You're someone in a little town with little problems and yet you just can't handle them. You're someone with such an acute sense of victimhood that you are exhausting. You get harder to be around every year, if you must know.'

'Why don't you leave me then?'

'That's right. Why don't I leave you? You certainly wouldn't have the balls to leave me. You never actually do anything. Is that why you're just sitting there, waiting to be left?'

'I'm not.'

'I have had such a nice evening, and I come home and you attack me. Probably for being happy.'

'That's not true.'

'It is true, Clive. You are a fundamentally unhappy man and it is *exhausting*. And your moods! You've been in this mire for months and then suddenly you turn round and you're all "would you like to go to bed?", as if that's going to solve anything. Of course I don't want to go to bed with you. What I want is for you to be happy. And then *we* can be happy.'

'Are you finished?'

'No, I am not finished. The sheer infectiousness of the misery that you bring into this house. Watching you as you absolutely fail to keep a lid on your anger. Us all looking on helplessly as you completely lose your temper with the toaster or whatever.'

'I think we both know that this isn't a conversation about the toaster.'

'It is a conversation about the toaster. It's a conversation about sex. It's a conversation about all of the things that we disagree on. Because all of the things that we disagree on are the things that make it harder for us to love each other. OK?'

Clive, though he was sitting back in an armchair, felt unbalanced. 'Another perfect evening,' he said.

'All this anger . . .'

'I'm not angry,' said Clive. 'I'm embarrassed.'

'By me?'

'By myself. You are so acutely aware of my failings that when I'm in your company I feel much more ridiculous than when I'm not. It's not an ideal atmosphere for a marriage.'

'I do love you, Clive.'

'I know,' said Clive. 'But I don't know why.'

'I have to go to bed,' said Helen. 'Can you undo my dress for me before I go up?'

'With pleasure.'

Helen turned her back on him and Clive got up and slowly lowered her zip, exposing those freckles that he had concealed just a few hours ago.

'We can talk in the morning.'

'Let's do that.'

'Goodnight.'

'Goodnight, Helen.'

Clive took the glass over to the shelf and filled it again one last time. Helen, as she went upstairs, wondered how she could ever persuade Clive that she still wouldn't want to be with anyone but him.

26

Immaculate. That was the word. Everything has to be immaculate. That's what the headmaster had told everybody
the afternoon before at the rehearsal. That there had to be
a rehearsal at all emphasised just how immaculate it had to
be. Everyone who was playing any part in the Speech Day
ceremony had been under strict instructions to be there,
at the marquee on the sports field. A vast and immaculate
white tent filled with rows and rows of neatly ordered,
empty seating, it would accommodate more than 2,000
people. There was a stage big enough to fit the entire staff.
And there were chairs set up to one side for every single
pupil who was receiving a prize. The staff didn't all have
to be there, of course, except a chosen few to help run the
rehearsal. Clive, inevitably, had been pressed into service.
He'd had to just hang around for the full rehearsal, making
sure that people were sitting in the correct order to go up
and receive their prizes, which they had to rehearse going up
to receive, shaking the hands of a few members of staff and
the headmaster. And then the headmaster's wife, who was
standing in for tomorrow's guest of honour, a former pupil
of the school who had had some sort overseas governmental
post and of whom everybody was, of course, tremendously
proud. The entire ceremony had been run through. Even the
very brief moment that involved Clive's active involvement.
Someone had to have the job of reading out the citation for
the winner of the school's Junior History Prize and Icke had
felt that Clive would be the perfect man for the job. Icke
had written the citation himself. The only things skipped

over in the rehearsal were the headmaster's speech and that by the guest of honour. Everybody had still had to practise the lusty applause that would follow these, though.

And now it was actually happening. It was the last day of the school year. The exams had all been sat. The sun was shining, the lawns were mown, the marquee scrubbed a gleaming white. The pupils looked smarter than they had at any other time of the year. So too did the staff, decked out in their academic gowns. The parents were all there, doubtless putting a brave face on to conceal the terrifying thought that they would now have to actually spend some time with their children for a couple of months. They were all dressed as well as they could afford, which in many cases was extremely. The guest of honour was due to speak, inevitably at length, about some hilarious events that had taken place in the Ambassador's Residence in Gibraltar and the marvellous things his years in diplomatic service had taught him. The head boy had given a confident account of how his time at Frampton had set him up for life. All the prizes (Clive had counted well over fifty in the programme) were yet to be handed out, and at this very moment Julian Crouch was up on his feet, pacing confidently up and down the stage in his pin-striped suit with his adoring staff lined up behind him, explaining to all assembled just how incredibly privileged and lucky they all were to be part of Frampton and for Frampton to be part of them.

Clive, sitting on the end of the front row, looked past the headmaster and out over the audience: the shiny little pupils, the smartly dressed fathers, the mothers in their hats. So many hats. He looked out over them all to the back of the marquee, the flaps of which were left open so that people didn't start collapsing in the oppressive atmosphere inside, and out to the gleaming playing fields where, once the school song had been sung, families would start competitively laying out their picnics in one last status battle before it all broke up. Some would have hampers and lay out lavish spreads on beautiful woollen blankets alongside their sports cars. Others would set up furniture and take chilled champagne from the boots of their Land Rovers. Boys who hated each other would be forced to make polite conversation while their parents were deep in discussion about how brisk business was or how much one can get for one's money in the Dordogne. Some families would sit glumly in the open boots of their dog-fur-lined Volvos, miserably eating cold sausages and talking to no one. Staff would wander about cadging free food and drink from the wealthier parents in exchange for a ready laugh at some dry wit and some complimentary remarks about their offspring's efforts. Clive caught a glimpse of Findlay sitting two rows from the front. It was almost funny to think how well they were getting on now. A week after the showdown with his parents, Clive had run into him in the chip shop again. Findlay had apologised to him. It hadn't been his idea to complain, he told him. It had been Icke, and his parents. And it had been Crouch. It was impossible to blame Findlay, really. In a way they were not so very different, he and Clive; they were just two bobbing corks in a sea of other people's agendas.

'You see, the thing that we must never allow ourselves to forget,' the headmaster was saying, 'is that what we have here at Frampton is completely and utterly *unique*. It's not just about the buildings and the grounds. Do you know, in many ways – and I'm sure my colleagues behind me will forgive me for saying this – it's not even about the teaching.'

Here the staff and parents laughed with varying degrees of polite unctuousness.

'No. It's actually about *you*. You, the pupils. And you, the parents. The uniqueness of the Frampton Character depends so much on what you bring us. On those you entrust us with. Yes, we can shape people. The pupils who leave Frampton today leave the school as well prepared for life ahead as they could possibly be. But it would be remiss of us not to acknowledge that's in large part because the – if you'll forgive the expression – *raw material* that first arrives here is already so very special. Interesting people, from interesting families. Good people, from good families. Strong people, from strong families. Creative people, from creative families. We are indebted to you, in the same way that in years to come we hope you will feel indebted to Frampton. We will shortly be presenting the prizes, we will hear from our guest of honour, and we will then finish, as is the rightful tradition, by singing the school song. Wonderful words, and a terrific tune. And I hope it means something to you, not just now but also in the future. Wherever you are in the world, and whatever befalls you, you should know that that song is something that you can always draw on. Sing it to yourself. Sing it with others. Take strength from it. Use it as a way to remind yourself that whatever life throws at you, you are and always will be a Framptonian. Thank you.'

The headmaster bowed his head to his audience, who began to clap enthusiastically. Cheers rang out. There was hollering. The headmaster smiled wryly at his staff as he made his way back to his chair, stopping on his way to shake the hand of the guest of honour. By the time he reached his seat, the opening bars of 'Jerusalem' were blasting out of the speakers and people were gathering up their verse sheets, standing and clearing their throats for another bit of pomp.

For the last few weeks Clive had been walking around in a sort of fug, as if he had been concussed again. A succession of completely unconnected thoughts had been tumbling around in his head in place of the thing that he was trying to think about. Sentences that he felt in complete control of would suddenly fall away at the end, disintegrating into nothing. How his pupils had fared in the exams they had just sat, he had no idea. And nor did he care.

*

The Junior History Prize was to be the thirty-fourth prize handed out during the ceremony. This had given Clive ample time to mull things over. As the winner of the Senior Biology Prize left the stage with his certificate, Clive stood up and made his way to one of the two microphones at the front of the stage.

'To read the citation for the Junior History Prize, Mr Clive Hapgood,' said the headmaster into his microphone. All of the citations were introduced in this fashion. The audience had clapped the first five or six times, but their patience had long since worn thin. Clive had the words written by Icke in his jacket pocket, but they could remain there for now.

'Thank you, Headmaster,' he said. Everyone spoke slightly too loudly into the microphones at first, and Clive was no exception. He took half a step back and began again.

'Thank you, Headmaster. It is a great privilege, ladies and gentlemen, to be asked to announce the winner of this year's Junior History Prize. And this year's recipient is an incredibly deserving one.'

This much had been written by Icke. He was sitting fifteen feet behind Clive's left shoulder and Clive was able to turn and smile curtly at him.

'Because history is all about revealing the truth. We can only truly learn where and who we are if we can first learn where we've been. The role of the historian is to question. New discoveries lead to new understandings; they lend themselves to fresh interpretations of events.'

Crouch, to Clive's right, was nodding sagely.

'The thing is,' said Clive, 'even the best historians will sometimes turn out to have been wrong. Because someone, somewhere, will always find more information. There are some people who think that once a history is written, it is finished. But history is a living subject. The accepted version of events is never necessarily the real version. That is why people must always question.'

If the audience in the marquee had been listening when Clive had started his citation, they weren't now. Programmes were being ruffled. The coughing was beginning. The headmaster was using his splendid eyebrows to appeal to Clive to get a move on. Clive, however, was not to be hurried.

'For instance,' he said, 'let us think about Frampton. And the Frampton Character. It's unique. That's what the headmaster has just told us. Of course, we already knew that. Because it's not the first time he's told us about it. He mentioned it at last year's Speech Day. And the one before that.'

Now the audience were listening; well, the parents were. The staff behind Clive were certainly listening.

'He mentions it to us in the staffroom most weeks. And there's a very good reason that he tells us about it so often. You'll all have heard it said that if you throw enough mud at someone then eventually some of it sticks. Well, in much the same way, if you repeat a lie often enough, people eventually start to believe it. The "uniqueness" of the Frampton Character is a lie. We all know, and the headmaster knows better than most, that there is nothing remotely unique about the Frampton Character.'

It was Crouch who coughed now. The microphone near him picked it up. Clive turned and smiled at him. He caught sight of Flora sitting among the staff. She looked like someone watching a mourner falling into a grave. He smiled at her too.

'Shiny schools like this are dotted all over this country, and they are, if we are honest with ourselves, much of a muchness. Yes, they have things that distinguish them from each other. Some get better academic results. Some have better sports teams, orchestras, architecture. Some produce more prime ministers. But what all of these schools have in common is something that should fascinate historians, junior or otherwise. People who go to schools like this generally leave with an innate capacity to be dishonest. It's ingrained. And why wouldn't it be? Because schools like this aren't built on values.'

Crouch coughed into the microphone again. It was deliberate this time.

'Schools like this are built on pretence. And artifice. We value A level results. Sports scores. We value these prizes. What we value is anything that gives the impression of success: a trophy, a certificate. Something that can be engraved or can have a number on it. But later in life, when you think about your time at school, do you remember the marks or do you remember the people? Does it matter if you made the first team for rugby or does it matter if you made friends?'

Clive looked out over the audience. The parents were still hooked. It didn't look as if the boys were listening though. A shame, Clive thought, as all this was really for their benefit.

'The headmaster is right about something though,' said Clive. 'You will all do well in life. By and large. And you will do so because you've been to Frampton.'

Crouch was relieved to hear something he could nod along to at last, and made good use of the opportunity.

'Sadly though,' said Clive, 'it won't be what you've learnt here that will help you do well, just the fact that you went to a school like Frampton. Out in the wider world that will be one of the few things about some of you that will be in any way remarkable.'

Crouch had stopped nodding now. Instead he was biting his lower lip and clasping his hands together so hard that his knuckles were whitening. The former Ambassador to Gibraltar, yet to speak, looked as if he was going to be sick.

'Yes, it's lovely to leave a hallowed place like this armed with great results,' Clive continued. 'Sadly, all some people seem to leave here with is a sense of entitlement. Some people arrive with one. It would be rather better if people eventually left here with kindness, honesty and integrity, if I can choose just three characteristics that our headmaster is entirely lacking in.'

Clive stopped here. The silence in the marquee was really quite something. Someone near the back sneezed and it was like mortar fire. He had only one more thing to say, but he needed the piece of paper in his jacket pocket to say it. He took it out and slowly unfolded it, then glanced through to check if there was anything else Robert Icke had written that might be worth throwing in.

'The winner of the Frampton Prize for Junior History is Richard Seddon.'

Richard Seddon, whoever he was, knew that he was going to receive the prize but hadn't yet stood up to come and receive it. Perhaps he didn't really believe that Clive's remarks had definitely come to an end. Clive looked out over the audience, and at last saw a boy near the back of the tent stand up. It was Mark Taylor who began the applause as Seddon started to make his way to the stage. Clive stood back from the microphone and joined in the applause, which was now gaining in volume. Amidst the hubbub, the headmaster took a few paces towards Clive, a certificate for the Frampton Prize for Junior History now clamped under his arm.

'I take it that was your resignation speech,' he hissed.

'Yes, it was,' said Clive.

'I hope you're not expecting a reference.'

'No, Headmaster. But can I just say something?'

'Yes?'

'You're a cunt.'

And with that, Clive Hapgood returned to his seat, and Julian Crouch had no choice but to try and get the show back on the road. Clive looked down the row of teachers sitting alongside him. Only Mark Taylor looked back at him. He wore a look of concern. Clive, though, smiled at Mark. He was glad Mark was happy. He deserved to be.

*

Helen was still asleep when Clive climbed out of bed at six the next morning. They'd barely spoken the night before, and that had been a shame. They still had lots to say to each other.

He showered and dressed and then went into the girls' room and kissed each of them on the head. They stirred quietly but didn't wake. He drank a glass of water in the kitchen and then washed up the glass and put it in the drying rack. Then he brushed his teeth in the little bathroom by the front door and placed his brush and the toothpaste in the side pocket of the bag that he had packed and left there the night before. It contained a few pairs of pants and socks, some shirts, two bottles of own-brand supermarket vodka, three novels he had been meaning to read and – on a probably pointless whim – his passport. He took his coat off the bottom of the bannisters and put it on, and then went and reread the note that he had left on the kitchen table. It was vague enough, he thought. But not so vague that she would fear the worst. Then he went back into the hall, swung the bag over his shoulder, took one last look into the sitting room and let himself out of the front door, which he closed quietly behind him before pulling open the gate and then turning right in the direction of town and the railway station. Beyond that he had no real notion of where he was going to go. He'd see which direction the first train was heading, he supposed. He would find somewhere to stay for a few days. He'd let the dust settle, and then he would ring Helen and tell her that it was final. He'd talk to the girls too. He'd tell them that he would see them soon and that he loved them very much. At the thought of the girls, the corners of his eyes started to fill, and so he took one last look back at the house before hurrying on.

Acknowledgements

I would like to thank Richard Roper, my editor at Headline, not just for the calm consummation of his duties but also his astonishing patience. Thanks too to Molly Wansell for getting the two of us to sit down together in the first place. Tara O'Sullivan's proofreading was thorough and exemplary, as was the thoughtful copy editing of Emma Horton, and I gladly thank Jo Liddiard and Antonia Whitton for the marketing and publicity. Thanks must also go to James Kettle and David Stenhouse for reading early drafts and saying the right things so nicely and the wrong things so constructively. All my remaining thanks are due to Rachel Boase for so many, many things.

MILES JUPP
Wales
February 2021